When Someone You Love Is Depressed

HOW TO HELP YOUR LOVED ONE
WITHOUT LOSING YOURSELF

LAURA EPSTEIN ROSEN, Ph.D.
XAVIER FRANCISCO AMADOR, Ph.D.

A FIRESIDE TRADE PAPERBACK
Published by Simon & Schuster

FIRESIDE
Rockefeller Center
1230 Avenue of the Americas
New York, NY 10020

Copyright © 1996 by Laura Epstein Rosen and Xavier Francisco Amador
All rights reserved,
including the right of reproduction
in whole or in part in any form.

First Fireside Edition 1997

FIRESIDE and colophon are registered trademarks
of Simon & Schuster Inc.

Manufactured in the United States of America

20 19 18 17

Library of Congress Cataloging-in-Publication Data

Rosen, Laura Epstein.
     When someone you love is depressed : how to help your loved one without losing
yourself / Laura Epstein Rosen, Xavier Francisco Amador.
         p.   cm.
     Includes index.
     1. Depression, Mental—Popular works.   2. Depressed persons—Family
relationships.   I. Amador, Xavier F.   II. Title.
     RC537.R638   1996
     616.85'27—dc20
                                                                                            96-5899
                                                                                            CIP

ISBN-13: 978-0-684-82407-9
ISBN-10:   0-684-82407-8
ISBN-13: 978-0-684-83407-8 (Pbk)
ISBN-10:   0-684-83407-3 (Pbk)

To my parents
Ellen and Leonard Epstein,
for your gifts of curiosity, love, and spirit of collaboration.
You taught me the true meaning of family.

L.E.R.

To Maria Christina Bielefeld and Aniceto Amador,
for giving me a new life.
To Bernard F. Bielefeld and Richard Eichler,
for showing me new ways to live it.

X.F.A.

Contents

Preface   vii

1. How Does Your Loved One's Depression Affect You?   1

2. How to Recognize If Someone You Love Is Depressed   14

3. When Your Partner Is Depressed   43

4. When Your Child Is Depressed   63

5. When Your Parent Is Depressed   86

6. Friendships and Depression   101

7. Constructive Communication   115

8. Is It Fair to Ask for What *You* Need?   134

9. When Your Help Is Turned Away   147

10. Alcohol and Drugs   163

11. Suicide   177

12. Psychological Treatments for Depression   200

13. Medical Treatments for Depression   214

14. Finding Help for Your Loved One and Yourself   231

Afterword   253
Recommended Readings   255
Recommended World Wide Web Sites for Dealing with Depression   256
Index   257

Preface

In many ways, the idea for this book was an inevitable outgrowth of our work as psychologists with the close friends and relatives of depressed individuals. As psychotherapists and teachers of people learning to become therapists, we have been struck by the many ways in which depression affects loved ones. On countless occasions when we have worked with a depressed person in psychotherapy, a friend or relative has inquired about meeting with us. Often they have questions about their depressed loved one's illness or about treatment, but inevitably they also have concerns about how best to interact with their loved one. They ask: "Should I push her?" "Should I leave her alone?" "I want to tell him how annoyed I am, but I am afraid because he's so down," and "Why won't she talk to me about what she's doing in therapy? I feel cut out."

Our work with couples and families made us aware that the friends and relatives of depressed individuals not only have questions; they too are experiencing ill effects from their loved one's depression, and their relationship with that person is suffering. Recent research on this topic supports our clinical experience. We could have written a book about depression and the most frequently asked questions loved ones have, but that would not do justice to what our clients have taught us. This book is not really as much about depression as it is about how depression affects relationships.

This book was written to help you identify the ways in which depression is affecting you, your depressed loved one, and your relationship with that person. Our ultimate goal is to help you to learn strategies to counter many of these effects. As you will see, inattention to depression's toxic effects on relationships can worsen a depression and leave you and your relationship vulnerable to other problems. For example, research has shown that the severity of depression worsens when there is tension in the depressed person's relationships, that people closest to a depressed person are more vulnerable to various disorders themselves, and that marriages in which one member is depressed are nine times more likely to end in divorce. The good news is that there is much you can do together with your depressed loved one to speed his recovery and to safeguard yourself and your relationship against the weight of the depression.

We provide you with information about depression, its treatment, and the help that is available. Moreover, we provide examples of common relationship problems when a loved one is depressed. Many of these topics may already be familiar to you; others are problem areas that you may encounter in the future. You will learn about the common responses and feelings elicited by the depressed person and how to avoid the pitfalls common in relationships with depressed people. Every chapter provides step-by-step guidelines for countering the negative effects of depression on your relationship, on you, and on your loved one.

Chapter 1 presents case examples and research to describe how depression affects you, your loved one, and your relationship. We introduce the stages all relationships go through in their adaptation to a depression and outline the strategies we will teach you throughout the book. Chapter 2 focuses on helping you to determine if your loved one is depressed and shows you how to use your relationship as a barometer for detecting depression. It sets out the stages relationships go through in their adaptation to a depression and lists the guidelines for countering the damaging effects of depression which are applicable to any relationship. Chapters 3 through 6 highlight particular kinds of relationships such as when a partner, child, parent, or friend is depressed. Regardless of the relationship you have with the depressed person in your life, we strongly encourage you to read all of these chapters. Although unique problems arise in these different scenarios, all of the strategies presented in each chapter will be relevant to your situation. Chapters 7, 8, and 9 teach you how to communicate effectively with a depressed man or woman, how to get your own needs met, and what to do if your loved one rejects your help. Chapter 10 describes what you can do in the special circumstance of a depression coupled with substance abuse, and

Chapter 11 focuses on guidelines to help you when your loved one is suicidal. The last three chapters examine the different types of treatment that are available for your loved one. These chapters also help you to deal with the feelings, reactions, and problems you may have to the treatment your loved one is receiving. Alternatively, if someone you love is depressed and is refusing to see a professional, these chapters will teach you ways to encourage him to get the help he needs. The last chapter also provides information on how you can get support for yourself. Because depression affects both men and women, we have used masculine and feminine pronouns in different chapters, depending on the gender of the depressed person in the case example.

Whether you are a daughter feeling overburdened by your elderly depressed mother, a parent worried about your withdrawn depressed son, a friend who is tired of always having to listen to problems, or a spouse upset about not being able to help, you will learn that you are not alone in how you feel. More important, you will learn how to cope better with your loved one's depression and not allow yourself, and your relationship, to become yet another one of this disorder's overlooked casualties. One of the most important lessons we have learned from our work with families and couples is the necessity of working together as a team with a depressed loved one. We hope that by following our guidelines, you will recognize the power of collaboration and work together with your loved one in the fight against depression.

There are many people who contributed to this book and whom we would like to thank. We learned so much from our patients and their families. Among the things they taught us was what worked and what did not. Above all, they showed us that where there is love, appreciation, and respect, anything is possible; no relationship problem is insurmountable. Out of respect for their privacy, names and specific details have been altered in our examples.

Our own families, friends, and colleagues also helped us in many different ways. For their support and belief in us, we thank Andrew Epstein, Ellen and Leonard Epstein, Barbara and Martin Rosen, Carin and Roger Ehrenberg, Rachele and Alan Price, Elena Taurke Joseph, Gil Tunnell, Rand Gruen, Chrysoula Kasapis, Judith Kiersky, Rich Keefe, Caren Gadigian Keefe, Jeff Foote, Paula Gadigian, Jack Gorman, Larry Welkowitz, Maria Christina Bielefeld, and Liz, Tom, Emma, and

Elana Brondolo. Marina Salazar's help copyediting the final manuscript was much appreciated. In particular, Barbara Fox provided an essential source of guidance and insight that made this book possible. And Larry Rosen's unconditional support and encouragement, as well as his much appreciated review of the book, was invaluable.

Special thanks go to our editor, Susan Arellano. Her professional acumen and personal passion for the topic helped to bring the book to life. She understood what we wanted to say and helped us to convey it. More important, perhaps, she understands that depression affects more than just the depressed person and believes, as we do, that with this knowledge, you and your depressed loved one can begin to make changes.

1

How Does Your Loved One's Depression Affect You?

Jane, a thirty-six-year-old advertising executive, has been feeling overwhelmed with her new responsibilities. In addition to her full-time job and two children, she has recently begun to take over many of her husband's customary chores, such as paying the bills, servicing their car, and fixing things around the house. For the past several months, her husband has not been sleeping well; he feels unmotivated and tired, and complains of feeling blue. Jane knows that he is not feeling well and feels sorry for him—but she is beginning to resent him.

Peter, a twenty-eight-year-old accountant, has not been sleeping and has been having trouble concentrating at work. Since the birth of their son four months ago, his wife has been moody and disinterested in sex. He misses the closeness with her and feels sad about the state of their marriage. He is reluctant to talk to her about his concerns because he does not want to make her more upset. Rather than express his feelings, he spends more time playing golf with his buddies.

Gail, a fifty-five-year-old homemaker, has not done any laundry or been food shopping or spent any time with her friends for several weeks. She has been preoccupied with worry about her elderly mother's worsening hopelessness and recent statement that "there is nothing left to live for." Because she is worried that her mother will harm herself, Gail travels an hour each day to visit and try to cheer her up. As a result, Gail is falling behind in her household chores, she feels that she is neglecting her friends, and her husband has begun to complain.

The specific details may be different, but Jane, Peter, and Gail all have something in common: They are affected by a loved one's depression. Jane feels overburdened and resentful. Peter is lonely and worried about his marriage. Gail's fear and guilt about her mother are taking her away from her other responsibilities. All of them want to help their loved one but are having reactions to the depression themselves. Because they are so busy caretaking, Jane, Peter, and Gail have not noticed how they too have been affected by depression.

When Peter first came to therapy to discuss his concerns about his wife, he spoke at length about her sadness and lack of energy. As a caring husband, he was understandably concerned about her adjustment to motherhood. He described all the ways in which her depressed mood had affected her personality, from her lack of interest in sex and her usual activities, to her irritability with their infant. When he was asked about how her depression had affected him, he paused and said, "I guess only in that I care about how she feels." When he was encouraged to think further about his reactions to her depression, he reluctantly revealed that he felt lonely and scared. Peter admitted that he had not been paying attention to how he was handling the situation because he was so caught up in his wife's problems. Only after he had begun to pay attention to his own reactions and feelings was he able to talk to his wife about the changes in their relationship and encourage her to seek help for her depression.

How Can Someone Else's Depression Affect You?

If you love someone who is depressed, you may be unaware of how the depression affects you. You may be so intent on helping the other person that you are blind to ways in which you are affected. Yet if you begin to reflect on your interactions with the depressed person, you may begin to recognize that indeed you do have important feelings and reactions. Perhaps you have felt frustrated with your spouse for being antisocial and overly pessimistic. Or maybe you have become annoyed or worried about your best friend who does not seem able to snap out of the blues. Our experience as therapists and the results of recent research studies have convinced us that everyone benefits when feelings and reactions to a loved one's depression are understood and acted upon constructively. In short, it is essential to your own emotional well-being and that of your depressed loved one that you pay attention to your reactions and feelings. If you recall your last interaction with the depressed person in your life, you will undoubtedly recall some feeling or reaction that you previously did not think about.

This shift in focus is a central part of our work as therapists. Experience and research have taught us that inattention to feelings and reactions is often at the root of many relationship problems people experience with a depressed loved one, and relationship problems almost always worsen a depression. In the chapters that follow, we will help you learn how to recognize the various ways in which you are affected by your loved one's depression. For some of you, it may be easier than it will be for others. For those of you who are natural caretakers, it may not be easy to think about yourself rather than focusing solely on the depressed person. However, it will be well worth your effort. It will give you the tools you need to help your relationship survive the depression.

As you read, you may discover that depression is affecting you in ways that you have not realized. But don't worry, we do not intend to leave you mired in this new knowledge without tools to do something about it. We will give you specific step-by-step guidelines as to how to use your reactions to get along better with the depressed person, to increase your sense of hopefulness, and to be a more skilled helper in the fight against the depression. Before we provide these skills, you will need to understand the various ways that depression can affect you and your relationship. We will describe in detail the most common effects of depression on relationships. After a brief review of new research on this topic we will end the chapter with a description of the four stages of adaptation to depression. In the following chapters we will teach you how to alter your passage through these stages to improve your adaptation and response to the depression.

Depression and Your Relationship

Depression is a devastating disorder for the depressed person. We all know that depression affects mood, sleep patterns, appetite, motivation, and even the will to live. But what many people do not realize is the extent to which depression affects relationships. If your partner is depressed, your marriage is nine times more likely to end in divorce than if you were married to a nondepressed person. This staggering statistic is not the only indicator of how destructive depression can be to relationships. The close relationships of depressed people are more stressful and conflictual than the relationships of nondepressed people, and arguments and misunderstandings are much more common. In this context, it comes as no surprise that depression, and sexual problems caused by depression, are the most common reasons couples seek marital counseling and that approximately 50 percent of depressed women complain of serious marital problems. The relatives of depressed people have also been found to suffer from increased worry, resentment, and exhaustion. In fact, people who live with a depressed person are more prone to depression themselves and have a higher risk for other emotional problems, such as anxiety and phobias.

Why should depression lead to such severe relationship difficulties and even harm to nondepressed family and friends? Think about it. If you are lonely and resentful because your wife has been blue for several weeks and never wants to do anything with you, you might respond to her request for help around the house by sighing and looking disgruntled. She senses your resentment and feels unsupported, more helpless, and more depressed—reactions that feed your resentment and loneliness. Researchers have described this kind of interaction as a downward depressive spiral in which your loved one's behavior and your reactions to it can worsen the depression rather than help to alleviate it.

The early stages of this downward cycle can take many forms. One possibility is that because you feel guilty about your resentment toward your wife, you do not readily voice your feelings, and she senses that you are not telling her how you feel. As a result, the communication between the two of you begins to break down. Or you may express your anger too freely, thereby lighting your spouse's already shortened fuse and making a constructive argument virtually impossible. As we all know, when fights are too hot, they resolve nothing. But what you may not realize is that these kinds of interactions may inevitably lead to increased depression and hopelessness, for both you and your loved one. It is almost like a dance pattern that both members of the relationship get locked into, with each member's step affecting the other's step. If you and your depressed loved one are having trouble in your relationship, chances are you are already interacting in this depressive dance.

If what we have said thus far does not ring true to your experience, perhaps a brief look at the relevant research literature will convince you that your loved one's depression is affecting your relationship with her in important ways. If what we have said already fits with your experience, read on anyway. We think this research will help you to identify further the ways in which your relationship is affected. It has only been in the past decade that mental health researchers have begun paying attention to the role of significant others in the lives of depressed people. Before that, depression was considered primarily a problem for the depressed individual, separate from others in their daily lives.

Recent Research on How Depression Affects Family and Friends

Data confirming the idea that depression affects people other than the depressed person initially came from studies of the interactions between depressed persons and strangers. If you are close to someone who is depressed, it is probably not hard for you to believe that when research subjects interacted for even a short period of time with a depressed person they never had met before, they reported feeling down too. More surprising perhaps, subjects who interacted with depressed strangers also reported more anxiety, hostility, and unwillingness to spend time with them in the future than did the subjects who interacted with nondepressed strangers. Researchers concluded that something about spending time with a depressed person, even a stranger, is intrinsically difficult and alienating to others. Importantly, these results showed that the depressed person's behavior was off-putting and held people at a distance. This finding is particularly bad news for depressed people because close, supportive relationships are essential to their recovery from depression.

If you mentally review your own interactions with your loved one, you may be able to pinpoint some behaviors that have been off-putting to you. It may be that your loved one seems withdrawn, uninterested in your company, or easily irritated. In the research studies with strangers, the participants particularly complained about the depressed person's "negative attitude" or "lack of energy." We have all had the experience of interacting with someone in a foul mood and know that mood can be contagious and that a depressed person can be unpleasant to be around. But what is it that is unpleasant? And what happens in more ongoing relationships? Are the effects that are seen in interactions with strangers even more pronounced in closer relationships?

Building on the studies of strangers, researchers next looked to the interactions of college roommates. They found striking differences between the roommates of depressed and nondepressed students. The roommates of depressed students reported significantly more conflict, increased arguing, and less direct communication. In addition, they described feeling frustrated, sad, and angry themselves. When asked about their relationship with their roommate, these students said that they were much less willing to spend time with this person and tended to socialize more with other friends, preferably outside the dormitory. The conclusion from this research was that depression clearly can affect those who live with a depressed person.

If you live with someone who is depressed, you too may feel frustrated, sad, and angry. You too may have worse arguments than before the depression and much less desire to spend time with her. As you might expect, these feelings can be amplified in ongoing, closer relationships than typically exist between roommates.

Only the most recent research has examined the intimate relationships of depressed people, with results similar to, but even more striking than, the studies of strangers and roommates. Although this may seem counterintuitive at first glance—you would think that there should be a stronger bond in intimate relationships—we think you will agree that these findings make a lot of sense. Marital partners, for example, spend more time together and have to resolve more daily life issues than do college roommates who may be living together for a limited period of time.

The research shows that people who are closest to a depressed person are often angry, discouraged, and strained by the depressed person's fatigue, lack of interest in a social life, hopelessness, and irritability. In addition, there is a much higher rate of anxiety and depressed mood in the spouses of depressed people than in the spouses of nondepressed people.

Both research and our clinical experience confirm that living with a depressed person frequently takes a serious toll on loved ones. Since we more or less spelled it out, it was probably clear to you that Jane, Peter, and Gail were affected by a loved one's depression. However, for all sorts of reasons, it is not always easy to recognize these same feelings and reactions in yourself. For example, when we first asked a husband of a depressed woman how her depression affected him and his relationship with her, he was surprised: "Affect me? I don't see how it affects me. She's the one who's suffering. I just want her to feel better." In the next section, we provide you with information that will make it easier for you to identify what effects the depression of your loved one is having on you and on your relationship.

Stages of Adaptation to Depression

We have found that the relationships of depressed people go through what we call the *stages of adaptation to the depression* (SAD). Just as an infant passes through developmental milestones, learning to crawl and then walk, so do relationships pass through stages in their response to depression. Like the infant's developmental stages, the SAD can occur at different times for different relationships, with the stages not always distinct and isolated from one another. Behaviors characteristic of a previous stage can persist into the next, just as a toddler who has learned to walk continues to crawl at times. Sometimes one can regress to an earlier stage. But the stages do progress in essentially the same sequence. At each level, decisions need to be made that can influence the course of the depression and its effect on your relationship with the depressed person. There are four stages:

1. *Trouble.* In this stage, one or both members in the relationship notice trouble in their interaction, some new difficulty has emerged, or an old one has intensified. The trouble can range from a change in the quantity or quality of time spent together to major arguments and communication breakdowns. For example, Jane noticed that she was assuming most of the household chores, Peter and his wife were aware that their sex life had practically disappeared, and Gail found herself spending much more time with her mother.

2. *Reaction.* The initial reaction to the trouble in the relationship may be conscious or unconscious—like a reflex. Regardless of whether

there is awareness, one or both members in the relationship react to the trouble, either constructively or destructively. Jane's reaction was to take up the slack and not to express her resentment. Peter's reaction was to be closed-mouthed with his wife and to spend more time with his friends in order to avoid the tension at home. Alternatively, Gail's reflex was to rush to her mother's side, spending more time with her than she really felt comfortable with.

3. *Information Gathering.* Information Gathering pertaining to the trouble can take the form of talking to each other or to people outside the relationship about their ideas of what the problem is. You may search your memory for similar experiences to confirm or deny ideas you have about what is causing the trouble. Depending on the idea you have about what is wrong, you might also read books like this one or seek professional advice. For example, Peter asked his friend who had a two year old if his wife had also been less interested in sex since the birth of their child. His friend told him that it was the same for them, but it eventually passed once the baby started sleeping through the night.

4. *Problem Solving.* Here, the information gathered is used to develop a new plan of action, which leads to a less automatic and more conscious response to the trouble. The members of the relationship may work on the problem together or separately. If the plan of action was based on the wrong problem (e.g., Peter's thinking his wife was simply exhausted), this stage will result in ineffective problem solving. If the cause of the trouble was correctly identified as depression, this stage results in an effective resolution to the trouble in the relationship. Gail eventually realized that her mother was clinically depressed and that she could not handle the situation alone. After sharing her concerns with her mother, together they decided to seek professional help.

In the chapters that follow, we will help you to identify when someone you know is depressed and even the type of depression they have. You will learn how to recognize your reactions to the "trouble" and how to build on your constructive reactions while redirecting your maladaptive efforts. We will provide you with specific guidelines to help you move through the SAD effectively. By following these guidelines, you and the depressed person you care about will learn how to interact with each other more effectively, reduce tension in the relationship, and seek appropriate treatment for the depression.

Using examples like those of Jane, Peter, and Gail, we will teach you how to use eight guidelines for your relationship with a depressed loved one:

1. Learn all that you can.
2. Have realistic expectations.
3. Give unqualified support.
4. Keep your routine.
5. Express your feelings.
6. Don't take it personally.
7. Ask for help.
8. Work as a team.

These guidelines will be most helpful during the Information and Problem-Solving stages. By remembering these guidelines and the SAD, you will be able to influence your trip through these stages. In brief, we will teach you how to learn all that you can about depression and its treatment; how to have realistic expectations about what you and the depressed person can do about the depression; how to give and ask for unqualified support; how to keep your routine despite feelings of guilt and fear; how to express your feelings to the depressed person; how not to take the depressed person's symptoms and reactions to the illness personally; how and where to ask for help; and perhaps most importantly, how to work as a team against the depression rather than as adversaries working at odds with one another.

Learn All That You Can

Let us return briefly to the examples given at the outset of this chapter to introduce you to the first guideline: Learn all you can. Chapter 2 gives detailed information that will help you to identify the various symptoms and syndromes of depression. There is, however, another important source of information about depression that you may not have considered. We like to think of it as an early warning sign, or an alarm of sorts that you can use to check out if the trouble in the relationship is due to depression. This early warning sign consists of your *feelings* and *reactions* to the trouble in the relationship.

If someone you care about is depressed, you will likely experience a wide range of emotions and reactions—from anger to grief, from withdrawal to critical statements like, "You just need to stop feeling sorry for yourself!" You are not alone in your thoughts and feelings about your loved one. Everyone who cares about a depressed person goes through some or all of the common feelings and reactions. They are absolutely normal and should be expected. You might be wondering whether we are saying it is normal for Gail to be angry at her elderly mother who is so depressed she wants to die. And are we suggesting that Gail should tell her mother she is angry or perhaps stop visiting? If Gail's situation were slightly different, we would not dream of suggesting she be that insensitive. Good social graces, if nothing else, require us to put aside our own needs and be sympathetic and helpful when someone is down. Indeed, if Gail's mother had been down for only a few days or even a week, then the situation would not warrant such blunt honesty. But in fact she had been feeling this way for almost a month, with no end to her suffering in sight. Because depression involves a lasting disturbance of mood, Gail and her mother were not just dealing with the everyday ups and downs that most people have. In fact, Gail normally did not feel burdened by her mother; they had a good relationship, and she loved her mother's company. The fact that she was now feeling overburdened and resentful was important information, but she was ignoring it. By not paying more attention to her feelings, Gail was slow to recognize that something unusual was going on and slow to get help for her mother and for herself.

Reactions to Watch For

Common reactions to a depressed person can run the gamut from the extreme of overfunctioning to help out to the other extreme of withdrawing and avoiding the depressed person. Gail's initial reaction was to overcompensate and travel hours each week to try and cheer up her mother. Jane was taking on some of her husband's usual responsibilities because they seemed too much for him. Peter did not want to upset his wife further, so he withdrew to avoid talking to her or initiating sex. In addition to these examples, there are a whole myriad of other common reactions. One natural reaction is to attempt to enliven the depressed person by suggesting or insisting that she be more active. One man had his depressed wife's social calendar so full that the two of them had no time to be alone or to simply unwind. He admitted that it was his way of "keeping her going." He believed that if she stayed home, she would "wallow in her sadness" and never feel better. Another typical reaction, which may seem counterintuitive at first, is to pick a fight with the depressed person. Some of us who are upset by our loved one's withdrawal and disinterest when she is depressed will find ourselves starting an argument just to get a rise out of her. So although these reactions differ widely, there is a common thread: They are all attempts, albeit often ineffective ones, to make the depressed person feel better.

Feelings to Listen To

The common feelings that trigger our reactions when someone is depressed also range from one extreme to the other. When someone first becomes depressed, you may be confused by the changes. As the depression continues, you may feel sad about the loss of the person's usual enthusiasm or interest, lonely or alienated from her, and probably helpless in your ability to make her feel better. And along with that sense of helplessness, you may feel frustrated and angry at the person for not snapping out of it, as well as guilty for having such feelings. Many family members of depressed patients tell us that they feel a whole range of feelings that can change quickly from one moment to the next. In our examples, Jane feels angry, Peter feels sad, and Gail feels worried and guilty. You may notice that your own feelings can shift very quickly, from sympathy for your loved one's sadness, to resentment that she will not join a social activity that you were looking forward to.

The feelings and reactions we described can be early warning signs of depression in a relationship. For example, Gail feels worried, and her worry propels her to drive to her mother's house each afternoon to check on her. Gail jumped to the conclusion that her mother was simply lonely and that she could help her best by keeping her company. Peter's frustration and worry account for his avoidance in talking to his wife about their relationship. He wrongly concluded that she needed to be left alone. If early on Gail had spoken to her mother about her feelings, and Peter to his wife, they could have begun a constructive dialogue resulting in recognizing that depression was at the root of the trouble in their relationship. They would have gotten the information they needed to meet each other's needs. By jumping to conclusions about what was going on and reacting without consulting with the other person in the relationship, Jane, Peter, and Gail delayed their recognition of the depression and ultimately delayed their entering into an effective Problem-Solving stage. Instead, they were stuck in the Reaction and Information-Gathering stages, assuming they knew what the trouble was about and how best to respond to it.

When Gail ultimately spoke to her mother about her resentment and worry in a constructive manner, her mother told her that she understood it was too much of a strain and that she need not bother coming anymore. Realizing that something very out of the ordinary was going on—her mother had *never* told her to stay away—she asked her mother about this statement. The two of them actually laughed together as they discussed this because the feelings and comment were so uncharacteristic of Gail's mother. Following this talk, Gail began to realize that what was happening was truly extraordinary and started her campaign to convince her mother to see a mental health professional for advice. In other words, she realized that it was unrealistic for her to expect that she could make her mother feel better by visiting more frequently. By recognizing her anger and worry and by talking to her mother about what she was feeling, Gail and her mother were able to get things pointed in the right direction. Gail realized her own limitations and in the end convinced her mother to see a psychiatrist. After three weeks on an antidepressant medication, Gail reported, with great relief, that her mother was back to her old self.

As you confront the possibility of depression in a loved one, learn all that you can to recognize it more quickly. Listen more closely to your feelings, become alert to dramatic shifts in your relationship, and be willing to discuss your feelings constructively. Because constructive communication is the key to successful negotiation of the SAD, we discuss it throughout this book and devote all of Chapter 7 to it. Of course, not all shifts or trouble in relationships are a consequence of depression. Nevertheless, certain changes can alert you to consider that depression may be responsible for the trouble. In the next chapter, we will tell you how to identify whether depression is the culprit at the root of the trouble.

2

How to Recognize If Someone You Love Is Depressed

William, a forty-two-year-old retail store employee, is married and has three young children. Over the past couple of months, William's wife and coworkers have noticed changes in his behavior. He was recently promoted from salesman to general manager of the store and put in the position of supervising coworkers with whom he has worked for years. Until this promotion, his coworkers had always considered him to be fair and easygoing. Soon after the promotion, however, they noticed that he was much more irritable and demanding.

When a salesman made a common billing error, William flared up at him and demanded that he work overtime to make up for the mistake. When a clerk called in sick, William questioned whether she was really ill and grumbled about how the store would be short staffed. In addition, William began arriving later and later at work each morning and did not seem as involved in the store. Rather than actively participating in the weekly staff meetings as he used to, he was withdrawn and forgot important details about a new shipment. When a coworker commented that he "wasn't acting like himself," William retorted, "Get off my case. I'm just tired. You don't know what it's like to have all my responsibilities!" Behind his back, the staff gossiped about how William's promotion had gone to his head. Some thought his new position revealed his "true" personality, and others wondered if William was worried about a medical problem. Most of the staff steered clear of him rather than risk confronting his anger and impatience, but several tried to reason with him to be "fair." William, however, refused to discuss his management decisions and began to spend more time in the back office alone.

At home, William was even more intolerant and irritable. He had always been easygoing with his wife and children but now began overreacting to everything. One morning, seemingly out of the blue, he angrily complained to his wife, Karen, "Your disorganization is driving me crazy!" and he stomped out of the house. Karen also noticed that William had been coming to bed much later than usual and was not interested in having sex with her. Initially, Karen wondered if William was upset about his new responsibilities at work. She tried to talk to him about the store, but he insisted that "everything would be fine if you'd stop making mountains out of molehills" and cut the conversation short by picking up the newspaper. Later that week, she noticed that when the children were around, he seemed even more disgruntled. Trying to come up with ways to help him feel better, she arranged for them to stay at her mother's and prepared a special dinner. Her anticipation of a romantic evening turned to disappointment when William arrived home, announced that he was not hungry, and escaped to the family room to watch television. That night she noticed that William's "spare tire" had disappeared, and he was looking thinner than he had been since before they were married.

Karen was baffled. Why was William behaving so differently, and why was he so uncommunicative? She had never seen him like this before. She felt that he was not attracted to her and that he had become increasingly uninterested in spending time with her or the children. She began to suspect that he might be having an affair. What else could explain his new behavior? With fears of his infidelity weighing heavily on her mind, she started to keep close tabs on William's comings and goings. He responded to her increased attention with irritation and ordered her to "stop being my watchdog." Although Karen did not discover any evidence of another woman, she fretted about the state of their marriage. As the weeks passed, Karen found herself becoming more irritable with William, and they argued more frequently. Although she continued to wonder about what was bothering William, she couldn't help but feel resentful that he was so difficult to live with.

Although neither Karen nor William's coworkers initially recognized it, William was depressed. His attitude and behavior had changed markedly over the course of a couple of months. His recent promotion may have contributed to his depression, but the promotion alone could not account for the kind of changes those close to him had noticed. William's withdrawal, irritability, loss of interest in his usual activities, and decreased appetite and sex drive are all symptoms of depression. Even if William was not experiencing depressed mood, these symptoms are enough for him to meet criteria for a diagnosis of depression. Nobody close to William considered that he might be depressed. Rather, they attributed the changes in their relationships with William to other factors, such as his recent promotion or the possibility that he was having an extramarital affair.

What neither Karen nor his coworkers knew was that William had been depressed twice before many years ago and probably had a biological vulnerability to become depressed under extreme stress. When he was in college and his parents had divorced, William had gone through a fairly severe depression. Later, when a serious romantic relationship ended, William suffered from another period of feeling down and unmotivated. William never thought of these two periods of sadness as anything other than a natural reaction to painful events. The recent promotion, which brought with it the added stress of more responsibility, combined with his tendency to become depressed under stress, probably accounted for the development of the current depression.

How Relationships Adapt to Depression

Returning to the SAD introduced in Chapter 1, we can identify how both Karen and William's coworkers moved through the various stages of Trouble, Reaction, and Information Gathering, without recognizing that William was depressed and ultimately without getting to the Problem-Solving phase. To illustrate how your relationship is adapting to the depression of a loved one, we will point out how William and those close to him got sidetracked as they moved through the SAD and how they could have improved their adaptation to the changes that they noticed.

Generally, the Trouble stage involves an observation that there is friction in the relationship. William's coworkers noticed his irritability and impatience with mistakes. Karen witnessed even more changes in her relationship with William; he was intolerant, detached from her and the children, and uninterested in their sex life.

If you have picked up this book, chances are that you and the person you are concerned about have already entered the Trouble stage. Like Karen, you may have noticed that the person is more distant or difficult to get along with. However, unlike Karen, you have suspected that the trouble in your relationship is related to depression. You are already one step ahead of the game in that you have considered depression as the culprit and want to learn more about it to protect you and your loved one from further harm. Not everyone recognizes the depression during the Trouble stage.

During the Reaction stage, Karen tried talking to William about what was upsetting him but then quickly jumped to conclusions when she was unsuccessful. In an attempt to lessen the distance between them, Karen made a romantic dinner for William. William's coworkers had different reactions. One salesman asked him what was wrong, while others tried to reason with him when he was impatient. These kinds of efforts are typical reactions to trouble in a relationship. When we are not getting along with someone, we naturally try to interact and resolve the differences. Karen and William's coworkers ran into difficulty when William was not responsive; he did not come out and say that he felt depressed. Very often we have to ask specific questions in order to determine if someone is depressed.

During the Information stage, the people close to William tested out different hypotheses about what was bothering him. They tried to educate themselves about what might account for the trouble in their relationships with William. Some of his coworkers gossiped and wondered if William had an overblown ego about his promotion. Others wondered if he was distracted by medical problems and watched to see if he took medication at work or spoke on the telephone to his doctor. Karen, suspecting that William was unhappy in their relationship, looked for clues of an affair. Because they lacked education about the signs and symptoms of depression, nobody close to William considered that he was depressed. Only by educating themselves with some basic information about depression would they have been able to identify what was going on with William.

Problem Solving is the final stage in a relationship's adaptation to depression. Neither Karen nor William's coworkers made it here. Effective problem solving would include seeking treatment for the depression and supporting the depressed person in specific ways designed to reduce the level of conflict in the relationship. In the chapters that follow, we provide specific advice about how to problem-solve effectively in a variety of different situations. But in many relationships, problem solving can be ineffective, particularly when appropriate knowledge about the problem is missing. Because Karen and William's coworkers did not have enough information about William's problems, they were not able to help him feel better or help themselves cope with the changes in his behavior. In addition, because they were acting on the wrong information, their actions served to raise the level of conflict in the relationship. We believe that only through a clear understanding of depression and its effects on relationships can you begin to cope with your loved one's depression. For that reason, although the rest of this book is aimed at helping you and your loved one work together against the depression, this chapter focuses on information you will need to identify whether your loved one is depressed.

In retrospect, although Karen and William's coworkers initially handled the first two stages of Trouble and Reaction with William adaptively (noticing the trouble and trying to talk about it), they reached a roadblock in the Information-Gathering stage. If they had been educated about depression, they would have recognized William's increased irritability, moodiness, difficulty sleeping, decreased appetite, weight loss, and lack of interest in usual activities as hallmarks of clinical depression. Without this recognition, they could not even begin to help him overcome the depression.

This is not an uncommon situation. Often when a loved one begins to act differently, we search for possible explanations, but clinical depression is not usually something we consider because we don't know enough about it or don't want to believe that someone we love is depressed. We might consider outside stressors, such as work or conflicts in the extended family. We wonder about medical illness. And many of us speculate about whether the person we care about is angry or dissatisfied in their relationship with us. In our practices, relatives and friends of depressed patients often tell us that they did not consider depression initially because the person did not "seem down enough" or "wasn't crying all the time." Some even report that until the person was diagnosed with depression, they thought depression was reserved for "crazy" mental patients or people who were suicidal. In fact, depression can take many different forms, with many different kinds of changes in personality and behavior. The good news is that once correctly diagnosed, depression can almost always be treated effectively.

That clinical depression can take on many different faces often makes it difficult to recognize. One of the problems is that the symptoms can intensify slowly so that the changes are not always immediately obvious. When we talk about the syndrome of clinical depression, we usually mean a group of symptoms that typically develop over several weeks. Your feelings and reactions are important tools that you can use to recognize such changes and identify the telltale signs of clinical depression.

What Is Depression?

The word *depression* can mean very different things to different people. In daily conversation, many of us say "I feel depressed" to describe everyday blues that come and go. These transient blues, also known as *dysphoric mood states*, are not what mental health professionals mean by the word *depression*. Clinical depression refers to a constellation of signs and symptoms that significantly affect a person's functioning and last for a substantial amount of time. Sadness is a natural reaction to common problems such as the end of a relationship, a disappointment about a job failure, or a conflict that cannot be resolved. All of us go through periods of dysphoric mood with some temporary symptoms of depression, but we usually continue to function normally and recover without treatment. A true depression lasts longer, usually has more extreme symptoms, and most often requires treatment to subside. It affects feelings, thoughts, behavior, and physical functioning.

It can be hard to identify this disorder because all of the symptoms occur periodically in just about everyone, and there are no definitive diagnostic tests. Although many studies report that one out of five patients who go to the doctor are seriously depressed, it often goes undiagnosed. The National Depressive Foundation reports that two out of three people with mood disorders such as depression do not get proper treatment because their symptoms are not recognized or are misdiagnosed. Depression can often be hidden or masked, by either the patient or family members, because it is hard to identify and often painful for people to admit that something is wrong.

Another problem in diagnosing depression is that it often goes hand in hand with other mental and physical illnesses. If someone is complaining of a physical problem, the depression may be overlooked. It has long been known that depression can co-occur with ailments such as heart conditions, cancer, and stroke. For years, physicians thought it was understandable that patients would feel down or stressed from their physical condition but did not see depression as something that needed treatment. Recently doctors have begun to realize that physically ill patients may also be clinically depressed. Studies have shown that there is a diagnosable depression in 50 percent of patients hospitalized after having a stroke, 15 to 20 percent of patients suffering heart attacks, and 8.5 to 27 percent of diabetic patients. The current thinking is that the depression needs to be treated as a separate condition because it is a real illness and can impair a patient's recovery and rehabilitation from the physical condition. Most mental health professionals insist on a medical checkup to rule out any physical conditions that could mimic or contribute to a depression. In turn, more and more physicians are becoming aware of the problem of depression and will assess for depression when doing a full medical workup.

At Karen's insistence, William finally went to the family doctor and complained of fatigue and difficulty concentrating. His doctor ordered some lab tests and prescribed vitamins and more rest but did not detect the depression. Part of this doctor's problem in correctly diagnosing William's difficulties as depression might have been that William did not identify himself as depressed. He may have recognized that he "wasn't himself," but the notion of being depressed did not occur to him, or if it did, he quickly dismissed it. For many people, admitting to being depressed may be akin to admitting that they are crazy or weak. Denial is particularly common in people who, like William, believe that they should keep their personal problems private. Not being able to snap out of the blues and acknowledging the need for help are particularly difficult for those who pride themselves on being self-sufficient and capable.

Family members or friends may not want to confront the fact that a loved one is depressed and may desperately look for other explanations for the changes in their relative's behavior. One man whose wife was depressed was convinced that if he could only make more money, his wife would not feel so bad. After he got a new job and began to earn significantly more yet his wife's symptoms persisted, he began to consider depression. He later admitted that he had avoided thinking about depression because he worried about what family members and friends would think about his wife's having a "mental illness." Unfortunately, psychiatric diagnoses still have a social stigma, and many people are not aware of how common and treatable depression is.

Of all psychiatric illnesses, depression is the most responsive to treatment. When properly treated, 80 to 90 percent of people with depression can be cured. Most of the other 10 to 20 percent achieve some reduction in their depressive symptoms. There is clearly hope for depression, but unfortunately, one of the major obstacles in treating depression is that it is often overlooked or ignored. Only by recognizing and acknowledging that someone you love is depressed can you begin to learn more about this complicated disorder and help both yourself and the person you care about.

What Causes Depression?

When we learn that someone we love is depressed, our immediate response is to wonder why. What caused it? Is it genetic? Is it something I did? All of these questions are natural. Fortunately, there has been a great deal of research devoted to the causes of depression over the past two decades.

Although the exact mechanism or mechanisms responsible for depression have not been isolated and controversy remains about whether biochemical or psychosocial factors are more significant causes, most mental health professionals now agree that usually a number of factors, both biochemical and psychological, work together to trigger a depression. Some people, because of their biochemical and genetic makeup, are inherently more vulnerable to depression when they experience life stress than other people who face the same stressors. (We return to the idea of biochemical versus psychological factors in our discussion of psychological and medical treatments for depression in Chapters 12 and 13.)

Depression has been linked to the improper functioning of certain neurotransmitters in the brain. Neurotransmitters are chemical messengers that transmit electrical signals from one nerve cell to another and ultimately control behaviors, thoughts, and feelings. A deficit of two particular neurotransmitters, serotonin and norepinephrine, is thought to be associated with depressive symptoms, although many other neurotransmitters, such as dopamine, are being studied and may play key roles in the development of depression. Other researchers have suggested that people who experience depression may have endocrine abnormalities. The endocrine system controls the production and functioning of the body's hormones. Some studies have linked depression to hypothyroidism, the reduced functioning of the thyroid gland.

Genetic studies have indicated that these kinds of biochemical difficulties may run in families. Families with an unusually high incidence of depression have led researchers to conclude that there is a genetic predisposition to depression, especially when depression recurs over many years. If one identical twin suffers from depression, there is a 70 to 80 percent chance that the other twin will also suffer from depression sometime during his life. Nonidentical twins, siblings, and parents or children of a person with depression run a risk of about 25 percent. Since identical twins have all their genes in common, the higher rates suggest a strong genetic factor. According to the American Psychiatric Association, depression occurs one to three times more often among those with a first-degree relative (parent, sibling, or child) affected with the disorder than among the general population. In studies of families in which several members were adopted, researchers have demonstrated that the genetic factors are more important than environmental factors in predicting depression. In other words, a genetic vulnerability plays a bigger role in the development of depression than do psychological stressors.

But what about stress? Recent research has shown that genetics is only one factor in causing depression. Among other factors, recent stress—

such as divorce, illness, or a death in the family—can trigger a depression in those who are genetically vulnerable to it. Stressors that contribute to depression tend to be major life events rather than more trivial and common annoyances like the rush hour commute. Even positive life events, such as William's promotion, can be factors in depression. All life changes, positive and negative, involve changes, and changes bring about stress. For a person who has a biochemical susceptibility to become depressed, a major life event can precipitate a depression. Other psychosocial factors that have been found to be linked to depression include a lack of social support, feelings of isolation, and belief that one is helpless. Yet in a significant number of cases, depression comes on suddenly, with no apparent stressor. Experts believe that depressions without a psychosocial stressor have a stronger biochemical component that triggered the depression, even without a stressful life event.

Is Someone You Love Depressed?

So how do you know if your loved one is depressed? First, it is important to recognize that depression can affect many aspects of personality, including mood, thinking, and attitude towards others. It also affects bodily functions, such as sleep patterns, energy, sex drive, and appetite. Most people exhibit disturbances in these areas from time to time, but having a particular combination of symptoms over a significant amount of time warrants a diagnosis of depression. Mental health professionals use specific criteria from the *Diagnostic and Statistical Manual of Mental Disorders*, fourth edition (DSM-IV), published by the American Psychiatric Association (1994), to make the diagnosis:

DSM-IV Criteria for Major Depressive Disorder

1. Depressed mood most of day, nearly every day, as indicated by either subjective report (e.g., feels sad or empty) or observation made by others (e.g., appears tearful),

and/or

2. Anhedonia (i.e., markedly diminished interest or pleasure) in all, or almost all, activities most of the day, nearly every day.

and four of the following symptoms:

1. Significant weight loss (± 10 pounds in a two-week period) when not dieting or significant weight gain, or decrease or increase in appetite nearly every day.
2. Difficulty falling asleep or staying asleep or sleeping too much nearly every day.
3. Being either restless or slowed down more than usual nearly every day.
4. Fatigue or loss of energy nearly every day.
5. Feelings of worthlessness or excessive or inappropriate guilt nearly every day.
6. Diminished ability to think or concentrate, or indecisiveness, nearly every day.
7. Recurrent thoughts of death, recurrent suicidal ideas, or a suicide attempt or a specific plan for committing suicide.

To qualify for a diagnosis of depression, a person must have either depressed mood or anhedonia (a loss of interest or pleasure in usual activities) and also have at least four other symptoms from the list for the same two-week period. In other words, a total of at least five symptoms, one of which must be either depressed mood or anhedonia, are necessary to make the diagnosis. The two-week period during which the symptoms exist must represent a change from the person's previous functioning and cause significant distress or impairment in social or occupational functioning. In addition, depression is not diagnosed if the symptoms are due to a medical condition or occur immediately after the loss of a loved one. When someone dies, a period of mourning, with many of the symptoms of depression, is normal. If the symptoms persist for longer than two months and are severe enough, a diagnosis of clinical depression should be considered.

We can use the DSM-IV criteria to make sense of William's behavior changes. Is he depressed? In general, mental health professionals will interview a patient directly and ask him specific questions about his mood, sleeping and eating patterns, and suicidal ideas, as well as personal and family history of mood disorders. They may ask family members or close friends what changes they have noticed in the patient. We do not have William's firsthand account of how he has been feeling, but we can try to identify whether he is depressed on the basis of what his wife and coworkers have noticed during the Trouble and Reaction stages. First, William appears to have a markedly diminished interest or pleasure in his usual activities, both at work and at home with his wife and children. Thus, he meets the first criterion for depression. He also has four additional symptoms that qualify him for a diagnosis of depression: His appetite is decreased, he has lost weight, he is having difficulty sleeping, and he is more fatigued than usual and is having difficulty concentrating at work. So, even without knowing how William would describe how he feels (e.g., feeling worthless, thinking about suicide), we can postulate that William is indeed depressed.

At this point, although we think that William is depressed based on the DSM-IV criteria, it would still be important for him to be evaluated by a qualified mental health professional to make an accurate diagnosis of depression and refer him for appropriate treatment. A diagnosis is made after a careful history of present symptoms, past symptoms, family history, observations of the professional, reports of family members, and a medical checkup. Sometimes the diagnosis might not be as clear-cut as in William's case and require more observation. If you have noticed that the person you care about is experiencing three or more of the symptoms of depression for at least a two-week period, especially either of the first two symptoms on the list, he should be evaluated for depression as soon as possible by a mental health professional.

If your loved one is having suicidal thoughts or has made a suicide attempt, it is even more critical that he been seen right away. In a crisis, always take him to a hospital emergency room for immediate attention. Suicide is a real and potentially fatal aspect of depression that cannot be overlooked. We will return to a more in-depth discussion of suicide in Chapter 11. You will be given both specific advice about how to recognize the warning signs of suicide in your loved one and guidelines about how to cope with suicidal ideas and/or threats.

The Many Different Faces of Depression

If the person you care about does not exactly match William's description, that does not mean he or she is not depressed. Depression can take on many different faces depending on a number of factors, ranging from the type of depressive disorder to the gender, age, and personality style of the person. Numerous subtypes have been identified in the research literature, based on differences in severity, symptoms, and responsiveness to different treatments. Professionals sometimes use different terms to describe them depending on who they are talking to, and many of the terms are overlapping: The category of mood disorders in the DSM-IV includes unipolar depression, bipolar depression, dysthymia, seasonal affective disorder, atypical depression, psychotic depression, and postpartum depression. The chart shown provides an overview of the different subtypes, with the most notable characteristics of each one. In the subsequent sections of this chapter, we discuss each of these subtypes in detail, giving you specific warning signs to look for in recognizing if someone you love is depressed.

The three most prevalent types are unipolar (also known as major) depression, bipolar (also known as manic) depression, and dysthymia. These different types of depression can look very different, with particular symptoms and distinct complaints. Before delving into the less common subtypes of depression, the following examples will illustrate these three major types of mood disorder. Because the specifics vary so much, you may question whether all of these people are suffering from the same illness. Yet each case illustrates one of the many different faces of depression.

Unipolar Depression

William, in our example at the beginning of this chapter, has a fairly typical case of what clinicians usually call *unipolar depression*—the type described by the DSM-IV criteria for major depression. Professionals also refer to it as *major depression* or *clinical depression*. Unipolar, meaning "one pole," reflects the fact that people who suffer from this disorder feel down (in bipolar depression, people experience both depressive and manic episodes at different points in time).

William, who recently was promoted at work, began to act differently in his relationships with both his coworkers and his wife, Karen. Those around him noticed trouble in their relationship with him and reacted to that trouble. William had experienced two previous depres-

Characteristics of the Different Subtypes of Depression

Unipolar depression. Depressed mood and/or markedly diminished interest as well as four other symptoms (e.g., sleep and appetite changes, loss of energy, feelings of worthlessness, and excessive guilt) for at least two weeks. Also known as major depression or clinical depression, this is the most common type of depressive disorder, affecting over 15 million Americans.

Bipolar depression. Extreme mood swings, alternating from depression to mania. In the depressed phase, the symptoms are the same as those of unipolar depression. In the manic phase, the symptoms are almost completely opposite (e.g., elevated or expansive mood, inflated self-esteem, more talkative, and racing thoughts). This disorder affects 2 million Americans.

Atypical depression. Type of depression characterized by chronic depressed mood, overeating, oversleeping, and sensitivity to rejection. It is more difficult to treat than other subtypes of depression.

Dysthymia. Chronic depressed mood for at least two years, with less severe symptoms than unipolar depression and without a break free of symptoms for more than two months. It affects 3–4 percent of the population.

Seasonal affective disorder. The form of depression related to seasonal changes in sunlight and lasting about five months. Symptoms are usually those associated with atypical depression rather than those associated with unipolar depression. Some evidence indicates that treatment with light frequencies can help alleviate symptoms.

Psychotic depression. Depression with delusions or hallucinations, usually with morbid or sad themes. Only 15 percent of people with a unipolar or bipolar depression develop a psychotic depression, which needs immediate psychiatric attention.

Postpartum depression. Occurs in 10 percent of new mothers in the week to six months following delivery and can interfere with the mother's ability to care for her new baby. The symptoms are the same as in unipolar depression.

sions earlier in his life and probably had a biochemical vulnerability to get depressed under stress. The promotion, a positive life event, was nevertheless stressful because of its added responsibility and may have contributed to the development of the unipolar depression.

Unipolar depression is the most common type of depression. Epidemiological studies have shown that in any given month, 2.2 percent of Americans experience a unipolar depression. In a measure of lifetime prevalence, the National Institutes of Health (NIH) has estimated that some 15 to 18 million Americans experience a unipolar depression sometime in their lives. The risk of unipolar depression is twice as high in women as it is in men. (Gender differences may account for this disparity, and we discuss this topic more fully later in this chapter.) Regardless of gender, unipolar depressions are usually episodic; they last for a given period of time and can recur. Estimates are that more than half of the people who have had one unipolar depressive episode will have a recurrence, many within two or three years of their first episode. The risk of recurrence rises with the number of episodes, to 70 percent after two episodes and 90 percent after three episodes.

Bipolar (Manic) Depression

Gloria is a forty-eight-year-old woman who had a period of feeling down and lethargic for a few months last year. Currently she describes her state as "just wonderful." She has more energy than she has ever had, has been working sixteen hours a day on her first novel, and reports that she has brilliant ideas for a screenplay. Acquaintances at the gym are impressed with Gloria's liveliness and stamina, but Gloria's close friends sense trouble in their relationships with her and are worried that she is doing too much. One friend comments that it seems as if she is on "high speed" all the time. Her husband complains of not getting along with her as well as usual and says, "I can hardly understand her lately because she talks so fast and jumps from one idea to another."

Does Gloria have a mood disorder? Gloria, her husband, and close friends have certainly entered the Trouble stage of the SAD. Her husband and friends have noticed changes in her behavior that affect how they interact with her. If we compare Gloria's symptoms to those of the DSM-IV criteria for depression, she certainly does not appear depressed: She is feeling energetic and has no complaints. But Gloria is experiencing an element of one of the subtypes of depression: She is manic. Bipolar depression, also known as manic depression, involves extreme mood swings or poles, alternating from depression to mania. According to the NIH, almost 2 million Americans suffer from manic depression each year. Unlike unipolar depression, bipolar depression affects men and women in equal numbers. Given Gloria's history of feeling depressed last year and her current manic state, we can postulate that she has bipolar disorder. In a depressed phase, people with bipolar disorder meet the DSM-IV criteria for major depression. When they are in the manic phase, their symptoms are almost completely opposite. The symptoms can include elevated mood, hyperactivity, aggressive behavior, irritability, grandiose beliefs, and poor judgment.

DSM-IV Criteria for Manic Episode

All four of the following criteria are required to make a diagnosis of mania.

1. A distinct period of abnormally and persistently elevated, expansive, or irritable mood, lasting at least one week (or any duration if hospitalization is necessary).
2. During the period of mood disturbance, three or more of the following symptoms have persisted and have been present to a significant degree:
   - inflated self-esteem or grandiosity
   - decreased need for sleep (e.g., feels rested after only three hours of sleep)
   - more talkative than usual or seems pressured to keep talking
   - racing thoughts or jumping from one idea to another
   - distractibility
   - increase in goal-directed activity (either socially, at work or school, or sexually) or increased physical agitation
   - excessive involvement in pleasurable activities that have a high potential for painful consequences (e.g., foolish business investments)
3. The mood disturbance is severe enough to cause marked impairment in occupational functioning or in usual social activities or

relationships with others. May necessitate hospitalization to prevent harm to self or others.
4. The symptoms are not due to the direct physiological effects of a substance or a general medical condition.

Casual observers often describe a manic person as euphoric, cheerful, or infectious, but those who know the person well usually recognize the behavior as excessive. Someone in a manic state may go off on an impulsive shopping spree or believe he can become a famous artist, without any particular talent or expertise. Gloria's husband and close friends noticed that she was not acting like herself and began to worry about her extreme behavior. Gloria, however, felt great and was reluctant to seek treatment. She called her husband the "crazy" one if he thought she needed to see a doctor because she had never felt better.

Regardless of how the person subjectively feels, however, it is important to realize that mania can be dangerous. When people are manic, they tend to overlook the painful or harmful consequences of their behavior. They can run up huge credit card bills, empty savings accounts, make poor decisions, and be sexually promiscuous. Some people in a manic state become psychotic and have delusions. As Gloria became more manic, she began to report hearing aliens tell her that she had a special mission on earth to save the environment. To fulfill her mission, she ordered thousands of dollars worth of dirt and insisted on "spreading the dirt" all over the sidewalk in the center of her town.

Just as there are a lot of variations in unipolar depression, there are many variations in manic depression as well. Some people have repeated depressions and only occasional manic episodes. Others have more frequent manias or episodes of varying length and severity. If someone you know suffers from manic depression, you may be interested in some of the Recommended Readings on bipolar disorder and lithium listed at the end of this book.

Dysthymia

Keith, a thirty-seven-year-old architect, describes himself as "chronically blue and ill-humored." For the past four years, he has felt down most of the time and experienced major doubts about his professional worth. When he comes to therapy, he explains that he feels as if he has a "chronic low-grade emotional infection." He has noticed that he does not get along very well with other people and worries about the trouble in his relationship with his girlfriend. A friend of his who was depressed says that he was "cured by Prozac." Keith begins his first psychotherapy session by asking if he should also take Prozac but notes that he is not as depressed as his friend, who was unable even to get out of bed in the morning. Keith has been able to work, see friends, and even keep up with his gardening. He wonders if he is doomed to feel blue for the rest of his life or if he is just a pessimist.

Is Keith depressed? Although he does complain about some of the symptoms of unipolar depression, his symptoms are less severe and more chronic. Keith suffers from *dysthymia,* a chronic, low-level depression. Dysthymia is diagnosed when one experiences depressed mood for most of the day, more days than not, for at least two years without a break free of depressive symptoms of more than two months. During these periods of depressed mood, there are some of the following associated symptoms: poor appetite or overeating, insomnia or sleeping too much, low energy or fatigue, low self-esteem, poor concentration or difficulty making decisions, and feelings of hopelessness. According to the National Institute of Mental Health, dysthymia affects 3 to 4 percent of Americans, most of them women. If the people close to Keith had been knowledgeable about the symptoms of dysthymia, they may have been able to use their own feelings and reactions to the trouble in their relationships with Keith to help them recognize that he was depressed.

Other Subtypes of Depression

There are numerous other types of depression that you may have heard about. As with any other kind of complicated phenomenon, researchers and clinicians have tended to divide up depression in an effort to understand how to treat this disorder better. Although it is beyond the scope of this book to provide an exhaustive description of all the subtypes of depression, we will mention a few of the other widely recognized forms.

Seasonal affective disorder, or winter depression, is a form of depression believed to be related to seasonal changes in sunlight. People with seasonal affective disorder report that their depressions usually begin in the fall and lift dramatically in the spring. Researchers believe that the reduced sunlight in late autumn triggers a change in brain chemistry that leads to depression. The average seasonal affective disorder episode lasts five months and is much more severe than the usual winter doldrums. Some preliminary research evidence indicates that treatment with particular frequencies of light can help to alleviate the symptoms. The symptoms are usually much more like those associated with atypical depression, as opposed to those of the more common unipolar depression.

Atypical depression is characterized by symptoms that are almost the antithesis of many of the symptoms of major depression. While depressed people typically sleep less and eat less than normal, people with atypical depression tend to sleep more and overeat, gaining weight rapidly. Atypical depression is more chronic rather than episodic and usually begins in adolescence. People who suffer from this condition are especially sensitive to rejection. For unknown reasons, atypical depression is often harder to treat with antidepressant medications or psychotherapy than are other types of depression.

Psychotic depression is depression with delusions or hallucinations, usually with themes of sad or morbid content. For example, a person may have a delusion that he has killed someone and cannot be forgiven. Only 15 percent of people with major depression go on to develop psychotic depression. This kind of depression is associated with the largest risk for suicide because of the person's lack of touch with reality and unawareness of the consequences of his behavior. Anyone who shows any of the signs of psychotic depression needs immediate psychiatric attention.

Gender and Depression

Depression can vary by gender. We have noticed that when couples seek treatment for depression, often the woman in the relationship is depressed. In fact, although the number one complaint of couples seeking therapy is sexual difficulties, the underlying problem is often that the woman is depressed. Statistics on the incidence of depression indicate that women are twice as likely as men to experience major depression. Studies have found that in the general population, one in four women, as opposed to one in eight men, are likely to experience a mood disorder at some point in their lives. Nevertheless, a growing number of mental health professionals believe that men are depressed just as often as women but that the number of depressed men is under-reported. It may be that men in our society are raised to be independent and strong, making it more difficult for them to seek help or admit weakness. Instead they tend to keep their sad feelings inside or try to distract themselves from their depression. Depressed men often admit that they became "workaholic" during the time they were depressed in an attempt to push away the depression. Some men report other means of distracting themselves from their negative feelings. As a result, it can be difficult to figure out if your husband is depressed or a true workaholic. Try to look for changes from your loved one's usual way of behaving and relating to you.

In William's case, those close to him did not even think that he was depressed. He did not even think of himself as depressed. Rather, his coworkers said he had a "stuck-up" attitude or perhaps was dealing with a medical problem. His wife thought he was having problems at work or even having an affair. William's depression was hidden from everyone, including himself. Rather than seeking help directly or talking to his wife, he kept his feelings inside and tried to distract himself from his depression. More and more research has suggested that William is not unique.

In particular, a growing body of research suggests that men are more likely than women to turn to alcohol or drugs. Clinicians use the term *masked depression* to describe when a person uses alcohol to "treat" sad feelings. (In Chapter 10, we focus more closely on the depressed person's use of alcohol and drugs and set out specific guidelines about how to cope more effectively with your loved one's substance use.) Although self-medication of depression may be more common in men, depressed men and women can turn to alcohol or drugs.

Yet despite the clinical and research data that indicate that depression is underreported in men, most clinicians still believe that depression is more common in women. According to the American Psychological Association's (APA) 1990 Task Force on Women and Depression, women are more depressed because of their experience of being female in contemporary society. The task force cites a variety of biological, social, and psychological factors that affect women in our culture: the hormonal changes that occur with miscarriage, pregnancy, and even the use of birth control pills and the stress of money problems, violence, rape, and conflicts between professional roles and roles as wives and mothers. In the APA study, the stress factors linked to a greater risk of depression were bad marriages or relationships, the absence of a husband, social isolation, and being homebound with young children or elderly parents. Women who have more social support and more help with child care were found to be less likely to suffer from depression. Some theorists believe that women are more affected by relationship stresses because interpersonal relationships are more central to a woman's sense of self-esteem than they are to a man's sense of his self-worth. In other words, the way women are socialized to be concerned about relationships puts them at a greater risk for depression.

To increase your knowledge about gender and depression, we will discuss both postpartum depression and depression that is related to the menstrual cycle and menopause.

Postpartum Depression

Although as many as 80 percent of mothers experience some period of postpartum blues that lasts a few days, postpartum depression lasts longer and is more severe. It can occur following both planned and unplanned pregnancies, as well as after the birth of first or subsequent children. The symptoms can include crying for no apparent reason, having trouble sleeping, developing extreme changes in eating habits, suffering from anxiety attacks, and becoming either overly involved with or not interested at all in the baby. Often the new mother with postpartum depression worries that she is defective because she lacks normal maternal instincts. The new father may feel guilty for having caused his wife's distress or angry at her for not being more excited about their child. These symptoms usually develop between one week and six months after the birth. Although some of these symptoms may be present in normal "baby blues," if several of them last for more than a few weeks, it should be cause for concern.

Jill was a thirty-year-old woman who sought treatment three months after the birth of her first child. Since the baby was born, Jill had felt exhausted and overwhelmed. Her mother reassured her that "new mothers always feel tired and you just need to adjust to motherhood," yet Jill continued to feel sad and less interested in caring for the baby than she thought she ought to be. She was often tearful and irritable when her husband finally got home from work. Her guilt over not being more excited about being a mother continued to bother her, and she found herself picking fights with her husband. He, in turn, felt guilty for being at work all day and leaving Jill with full responsibility for the baby. At her next appointment with her obstetrician, Jill brought up her experience, and her doctor suggested that she see a therapist to determine if she was suffering from postpartum depression.

Postpartum depression can be incapacitating and interfere with a mother's ability to care for her new baby. If it is not treated, it can last for months or even years, and the long-term effects on the attachment between mother and baby and on the child's development can be severe. Many of the treatments for depression that we discuss in Chapters 12 and 13 can be effective in treating postpartum depression, and most mothers who get treatment show significant improvement within weeks. The problem is that postpartum depression is often misunderstood. Many women who suffer from it do not recognize their symptoms as an illness or do not know where to seek treatment. They often assume that they are "bad mothers" because they are not happier about the birth of their new baby.

Jill was wary of seeing a "shrink," but with encouragement from her husband, she reluctantly made an appointment. From her first session, it was clear that Jill was indeed suffering from postpartum depression. For several weeks before her therapy appointment, Jill blamed herself for not being able to snap out of her bad mood. She assumed that her sadness indicated that she did not love her child. Her husband also wondered if he was somehow letting her down by not being a more involved father, but her negativity was off-putting, and he found himself avoiding her by spending more time than usual at work. After psychotherapy and a course of antidepressant medication, Jill felt much more able to handle the adjustment to being a mother and said, "If I had only known what was happening to me, I would have felt so relieved." Her husband also reported feeling much less guilty after he understood that Jill was depressed. Once he did not feel so responsible for her sadness, he began to spend more time helping her take care of the baby.

In very rare cases, postpartum depression can develop into a more serious condition, *postpartum psychosis*. This occurs in only one or two out of 1,000 new mothers. The symptoms can be severe: hallucinations (seeing or hearing things that are not really there), delusions (running the range from believing that the baby is somehow possessed by evil spirits to worrying that someone is after the baby), suicidal thoughts, and attempts to harm the baby. A mother who is suffering from postpartum psychosis has great difficulty distinguishing between reality and fantasy. She requires immediate psychiatric care, for both her sake and the welfare of the baby.

Before much research was done in this area, most mental health professionals believed postpartum depression was caused by ambivalent or anxious feelings about being a new mother. As a result, many women felt guilty about their depression because it implied that they were unhappy about motherhood. Now, based on recent research, we know that postpartum depression is like other forms of depression and probably related to both psychological factors and biochemical factors. The hormonal changes that occur when a woman goes from pregnancy to the postpartum period probably make women more vulnerable to depression. And in women with a preexisting genetic or biochemical vulnerability to depression, the hormonal changes and demands of new motherhood increase the risk of depression even further. The results of recent studies have indicated that women who are depressed during pregnancy or have a history of depression are more likely to develop a mood disorder after childbirth. More research in the area of postpartum depression and how it relates to women's biological and social factors is needed, but what we do know is that it is treatable. Women with postpartum depression can go on to be loving and stable mothers.

Fathers too can suffer from a type of postpartum depression. A recent British study found that in a survey of 200 new fathers and mothers, 9 percent of the men reported a general feeling of sadness, worry, a loss of sex drive, or disturbed sleep for six weeks after their baby's birth. About 5 percent had symptoms that lasted for up to six months. It may be that new fathers are reacting to the changes in their relationship with their wives after the baby is born or that they also experience biochemical changes after the birth of a baby. Depression after the birth of a baby is not uncommon for both men and women and may require treatment just as depressions do at other points in life.

Many couples are tremendously relieved to know that the spouse is experiencing a treatable depression and not just having trouble with parenthood. If you think someone you love is suffering from postpartum depression, talk to her about seeking professional help. She may feel too overwhelmed with the new baby to seek treatment herself or may feel that such blues are to be expected and will pass. But if the symptoms persist for more than a few weeks, sit down with her and explain your concerns. If she understands that you are worried and want to help her, she may be more willing to get professional help. A loved one who shows any of the signs of postpartum psychosis needs immediate professional help, even if she is unwilling to go to the doctor.

Premenstrual Syndrome and Menopause

Other hormonal changes have also been linked to depression and can affect relationships. Many women are familiar with the depressed mood and irritability that accompany premenstrual syndrome (PMS). Women who are prone to PMS usually find that their mood symptoms worsen prior to the onset of menses. Some 3 to 5 percent of menstruating women experience a more severe cyclic mood disorder known as *premenstrual dysphoric disorder*. The symptoms are more extreme than the common PMS mood changes and usually last for a week or two around menstruation each month.

Research indicates that couples dealing with PMS or premenstrual dysphoric disorder exhibit increased friction during the time just prior to menses. Women with PMS are more easily annoyed, less patient, and more likely to respond in an angry manner than at other times during the month. Their loved ones find the premenstrual period trying because nothing they do seems to help. If you notice intermittent trouble in your relationship that worsens on a monthly cycle around your loved one's menstrual period, then the two of you may be dealing with PMS-related depression. Help, particularly antidepressant medication, might alleviate many of these hormonally triggered depressive symptoms.

Many people also associate menopause with mood fluctuations and especially with depression, although a growing number of researchers and clinicians argue that menopause generally does not lead to depression. They point out that many of the symptoms of menopause itself, such as difficulty sleeping and irritability, are easily confused with the signs of a clinical depression. Women who are going through menopause are often instructed to "bear with it" and expect the symptoms to pass in time. Only if depressive symptoms persist do these professionals recommend treatment.

On the other hand, many clinicians agree that menopause is related to depressive symptoms such as sadness, fits of crying, and extreme irritability. Menopause does involve significant hormonal changes, and some women may be prone to experience depressed mood during this period, just as some women are more sensitive to the hormonal changes during the premenstrual or postpartum period. Recent research has found that women with a history of depression (either hormonally related or not) are twice as likely to report depression during menopause. These women are also more likely to complain of menopausal symptoms, such as hot flashes, and to seek medical help.

Clearly, psychological factors can account for increased depression in middle-aged women. Many women understandably have a hard time accepting the loss of their reproductive abilities. In addition, many women are simultaneously coping for the first time with an empty nest, when their children grow up and leave home. One woman, whose youngest child had recently left home, talked about how barren and unproductive her life felt now. She felt as if her role in life had been taken from her. The loss of maternal role may help explain the association between menopause and depression. Some women may also experience a midlife crisis when they begin to look back over their personal and professional lives and regret decisions that they made.

If your loved one is going through menopause and experiencing depression, you should learn more about the association between reproductive factors and depression. (For suggestions on further reading, see the Recommended Reading section at the end of this book.)

Life Stages and Depression

The stage of life can also affect how depression appears. For example, depression took on very different faces in the following two patients. Jonathan, a five-year-old boy, was withdrawn and brooding, refusing to play with his peers. Adele, an elderly woman, was irritable, complained of difficulty sleeping, and reported that she had frequent thoughts about death. Although they had different symptoms to the outside observer, both Jonathan and Adele were depressed.

When trying to assess whether someone you care about is depressed, consider their stage in life. Children are less likely to display the typical signs associated with depression; they rarely complain of depressed mood. Instead, childhood depression is more often acted out through the child's behavior. Detecting whether your child is depressed requires special skill. Chapter 4 is devoted to recognizing childhood depression and teaches you specific skills so you can cope more effectively when your child is depressed.

Depression in the elderly may also look different from depression in young adulthood. It is widely recognized that older people in institutions, whether nursing homes or hospitals, are often severely depressed. The National Institute of Mental Health estimates that between 10 and 20 percent of the elderly have major depression. Often older people do not seek help for depression. It is often up to adult children to recognize that something is wrong. There are specific signs to look for in older adults that may help you identify whether someone you care about is depressed. Chapter 5 focuses more closely on this life stage and helps you to respond to a parent's depression.

Using the Trouble in Your Relationship to Identify Depression

To recognize if someone you know is depressed, we cannot stress enough the importance of paying attention to your own reactions to the trouble in your relationship. Because depression is such a complicated and varied illness, your observations and feelings can be early warning signs. If you are currently in the Trouble or Reaction stages of the SAD, try to think about what you have noticed, and use your reactions as a guide. For example, have you felt more angry than usual at your loved one? Do you feel lonely even when he is around? Have you felt as if he is more withdrawn than usual? Are you worried about him? Do you wish he'd snap out of it? Have you been less patient with him? All of these thoughts and feelings are common, natural reactions to the trouble in a relationship and could indicate that your loved one is depressed. We have often seen family members or friends of depressed people who ignored their own intuition that something was wrong. Only after the diagnosis was made do they realize that they overlooked important indicators that the person was depressed.

If you notice trouble in your relationship and suspect that your loved one is depressed, you are ready to move from the Trouble and Reaction phases of the SAD into the Information-Gathering phase. It is time to learn all you can about depression, its effects on your relationship, and ways to respond adaptively. Read the rest of this book, read this chapter again, or refer to some of the Recommended Readings listed in the back of the book. Using your own observations, try to determine whether your loved one is depressed. If you suspect that he is, seek an evaluation with a mental health professional. Chapter 14 provides advice about how to get help, for both your loved one and yourself. If someone you love is depressed, you need to ask for help too, from friends, family, or professionals. Remember not to overlook your own needs as you cope with a loved one's depression.

The questionnaire shown will help you to determine whether or not your loved one is depressed. It is based on the diagnostic criteria we discussed in this chapter. Although this questionnaire is designed to help you detect depression, remember that you should always seek the advice of a trained mental health professional for an actual diagnosis of depression. A mental health professional will use a wider range of information than is available to you to make a diagnosis.

In William and Karen's case, Karen told us that she had sensed that something was wrong but could not put her finger on it. After reading about depression in a magazine, she began to suspect that William was depressed. When her suspicion was later confirmed, she remarked, "I wished that I had known more about depression when all this started. Given the way *I* was feeling, the only possibility I could consider was that he was cheating on me!" Karen acknowledged having felt distant

Is Your Loved One Depressed?

Answer the following questions based on how your loved one has been doing in each of these areas **in the past two weeks.**

1. Yes No Does he/she complain of feeling "down," "blue," "sad," or "depressed," for much of the day, more days than not?

2. Yes No Does he/she seem significantly less interested in his/her usual activities?

3. Yes No Does he/she appear to take less pleasure in activities that are usually pleasurable?

4. Yes No Have you noticed any significant weight loss or gain, when he/she has not been dieting, or any decrease or increase in appetite?

5. Yes No Does he/she have difficulty falling asleep or staying asleep or sleeping too much?

6. Yes No Does he/she seem either restless or slowed down more than usual?

7. Yes No Does he/she seem to feel more fatigued or low on energy?

8. Yes No Does he/she appear to feel worthless or excessively guilty?

9. Yes No Does he/she have trouble thinking, concentrating, or making everyday decisions?

10. Yes No Does he/she express recurrent thoughts of death or suicide, have a plan to commit suicide, or made a recent suicide attempt?

Scoring
Count the number of times you circled YES to questions 4 through 10.

If you answered **YES to any of the first three questions,** use the following scoring key:

Definitely depressed
6 or 7   Your loved one is most likely seriously depressed and should seek immediate professional help if he/she is not already in treatment. He/she is exhibiting many of the key signs of major depression.

Probably depressed
4 or 5   Your loved one is probably depressed and should make an appointment to be evaluated for depression. You have noticed many of the signs of depression and need to consider that he/she may indeed be depressed.

(con't.)

Is Your Loved One Depressed? (con't.)

Possibly depressed
3 or less   Your loved one probably has a milder form of clinical depression and would benefit from seeing a mental health professional. He/she is experiencing several symptoms of depression and may be in the early stages of a major depression.

If you answered **NO to all of the first three questions**, use the following scoring key:

Possibly depressed
4 to 7   Your loved one may be depressed or in the early stages of developing a full-blown depression. He/she may be experiencing some symptoms that you have not yet detected.

Probably not depressed
2 or 3   Although your loved one may be experiencing some of the symptoms of depression, they are probably due to other causes. However, if you answered YES to question 10, you should stay alert to your loved one developing other signs of depression or a worsening of suicidal feelings.

No signs of depression
0 or 1   Chances are that your loved one is not depressed.

from William, angry at him, worried about him, and distrustful of him. Once she understood that her feelings were a natural response to depression in a loved one, she was able to acquire the information necessary to help William and herself. In the chapters to come, we will show you how to use your reactions to respond more quickly and effectively to the depression as you enter the Problem-Solving stage of the SAD.

3

When Your Partner Is Depressed

After six years of marriage, Joan and Eric noticed worrisome changes in their relationship. When they first met, they spent all their free time together and enjoyed an active and satisfying sex life. Despite some normal ups and downs, they both described the early years of their marriage as very happy. When one of them was having problems at work or with a friend, they knew that they could always turn to the other for loving support and advice.

They came to couples therapy, however, because of concerns about their compatibility. Eric said, "I don't know if we can work this out because Joan can't stop herself from nagging me about everything." Joan griped that "Eric has been so distant for the past few months that I am beginning to feel alone in this marriage." His complaint was that she wanted him to be more productive at his job and make more money but that she did not understand what he was going through. Recently he had been feeling depressed and unmotivated to do much of anything at work or around the house. Her constant badgering to "get up and do something" made him feel as if she did not care about his feelings. He had been depressed before and knew that he needed some time to get back to his "old self." Joan acknowledged that Eric had been feeling sad and understood that he was suffering from a depression, but she did not understand why he would not let her help him. She complained, "Whenever you get depressed, you push me away." She explained that she was trying to be a "good wife" by offering advice but that he was shutting her out and was not willing to accept her help.

In their first session, Joan and Eric reported that they were bickering constantly and had not had sex in weeks. Joan complained that Eric did not seem interested, always said he felt "too tired," and when they did have sex, he had difficulty maintaining an erection. He countered that she was too focused on sex to the exclusion of the rest of their relationship. Whenever they tried to talk, their discussions quickly escalated into shouting matches.

Bennett knew that his wife, Leslie, was depressed. Over the past several months, he had observed dramatic changes in her mood and behavior. They had been married for over twenty-five years, and he had never seen her so down and listless before. He figured that it would be hard when the last of their children went off to college, but he did not realize that Leslie would take the empty nest so hard. She had been moping around, mostly complaining about having nothing to do. Although Bennett was a traditional man who believed women belonged at home, he even suggested that Leslie take a course at the local college or get a part-time job. He was surprised at her response: "You just don't understand. I don't feel like it. I can barely get all my housework done now." He noticed that they talked to each other much less in the evenings than they used to, and when he tried to initiate sex, Leslie pushed him away with, "Why would you want to make love with an old bag like me?" and broke into tears, crying inconsolably. She did not believe him when he told her that he was still very attracted to her, and she refused to talk about it.

His concerns about her depression grew, but each time he tried to discuss it with her, she told him that he did not understand and to give her time to adjust to life without the children. But when Thanksgiving came around and their children came home from school, Bennett noticed that Leslie did not snap out of it as he thought she would. She spent most of the holiday weekend sitting quietly alone, withdrawn from everyone. Bennett wanted to suggest that Leslie get some help for depression but worried "how she would take it." If he suggested that she see a psychiatrist or psychologist, would it upset her and make her think that she was "crazy"? When he finally approached her, she was reluctant but agreed to learn more about depression and consider getting help.

If your partner is depressed, some of Joan and Eric's story or Bennett and Leslie's story may sound familiar. There can be different signs of trouble in the relationship. You may find yourself having less patience for his moods. Or you may feel helpless that you cannot help him feel better. You may find that you are fighting with each other more than usual or spending less time together. If this is the case, you need to understand what is unique about how depression affects couples. Then you need to learn how to problem-solve effectively and in collaboration with your loved one.

What Is Special About Being a Couple?

Almost all couple relationships—ranging from heterosexual to homosexual, from monogamous to sexually open, and from committed to casual—are more intimate than other relationships, both physically and emotionally. Many people express feelings with a partner that they do not reveal to other people in their life. In sex, partners experience physical closeness and a special kind of vulnerability with each other. Partners also tend to make a commitment to each other, whether it is a lifelong commitment of marriage or a more short-term commitment such as plans to go to a baseball game next week. Partners often share responsibilities too, for child care, food shopping, or even remembering relatives' birthdays. There are often unspoken agreements as to who is responsible for what. For example, although they had never explicitly divvied up responsibilites, Eric took care of the car tune-ups while Joan handled their social life. In Leslie and Bennett's relationship, she had always taken care of the house, and he was the breadwinner for the family.

Joining your life with someone in these ways makes a couple relationship special and makes the details of traveling through the SAD different from the typical pattern seen in other relationships. Given the closeness and intimacy of a partner relationship, all of the stages, from the initial Trouble stage to the eventual Problem-Solving stage, can be more intense. There is often a case of the *ripple effect* in couple relationships, that is, one aspect of the couple's relationship, such as their sex life, can ripple and have strong effects on the rest of their relationship. Whenever you are in a partner relationship, it is important to recognize how all the aspects of your relationship are intertwined.

We describe two subtypes of depression that are common in couple relationships and provide guidelines to assist you as you move through the SAD with your partner. Finally, we focus on sexual difficulties, a common problem in couples with a depressed member that often has a ripple effect on other aspects of the relationship.

How a Partner's Depression Affects You and Your Relationship

Changes in Roles

Researchers interested in the intimate relationships of depressed people have found that a partner's depression can have far-reaching effects on you and your lifestyle. Depression changes the underlying structure of your relationship. Couples often tell us that as one of them began to get depressed, their roles in the relationship shifted. For example, if you and your partner have always had a relatively equal relationship in terms of lending a sympathetic ear at the end of the day, you may find yourself becoming more and more the listener as your loved one sinks into a depression. Or if she typically handled the grocery shopping for the two of you, you may suddenly find yourself pushing a shopping cart on the evenings you used to relax at home.

Financial Changes

Depression can change your relationship not only in the time and energy needed to take care of your partner but also in financial terms. If your partner is too depressed to work, you may find yourself responsible for more of the household income. Many spouses of depressed people report having to get a job for the first time, or even holding down a second job, to compensate for the lost income. Additional child care costs or other services may be needed when a partner is depressed and can no longer keep up with usual activities. If your partner has bipolar disorder, you may also have to keep a careful watch over your joint finances to make sure that excessive spending is not a problem. One wife of a manic-depressive man told us that she monitored her husband's shopping sprees by calling their bank several times a week to check the balance of their savings account.

Changes in Routine

Your partner's depression may affect your routine and lifestyle in a myriad of ways. You may have less time to pay attention to other family members or take care of yourself. You may not be able to continue your usual activities, like working out at the gym or doing errands. If you are needed more at home, you may find yourself leaving your job earlier or coming in later. Bennett started calling home more frequently to check in on Leslie. When he was offered a business trip that would have been good for his career, he turned it down because he felt that he had to be near home for Leslie. He worried that she would feel more lonely and isolated if he were away, even for a couple of days.

Changes in Social Life

If your partner is not as interested in seeing friends, your social life will change too. Going out requires energy that your depressed partner may not be able to muster. Inviting friends over may not be possible because of your partner's irritability or withdrawal. Friends can pick up on the depression and avoid getting together with you. As you probably know, it can be hard to be around a sad person, and without their even consciously realizing it, friends may begin to make other plans that do not include the two of you. As a result, you may suddenly find yourself out of touch with many of the people you used to socialize with.

If you try to make plans for just you and your partner, you may have to postpone or cancel them if he is not feeling up to it. Joan complained that Eric spent night after night in front of the television when he was depressed, refusing to do anything she suggested. She felt angry that they did not "do anything together anymore." Eric's response was that Joan did not seem to understand that he had no interest in going out.

How These Changes Affect You and Your Relationship

These kinds of changes are a strain on even the healthiest and most well-adjusted relationships. Any issues that you had in your relationship before will become more pronounced when your partner is depressed. When one or both of you notice these new difficulties, you are in the Trouble phase of the SAD. Recent research into the relationship between social support and depression has found that having an intimate relationship can protect one from becoming depressed or help one to overcome depression more easily. Even more impressive research has shown that having a conflictual relationship with your partner can be worse than having no relationship at all. In other words, if your relationship with your partner is conflictual and difficult, it can worsen the depression. If not for yourself, then for your partner, pay close attention to the trouble in your relationship when your partner is depressed.

Joan and Eric admitted that their arguments had always centered on her being a more active person and having a more intense sex drive than Eric, but their different styles seemed even more exaggerated when he was depressed. Although they argued in the past on how to spend their free time, the fights had recently become much more frequent and extreme. Part of the problem is that like most other couples, Joan and Eric had established a pattern of resolving issues that more or less worked for them until Eric got depressed. When they argued in the past about what Joan called his "inertia," he would eventually agree to do something active, such as make plans with friends next week, and she would accept the compromise of staying home if plans were made for the near future. When Eric was depressed, however, he no longer offered to make such compromises, and their arguments would end in a stalemate rather than a resolution.

In the Reaction phase, both you and your partner experience reactions or responses to the trouble in your relationship. Perhaps your reactions to your partner change over the course of his depression. Initially, you probably will feel sympathy, and you honestly want him to feel better. Perhaps you feel as if you would do anything to make him happier. But as time goes on, you may begin to resent your partner's depression and the way it is affecting you. You feel angry, unloved, and maybe even depressed yourself as the depression becomes "contagious." Bennett admitted that he initially felt sympathetic with Leslie. He too missed their children and felt pangs of loss from their new empty nest status. However, as Leslie continued to be depressed and did not snap out of it, Bennett felt annoyed and angry at times. He wished that "things could be back to normal."

Although many of these same feelings and reactions can arise if a partner has a heart attack or a chronic illness, depression tends to be harder to confront because we feel angry about it, as though it is a willful or purposeful thing that a loved one does to us. We wonder whether our partner is "getting back" at us for some past wrongdoing. We also worry about what others will think if we reveal that our partner is depressed. Bennett avoided confiding in his close friends because he was embarrassed and feared that they would think Leslie was "a mental case."

Many of the misconceptions about depression come from a general ignorance about what depression is. Depression is not willful. Depression is not a way that someone gets back at us. And it does not mean that someone is crazy. Depression is a complicated and often serious emotional disorder that can almost always be treated effectively once it is recognized.

The first step is to recognize the trouble in your relationship and begin to monitor your own reactions to your partner. Then you will be in a better position to gather relevant information about what is going on with your loved one and work together with him to solve the problems. If you isolate yourself and do not work collaboratively with your partner, it is likely that your relationship will suffer from taking the same kind of wrong turns taken by Joan and Eric or Bennett and Leslie as they moved through the SAD.

How to Problem-Solve When Your Partner Is Depressed

Now that you know the details of how your partner's depression can affect you and your relationship, what can you do about it? Can you problem-solve in a more effective way? If you have read this far, you probably have already noticed trouble in your relationship. You and your partner have already had initial reactions to the trouble. You picked up this book, presumably to gather information about depression and its effect on your relationship. You have successfully navigated through the Trouble and Reaction phases and entered the Information-Gathering phase of the SAD. As you interact with your depressed partner, try to remind yourself of the following guidelines.

Have realistic expectations. Many of us with a partner who is depressed expect that we should be able to provide a remedy for the depression. If only we could make him laugh. If only she would get up and go out. But depression is a complicated and often serious emotional illness that cannot be cured overnight. Do not expect to alleviate it magically. Thinking that you can "cure" the depression is not realistic. Be patient and have sensible expectations for what you can and cannot do. Your partner's depression is not your fault, and although you can help him, you cannot make it go away. Only time and the proper treatment can do that.

Over the course of Leslie's treatment, Bennett struggled with his expectations for Leslie's recovery. First, he thought that he could cheer her up by suggesting that she find a part-time job or by planning a vacation. When that did not work, he thought that having the children home for Thanksgiving would make her feel better. Only after he learned more about depression and its treatments did he realize that neither he nor their children could cure the depression. Instead, he recognized that he could help her by being there for her and helping her get the proper treatment. His knowledge about depression enabled him to have much more realistic expectations about when she would recover. He learned that he had to tolerate not being able to "make it all better" for her.

Offer unqualified support. What your depressed partner needs more than anything is your unconditional love and support. He needs to know that despite his recent moodiness and irritability, you will be there for him during this period. You need to convey that you will work as a team to conquer the depression and that you do not blame him, or yourself, for what is happening. Despite all our best intentions, however, depressed people often turn down our offers of support. Like William or Leslie, they complain that we "don't understand" or are "nagging" them.

So how do you continue to offer unqualified support when your loved one is not accepting your help? It is difficult, but possible. Chapter 9 focuses exclusively on the issue of what to do when your help is turned away. The key strategies are to communicate to your loved one that you are there to help but not to come on too strong and not to take the rejection of your support personally. Joan complained that Eric always pushed her away when he was depressed. Through discussion in their couples therapy sessions, Joan learned that Eric's rejection was part of his depression and did not reflect his true feelings for her. She tried to continue to offer support to him but not bombard him with constant advice and suggestions. She also let him know how it made her feel when he would not accept her help. After these discussions, Eric recognized that Joan just wanted to help and was better able to listen to her suggestions without getting defensive.

Maintain your routine as much as possible. When your partner is depressed, try to maintain your regular routine as much as possible. Keep up with friends and do as many of your usual activities as you can to keep the depression from becoming contagious. Make time for yourself so that you are refreshed and better equipped to help your partner through his depression. Maintaining your usual patterns can be hard, especially when someone close to you is depressed for an extended period of time.

Bennett found that he was not keeping up with work when Leslie was depressed. It made sense to him that he turned down the business trip opportunity because he did not want to leave Leslie alone, but then he began to slack off on his other work responsibilities. His boss questioned his commitment to the business. In addition, Bennett gave up his weekly tennis game with his best friend. As time went on, he became anxious about work and felt out of shape from not playing tennis. His annoyance with Leslie grew, and he was less emotionally available for her. Once Leslie got into treatment for her depression, Bennett realized how much of his usual routine he had given up. He was able to get back on track with work and reestablish his weekly tennis game. Once he returned to his usual activities, Bennett felt better able to support Leslie and problem-solve with her rather than feel resentful for taking him away from his routine.

Share your feelings. It is absolutely imperative that you let your partner know how you feel. Communicating your feelings directly is the best way to avoid the kind of misunderstandings that arise when your partner is depressed. Many partners of depressed people feel as if it is not fair to burden their loved one with their own problems. Bennett worried that telling Leslie about his fears would only deepen her depression. He was wrong. Even when your partner is depressed, you need to let him know what you are thinking and feeling. Sharing your experiences is vital to the kind of collaborative dialogue with your partner that you need to solve problems together. Part of coping with having a depressed partner is learning to tolerate some of the negative feelings toward him. Being able to talk about these feelings makes that coping much easier.

There are better and worse ways to communicate. In general, let your partner know how you feel without attacking him or blaming him for the depression. You do not need to say things that will be hurtful as a way to "get back at him" for his depression. Be honest but sensitive to how your partner will hear what you say. For example, Joan usually told Eric how she felt by complaining about their "sexless marriage" and then chastising him for not "getting up and doing something" with himself. Eric became defensive and would counterattack by calling her a "nag" or walking away. In the course of couples therapy, they learned new communication strategies. Joan was able to tell Eric how she felt by saying, "When you aren't interested in sex, I feel as if I am unattractive" or "When you lie on the couch like this, I worry that you won't be there for me if I need you." Eric now reacted to these statements very differently than he did previously. Instead of his guard immediately going up, he responded, "I didn't realize that it made you feel that way. Let's see if we can figure out a way to both feel okay about this issue." If you are having trouble sharing your feelings with your loved one, turn to Chapter 7 for advice on how to improve your communication with the depressed person.

Try not to take the depression personally. Your partner is not "doing this to you." If your wife is depressed and does not want to go out to dinner, it is not because she does not want to be with you but because she does not feel up to it. Constantly remind yourself that your partner's actions are part of the depression rather than intentional. When he does something annoying or irritating, consider whether it could be the depression, not your partner, that is upsetting you. Realize that you did not cause the depression and should not feel guilty for not being depressed yourself.

When Leslie became depressed, Bennett felt hurt. He knew that having their youngest child leave home would be hard for both of them, but he did not expect Leslie to be depressed. In fact, he thought that now they would have a lot more time and energy to devote to their own relationship. He envisioned more free time for them to travel, see friends, and spend time together. Instead, Leslie did not feel like doing anything. Bennett wondered if perhaps he was not enough for her. Maybe she did not love him anymore and was depressed about being "stuck" alone with him. He took her depression personally. He also felt strangely guilty that he too was not depressed about the children's leaving home and was looking forward to freedom and flexibility. Fortunately, Bennett recognized that Leslie's depression was getting worse, and he helped her get the appropriate treatment. After the depression lifted, Bennett realized how much he had personalized it. He said, "If I had only known that it was the depression and not me that was making Les feel that way, I could have coped with it much better and blamed myself much less."

Ask for help. When your partner is depressed, you need support and help for yourself too. Your loved one needs to be evaluated by a mental health professional and treated for the depression, and you may want to seek help for yourself. Reach out to family members and friends. Confide your concerns in people whom you trust. Many partners of depressed people assume that once they have gotten their loved one into treatment, their work is done. It is not. Living with a depressed person, whether he is in treatment or not, can be very stressful and can take a toll on your work, your social life, your health, and your emotions. Getting help for yourself is an integral part of your relationship's adaptation to the depression.

When Eric became depressed, Joan and he began to have marital problems. They were fighting more than usual, having sex much less than usual, and feeling very distant from one another. Joan was initially resistant to couples therapy. If he was the one who was depressed, why shouldn't he be the one to get the help? But when Eric explained that his depression affected both of them and how they related to each other, Joan agreed to try a couples session. In therapy, both Eric's depression and how it affected their relationship was addressed. Eric felt that he got help with the depression and learned how to stay close to Joan during this period. Joan felt very supported by the therapist and gained new skills in communicating effectively with Eric. Some partners of depressed people have also found it helpful to be in individual therapy or part of a support group when their partner is depressed. Others feel that they do not need professional help but find it useful to talk to friends and acquaintances and read more about depression to educate themselves as much as possible.

Work as a team with your partner. You have a much better chance of constructively solving problems if you and your partner function as a team. You are on the same side in the fight against depression. Rather than becoming adversaries at odds with one another, try to work collaboratively to discuss issues and come up with solutions to problems. Set aside time to talk and share your feelings.

For Leslie and Bennett, it was important for them to collaborate. She was feeling a void in her life after the children left, but she also felt that it was important to Bennett that she stay at home and care for the house. He had always been a traditional man, and she was certain that he would not want her to work. When she was depressed and he suggested that she get a part-time job or take a course, she thought he was feeling sorry for her and did not really mean what he said. When they finally sat down to problem-solve together, she revealed that she had been somewhat bored at home and wondered if she would be a good piano teacher. She had played the piano for years and always thought about teaching. Bennett was able to understand that it was important for Leslie to feel fulfilled, and he supported her decision to give piano lessons at the local high school. He even helped her print flyers advertising her lessons and let her know that it was all right with him if she worked. Although Leslie was not home as much as before, she was much happier and Bennett was glad that they had "put their heads together to come up with something."

Leslie reported that she could never have taken the step to start "without working with Bennett on it."

Sexual Difficulties

Sexual difficulties can become a major issue when your partner is depressed because depression affects sexual desire and performance. And as sexual difficulties become a major issue, you may notice that other aspects of your relationship become more problematic as well.

Recall that both of the couples that we introduced to you at the beginning of this chapter experienced sexual difficulties, as well as other trouble in their relationships. Leslie and Bennett were having sex much less frequently, and she tended to push him away when he tried to initiate sex. Joan and Eric were concerned about the changes in their sexual relationship and came to couples therapy for specific help with their sexual difficulties. In our practices, sexual problems are the most prevalent complaint of couples when one partner is depressed. Joan worried that Eric did not find her attractive anymore, and she resented always being the one to initiate sex. Eric was troubled by his lack of interest in sex and wondered if there was something physically wrong with him that was causing his frequent impotence. Whenever they discussed their sex life, both of them tended to get very defensive and blame the other. Joan told Eric that the problem was that "you can't loosen up enough," and Eric complained to Joan that she expected sex too often. These discussions often ended in heated arguments, with nothing resolved. When they came to couples therapy, they were having great difficulty talking to each other about their sex life.

Depression itself can lower sex drive. Low libido, fatigue, and negative feelings about one's body are all associated with depression and can contribute to sexual problems. Men who are depressed often report problems with impotency and their ability to have an orgasm. Depressed women may have difficulty getting physically aroused and need more stimulation than usual to achieve orgasm. If you imagine for a moment what it must feel like to be depressed with low energy and feelings of worthlessness, you may be able to understand why your loved one is less interested in sex than usual. Eric told us that during his depression, he felt as if he was "swimming through molasses" all day; sex seemed to require too much effort. Often people who have been depressed tell us that they felt so unattractive during the depression that they could not believe that their partner would even want to be close to them. Leslie told Bennett that she couldn't believe he would want to "make love to an old bag like me."

Many antidepressants have potential side effects that include impotence and difficulty achieving orgasm. (We return to a more thorough discussion of these side effects in Chapter 13.) Usually, though, depression results in decreased sex drive, and antidepressant medication, by treating the depression, usually restores the sex drive to normal. Nevertheless, some antidepressant medications can lower the sex drive, cause impotence, or make it more difficult to achieve orgasm.

So if your partner is uninterested in or unable to have sex with you, you may notice the trouble in your relationship. You may have strong feelings and reactions. But as you probably know from your own interactions with your partner, sometimes first reactions do not help problem-solve with our mate. We may become angry and lash out or make our partner feel guilty for not being able to perform sexually. These are all natural reactions to a difficult situation but do not help in the SAD.

The following guidelines are adapted from our general guidelines to help you through the Information-Gathering and Problem-Solving phases of the SAD when you have sexual problems with your partner. These guidelines may look very familiar at first, as they are the same guidelines you've seen before, but they are now geared toward the specific problem of sexual difficulties in your relationship.

Have realistic expectations. Depression has an effect on sexual functioning, so do not expect your depressed partner to be as interested in sex as in the past. His sex drive may be lower, or he may have difficulty achieving an orgasm, or both. Be realistic about what he can and cannot do during this period of time. Do not build up hopes that if you talk about sex, it will automatically get better. It may take time until your sex life is back to normal. Many couples have told us that their sex lives are actually better after one of them has been depressed. Perhaps the period of abstinence or less frequent sex accounts for more intense lovemaking once the depression has lifted. Whatever the case, you need to understand that depression can and often does affect a couple's sex life.

Offer unqualified support. Many depressed people feel so worthless and unattractive that they pull away from being touched. It is hard to initiate sex with someone who continually rejects your overtures; however, it is important to continue to touch and offer unqualified support to your loved one. Reaching out will help to make him feel loved and attractive. Be sure to make time to touch and cuddle without any expectation that it will end in having sex. Be persistent but patient. Let him know that you understand how he feels and that you will be there when he feels ready. If you can create an atmosphere in which there is less pressure to perform and more freedom for your mate to discuss his concerns, the rewards will be not only an improved sex life but also a strengthening of your relationship. As a result, you will be in a much better position to conquer the demons of the depression together.

Maintain your routine as much as possible. The experience of craving sexual release and having a partner who is not interested in sex can be very frustrating. It is important to acknowledge your sexual needs. If you cannot have sex with your partner, one solution is autoerotica. People vary in their comfort level with masturbation; some readily turn to self-stimulation, and others are more reluctant. If your partner is uninterested in sex during the depression and you are comfortable with masturbation, you can masturbate if you need sexual release. Although masturbation provides a release from sexual tension, it does not provide real closeness and intimacy with another person. We recommend using masturbation as a short-term solution to a decreased sex life with your partner but continuing to work together to improve the relationship.

Share your feelings. Let your partner know how you feel about the changes in your sex life. When your partner is depressed, you may feel that you are being insensitive and selfish for wanting sex—a guilty feeling that is common but not rational. It is absolutely natural to want to make love with your partner. Even though you are upset about the trouble in your relationship, you may still crave the intimacy and physical stimulation of sex. If you can begin to share your feelings with your partner, the two of you stand a better chance of recapturing sexual closeness. Try to let your partner know how you feel in an honest and direct way. Rather than isolating yourself as Joan did, discuss sex as openly as you can. Most people, even in close relationships, feel uncomfortable talking about sexual needs, but it is important to share your feelings with your partner. If you are worried that your partner will feel guilty or defensive if you bring up sexual problems, we recommend using "I statements," which we will tell you more about in Chapter 7 when we discuss constructive communication. Basically, an "I statement" is a way of saying something that focuses on your experience, not on what your partner is doing wrong. For example, instead of saying, "You never want to have sex," you could rephrase that statement as, "I feel sad and unattractive when you don't want to have sex." The focus is on how you feel rather than a direct criticism of your partner, and he may begin to understand how you are affected by his behavior rather than react defensively.

Try not to take the depression personally. Tell yourself that it is the depression that is causing your partner to pull away and not you who is being rejected. Don't take it personally. A partner's lack of interest in sex can sometimes be contagious. If you take your partner's withdrawal from you personally, you are especially likely to be resentful and uninterested in sex yourself. If your partner continually rejects your attempts to initiate sex, you might eventually lose interest in pursuing him. Try not to take your partner's lack of interest in sex or sexual problems personally. The difficulties are not about you or your attractiveness but stem from the depression.

Ask for help. If you have followed the other guidelines and the sexual problems with your partner do not resolve, seek the help of mental health professionals who are specially trained in both couples therapy and sex therapy. Over the course of their couples therapy, Joan was able to tell Eric how his lack of interest in sex made her feel undesirable and how she needed his reassurance. He was touched by her feelings and understood how he had misinterpreted her reaction to recent changes in their sex life as nagging rather than as her genuine sadness and worry about his feelings for her. When these issues were brought out in to the open, both of them felt a tremendous sense of relief and were able to reassure each other that the problem was not that they were no longer in love. With guidance from us, they began to problem-solve and practice some sex therapy exercises, with good results. They were relieved to have a satisfying sex life once again.

Work as a team with your partner. You and your partner need to work together to solve your sexual difficulties. The first step is to acknowledge the problem and begin to express your feelings about the changes in your sex life. Once the lines of communication have been reopened, more collaborative problem solving is possible. For example, massage is often an effective entry way into sex or can even be used as an end in itself. Work as a team, and take turns touching and exploring each other's bodies.

Sex therapists often prescribe sensate focus exercises to clients with sexual difficulties: The couple refrains from intercourse and orgasm for several days or weeks and focuses instead on gently caressing each other's bodies and genitals. The idea is that by prohibiting sexual intercourse and orgasm, the pressure to perform for both members of the couple is decreased. Then partners can become reacquainted with each other's bodies and focus on giving and receiving sensual pleasure again. Once couples are comfortable with each other, sexual intercourse and orgasm are slowly reintroduced.

If you and your partner have been having sexual difficulties, try to focus on touching each other's bodies, rather than on the goal of orgasm. This exercise can reduce the pressure on both you and your depressed partner and shift the focus from two opponents to collaborative partners. Holding each other does not have to be a preface to sex but can help you begin to feel sensual and connected to one another again.

This chapter has focused on the effects of your partner's depression on you, your partner, and your relationship. If you are still wondering if your partner's depression has caused trouble for you and your relationship, you can take the quiz on page 60. It was designed to help you assess the extent to which you and your relationship may be suffering from the secondary effects of your partner's depression. Remember to

How Much Trouble Has Your Partner's Depression Caused You and Your Relationship?

Answer each question by circling "Yes" or "No."

1. Yes No Do you feel less attractive or unsure of yourself sexually because he/she has been less interested in having sex with you?

2. Yes No Are the two of you having other sexual problems?

3. Yes No Are you feeling less interested in spending time with him/her?

4. Yes No Do you feel frustrated because your attempts to help are pushed away?

5. Yes No Do you find yourself spending so much time with your partner that you no longer have time for other people and activities?

6. Yes No Are you experiencing any signs of depression yourself such as feeling down, less interested in your usual activities, taking less pleasure in life, trouble with sleep, weight, appetite, concentration, energy level, and/or feelings of worthlessness?

7. Yes No Are you and your partner arguing more intensely and/or more often?

8. Yes No Are you "picking up the slack" so much that you feel overburdened?

9. Yes No Are you feeling more stress at work or school?

10. Yes No Are you feeling isolated and more lonely than usual?

11. Yes No Do you feel more tense and anxious?

12. Yes No Have you and your partner been considering separation or divorce?

13. Yes No Have you and/or your partner been drinking or using drugs more than usual?

14. Yes No Have you or your partner lost income, either to job loss or missed work, since the depression started?

15. Yes No Do you worry a lot of the time that your partner no longer has the will to live?

16. Yes No Are the two of you having communication problems such as frequently interrupting each other, putting each other down, and not listening to one another?

17. Yes No Are you and your partner more competitive with each other than usual?

18. Yes No Are you having more physical problems than usual?

Scoring

Count the number of times you circled Yes to get your "Trouble with Depression" score.

<u>Severe trouble: time to seek help</u>

18 to13   You and your relationship are definitely affected by your partner's depression. You are experiencing many of the classic secondary effects of depression and are at risk for depression yourself. Your relationship is also suffering significantly from your partner's depression and the negative interactions between the two of you will likely result in a worsening of his/her depression. Your relationship may be at risk for several severe problems such as communication breakdowns, separation, or even divorce. You and your loved one should definitely gather more information on depression's effects on loved ones and relationships. You should also consult with a mental health professional for both yourself and your relationship.

<u>Moderate trouble: time to be concerned</u>

12 to 7   You and your relationship are affected by your partner's depression. You may be feeling overburdened, resentful, stressed, and/or distant from your partner. The two of you may be arguing more frequently and intensely. You should gather more information about depression and its secondary effects. You may also want to consult with a mental health professional for the sake of both yourself and your relationship. If you act now you can neutralize depression's toxic effects on you and your relationship before you reach the Severe trouble stage.

<u>Little or no trouble: keep your eyes open</u>

6 or less   Although you and your relationship may be experiencing some difficulties, depression is no more likely than other factors to have caused the trouble. However, because depression is so common and its effects on loved ones and relationships are so pervasive, it is always a good idea to keep your eyes open to the warning signs described in this questionaire.

---

use your own feelings and reactions as a guide in answering these questions.

If you discover that your partner's depression has caused trouble for you and your relationship, use the guidelines suggested to improve your adaptation to the depression. Follow our suggestions on how to prob-

lem-solve with your partner. If there is little or no trouble in your relationship at this time, you are lucky, but problems may develop as your
partner's depression continues or recurs. Read on for more specific advice about how to communicate with your partner. Although the next
several chapters focus on particular problems that are common to
other relationships such as with a depressed child, friend, or parent,
you will also find information relevant to any relationship with a depressed person.

4

When Your Child Is Depressed

Brian Walker, now twelve years old, lived with his parents and two younger sisters. According to Mrs. Walker, Brian had always been "kind of moody," but she had begun to notice changes in his attitude and behavior. He could not be relied on to do his chores and seemed not to care about getting into trouble. He often talked back to his parents and had been starting fights with his sisters. When asked about what was bothering him, Brian replied, "I'm just tired" or "I don't feel well." Mrs. Walker was having a harder time getting him up in the morning to get to school on time. His teachers reported that although he was very bright, he seemed to be daydreaming a lot, and his homework assignments were poorly done. Brian was intolerant of his parents and constantly accused them of being unfair. When Mr. Walker suggested that he and Brian go to see their favorite basketball team in the playoffs, Brian refused and stated, "I don't really like basketball much anymore."

These changes in Brian's behavior were dramatic. He had always gotten along fairly well with his sisters and enjoyed going to school. When his parents discussed the changes that they noticed, Mr. Walker thought that Brian was "just being a typical adolescent" and told his wife that she was worrying too much. He recalled his adolescence and how much he disagreed with his own parents. Mrs. Walker acknowledged that Brian's behavior might be normal for his age but continued to worry that something more serious was wrong.

One evening, Brian and one of his sisters got into a heated fight over the TV remote control in the family room. His sister argued that he "always gets things," so that it should be her turn to change the channels. Brian reacted by saying, "Well, maybe you'd all be better off without me. See how you feel when I'm dead!" and ran out of the room. Alarmed by this comment, Mr. and Mrs. Walker talked to Brian and he admitted wondering if he should just die to make everyone else happier without him. He told them that he had even considered jumping in front of a bus on the way to school. At this point, Mrs. Walker convinced Mr. Walker that they needed to make an appointment for Brian to be seen by a psychologist.

Brian was indeed depressed and needed treatment. Fortunately, his parents recognized the trouble in their relationship with Brian and were able to get him help before he hurt himself. His father's initial reaction to the changes was to chalk it up to adolescence, while his mother was more concerned that something was seriously wrong. When he spoke of hurting himself, they recognized the danger and got help for him. They also learned more about depression, how to have realistic expectations for Brian, and how to work as a team against the depression.

Research on Childhood Depression

Many parents and even many pediatricians do not recognize childhood depression, instead attributing the signs of this disorder to normal development. Part of the problem is that until recently, information on depression and suicide for children before puberty was not available. It was widely believed that childhood depression didn't exist. Many medical and even mental health professionals assumed that children had only short-lived bad moods but could not experience clinical depression. Recent research, however, has revealed that in the United States, between 3 and 6 million people under the age of eighteen suffer from clinical depression and more than 2,000 children between the ages of five and fourteen commit suicide each year.

The rate of depression in children varies with age and with sex. In infancy, depression is very rare and hard to detect, yet some researchers believe that it may be an underlying factor in babies who fail to thrive—that is, do not develop at a normal rate, usually with no apparent cause. It turns out, however, that many failure-to-thrive infants were separated from their mothers or did not receive adequate care during the first few months of life. As a result, they became depressed, with the depression expressed in slower-than-normal development.

In preschool children, the rate of depression climbs to about 1 percent. In school-age children, the rate goes up, with recent studies indicating that more than 2 percent of children ages seven to twelve are depressed. After puberty, the rate jumps dramatically, to over 8 percent for boys and 10 percent for girls. Through adolescence, the rate of depression continues to rise more steeply for girls, until it reaches the adult rate of twice as many depressed women as depressed men. The gender difference in teenagers may stem from the changes during adolescence in our society that are experienced as more stressful for girls. Several studies have found that while boys tend to be pleased with the physical changes of puberty, girls are more likely to be disturbed by their development and worry more about being accepted by their peer group and becoming sexually active.

The best explanation as to why so many childhood depressions go unrecognized and untreated is that children do not always exhibit depression in the same way as adults. For example, rather than the loss of interest in usual activities or decrease in sex drive noticed by adults, children may show subtler signs of apathy. Clinicians often talk about childhood depression as *masked*, meaning that the symptoms are hidden and usually shown through behaviors and signs not associated with depression. For example, Brian did not appear sad and tearful as we might expect a depressed child to be; instead, he exhibited increased aggressive and negative behaviors with his family, problems in completing his schoolwork, and a loss of energy. Many of these symptoms can be easily confused with typical behavior, particularly in preadolescent and adolescent children. For Mr. and Mrs. Walker, Brian's talk of suicide clued them in to the seriousness of Brian's condition. If you are aware of what to look for, you can detect your child's depression long before it reaches that point.

Is My Child Depressed?

Keep in mind that children who are depressed may not look sad. Some children may be able to tell their parents that they are depressed, but the majority cannot. Some children show acting-out behaviors like Brian; others become strikingly withdrawn and quiet. Regardless of whether your depressed child is acting out or withdrawn, he will also exhibit other signs of depression. If you suspect that your child is depressed, pay attention to the trouble in your relationship with him and look for these eleven important warning signs based on the DSM-IV criteria for depression:

1. *Lack of interest in things that previously seemed important.* Your child seems to be always daydreaming or not paying attention. Brian was no longer interested in his favorite basketball team and was daydreaming a lot in school.

2. *Negative self-image.* Your child may put himself down and express feelings of worthlessness. He may say that he feels unloved and unwanted by everyone. He may be self-critical and believe everything he does is wrong. Brian felt that no one in his family wanted him around and believed that he was a burden to his parents.

3. *Changes in sleep habits.* Your child may sleep restlessly, not be able to fall asleep at night, or wake up in the early morning hours and not be able to fall asleep again. You may notice that your child is sleeping much more or much less than usual. Many teenagers sleep late on weekends, but if your child sleeps whenever possible and still seems fatigued when awake, that is cause for concern.

4. *Difficulty concentrating.* You may notice that your child's attention span is decreased, and he has difficulty remembering directions or instructions. Brian had trouble paying attention at school and became much more forgetful.

5. *Changes in appetite.* Look for extreme changes from his usual food habits—eating too much or too little. Some children use food as a way to self-medicate feeling bad and overeat. Others eat less, fail to gain weight, and grow more slowly than normal.

6. *Extreme fearfulness.* You may notice that your child is much more afraid of things than he was in the past and avoids doing usual activities because of his fears.

7. *Lack of energy.* Your child may lie around, resist doing any activities, and put off tasks until later. Brian's energy level was much lower than usual. He spent most of his time sitting around the house and avoided doing his chores.

8. *Thoughts of death or suicide.* Your child may talk or write about morbid death themes or show great interest in terrorists or murderers. Brian's mention that they would "be better off without me" clued his parents in to the seriousness of his depression. If you sense that your child is preoccupied with death or suicide, seek professional help immediately. (Chapter 11 provides you with more specific advice about how to deal with a suicidal loved one.)

9. *Aggressive behavior.* Your child may be more irritable than usual, pick fights with siblings or friends, and talk back to you. He may be destructive and seem to "look for trouble," without regard for the consequences of his actions. Brian, who had always been a well-behaved boy, became much more aggressive when he was depressed. He picked fights with his sisters and did not seem to care about getting punished.

10. *Physical complaints,* especially ones that do not seem to have a physical cause. Your child may complain about vague aches and pains. He may also want more attention and comfort than usual.

11. *Hyperactivity.* Although most depressed children lack energy, some mask their depression in a whirlwind of activity that may function to keep the depression away, though only in the short term. Also be on the lookout for risk taking, truancy, and other behaviors linked to hyperactivity.

All of these signs can come and go in all children, regardless of whether they are depressed. But if several of these signs persist for at least two weeks or more, it is time to seek professional help. As you think about whether your child is depressed, use your own reactions to the trouble in your relationship. During the Trouble and Reaction phases of the SAD, your feelings are always an important indicator. Often parents tell us that they noticed changes in their children as they became depressed but disregarded their concerns and believed it was "just part of growing up." Watch for behavioral changes, pay attention to your own reactions, and carefully consider whether your child has a depression.

What might you see or experience during the Trouble and Reaction stages? With an infant, you might notice your baby withdraw, lose interest in activities around him, and stop eating. A preschool child might throw temper tantrums, cling more to you, or regress in speech and toilet training. A school-age child might become more aggressive or withdrawn, or both, and complain about aches and pains. Because many children act in these ways anyway for a million different reasons, ranging from physical pain to normal developmental phases, depression in children is difficult to diagnose and must be evaluated by a trained professional.

Some children who seem depressed really have behavior disorders, and other children who appear to have behavior disorders might really be depressed. Given these ambiguities, mental health professionals are specially trained in differentiating between different kinds of problems. For example, depression in children is often diagnosed on the basis of irritability rather than expressed sadness. When Brian's family brought him to see a psychologist, she took a careful family history, listened to their story of Brian's recent behavior changes, and then spoke to Brian about how he had been feeling lately. Only after a careful evaluation did she make a diagnosis of depression and discuss treatment options with his parents. Fortunately, Mr. and Mrs. Walker were able to pay attention to their own feelings and reactions during the Trouble and Reaction stages and move into the Information-Gathering stage by seeking professional help.

Is My Teenager Depressed?

It can be even harder to detect depression in teenagers because many of the hallmarks of depression are common in normal adolescence. Most of us remember feeling irritable and withdrawn during our own teenage years, and we all know that normal, nondepressed teenagers appear angry and moody at times. Detecting depression in teenagers is tricky business, but if you are concerned that your teenager is depressed, look for extreme changes in their behavior or outlook. In addition to the eleven warning signs of childhood depression, keep an eye out for cutting school, dropping out of favorite activities, substance use, running away from home, and extreme isolation. You may also notice that your depressed teenager does not pay as much attention to his physical appearance and may resist showering or changing clothes.

Why Is My Child Depressed?

Children and teenagers get depressed for the same reasons that adults do: genetics, biochemistry, and psychosocial factors. Researchers have found, however, that there are some particular stressors associated with an increased risk of depression in children: the death of a parent or sibling, living with an abusive parent, moving to a new place, breaking up with a girlfriend or boyfriend, or suffering from a chronic illness. In particular, children who have lost a parent at a younger age or have a family history of depressive disorder are more susceptible to depression. Although it is not yet entirely clear, there is also preliminary evidence that a conflictual parental relationship or difficult divorce can increase the risk of depression in children. What we do know is that when parents leave (through either divorce or death), many children conclude that if they had been more lovable or different, the parent would have stayed. It is important for children to be reassured that the parent did not leave because of them.

Some researchers have also pointed to the high incidence of depressed children in families with a depressed parent and suggested that depression is a learned response to stress. That is, children respond to stress in their own lives in much the same way that they have seen their parents do. When their parents react to pressure and frustration with depression, the children will do the same. However, it is important to note that the increased risk of childhood depression in the offspring of depressed adults probably also has to do with inheriting a genetic vulnerability to develop the disorder. In other words, just as the parent was susceptible to depression for biochemical reasons, so is the child. For that reason, when a child is evaluated for depression, the mental health professional will always ask about family history of mood disorder.

Although neither of Brian's parents had ever suffered from depression, there was a strong family history of depression on his father's side. Brian's paternal grandfather and two aunts had experienced recurrent depressions throughout their lives, and one of the aunts had committed suicide. When the psychologist asked the Walkers about any family history, Mr. Walker recalled that his father and his aunts had been depressed. Until that moment, it had not occurred to him that Brian's problems could be related to a family history that was a whole generation removed. The psychologist explained that genetics can play a role in the development of depression by making someone more susceptible to depression, but that there was probably also some stressor in Brian's life that contributed to the depression. As the Walkers later learned, Brian was having great difficulty at school because of a falling out with his best friend. The combination of his genetic vulnerability and the current stressor in his social life presumably led to his depression.

How a Depressed Child Affects You and Your Family

Having a depressed child is difficult. It affects you and your family in a multitude of ways. During the Trouble phase of the SAD, you will notice difficulties in your relationship with your child and possibly in your relationship with other family members. Up to now, we have focused on how depression affects your relationship with the depressed person but not how it can affect your relationships with the other people in your life. For example, you and your spouse might not get along as well. As time goes on, you will enter the Reaction phase of the SAD and notice changes in your actions and behaviors as you respond to the trouble. First, as you are probably already aware, there are the additional time commitments, ranging from meetings with school personnel and going to medical appointments, to time spent trying to solve problems at home. It is hard to keep your regular routine when your child is depressed. Second, your social life can be affected. Having a depressed child at home may make it more difficult to keep up with your friends. You make excuses about not going out because you feel you are needed at home. You may be self-conscious about how your child is doing and not want to admit to friends that your child is depressed. You may feel apologetic and defensive, perhaps even embarrassed, and you may think that it is your fault.

During the initial Reaction stage, many parents report telling their spouse that the depression must come from "your side of the family." Parents often wonder why their child is depressed and worry about the effect of the depression on their other children and their marriage. You and your spouse might begin blaming each other for doing something to trigger the depression. When you cannot cure your child's depression as you can help other childhood woes, you will probably feel incompetent and useless. As time goes on, you may feel depressed too.

One of the biggest effects of a child's depression is the worry that the child might hurt himself. As a result, many parents become even more watchful and protective. Mrs. Walker, who had always been an involved parent, now kept an eagle eye on Brian. If he was five minutes late coming home from school, she was ready to call the police. Mr. Walker told us that he began to feel as his entire life was organized around making sure that Brian was safe. He gave up his Saturday golf game to watch Brian while Mrs. Walker did the grocery shopping. Although both Mr. and Mrs. Walker were appropriately concerned, they also began to feel some resentment and anger that their world was revolving around Brian's depression.

Having a depressed sibling can also be hard on the other children. Children often assume they are the center of the universe and may feel all-powerful in having caused the depression. One of Brian's sisters felt guilty when Brian talked about hurting himself. She assumed that arguing over the remote control had upset him to the point that he wanted to kill himself. Because her parents were so concerned about Brian, she kept her feelings of guilt inside. Only after the family took part in family therapy did they begin to realize the extent to which Brian's depression had affected all of them. Once they talked about it, his sister felt relieved and was able to articulate her feelings of having caused Brian's depression.

Siblings of a depressed child may feel abandoned, as if their parents are giving all their time and attention to the depressed one. Brian's youngest sister admitted resenting him and wanting to act "sad like him" to regain her parents' attention. Brian's other sister confessed that she felt ashamed by Brian's depression. She worried that he might embarrass her by sitting alone in the playground. Other siblings have told us that they miss what the depressed child used to be like or what the family was like before the depression.

Many of these feelings and fears come from a lack of knowledge and misunderstanding of what depression is. One brother of a depressed adolescent confessed that he worried that he would "catch" it from his sister. He assumed that "craziness" ran in his family because an elderly uncle had been hospitalized for a "nervous breakdown." It was important for him to understand that although he does have a slightly higher risk of getting depressed because of genetics, depression is absolutely not catching like the flu. In family therapy sessions, this young boy learned some of the specific strategies that we discuss in Chapters 7, 8, and 9 to "inoculate" himself against his sister's depression and to help her feel better at the same time. For example, he learned how to not take her depression personally, how to communicate with her more constructively, and how to deal with his own feelings of anger and frustration.

If you are still unsure whether your child's depression has caused trouble for you and your relationship, you can take the quiz shown. It was designed to help you determine the extent to which you and your relationship with your child may be suffering from the secondary effects of his or her depression. Once again, remember to use your own reactions and feelings as a guide to answering the questions.

Treatment for Your Depressed Child

If you suspect that your child is depressed, he should be evaluated as soon as possible by a mental health professional or pediatrician experienced in working with children and depression. If your child denies that he is depressed, that does not mean that you can ignore the signs, even if they are subtle. Depression in children can be every bit as severe as in adults, even leading to suicide in some cases. Rapid diagnosis and treatment are especially important, considering the critical stages of development children are passing through. Early childhood, preadolescence, and adolescence are periods that have profound effects on one's adult sense of self. Personality and social competency develop along with physical characteristics. Many adolescents who recover from depression feel that they missed out on an important part of their life during high school because of the depression.

Although we go into more detail about the various psychological and medical treatment approaches in Chapters 12 and 13, we focus here on some of the forms of treatment that are most effective with children. As part of the Information-Gathering phase of the SAD, it is important to learn about treatments tailored especially for children.

How Much Trouble Has Your Child's Depression Caused You and Your Relationship?

To determine the extent to which you and your relationship with your child may be suffering from the secondary effects of his/her depression, answer each question by circling "Yes" or "No."

1. Yes No Do you feel especially unappreciated or disliked by your child?

2. Yes No Are you less interested in spending time with him/her?

3. Yes No Do you feel frustrated because your attempts to help are being pushed away?

4. Yes No Do you find yourself spending so much time with your child that you no longer have time for other people and activities?

5. Yes No Are you experiencing any signs of depression yourself such as feeling down, less interested in your usual activities, taking less pleasure in life, trouble with sleep, weight, appetite, concentration, energy level, and/or feelings of worthlessness?

6. Yes No Are you and your child arguing more intensely and/or more often?

7. Yes No Do you feel overburdened by your child's needs?

8. Yes No Are you feeling more stress at work or school?

9. Yes No Are you feeling isolated and more lonely than usual?

10. Yes No Do you feel more tense and anxious since your child has been depressed?

11. Yes No Have you been spending more and more time disciplining your child or dealing with his/her problems at school and with other children?

12. Yes No Have you been drinking or using drugs more than usual?

13. Yes No Have you missed a significant amount of work, since your child's depression started?

14. Yes No Do you worry that your child no longer has the will to live?

15. Yes No Are you and your child having communication problems such as frequently interrrupting each other, putting each other down, and not listening to one another?

16. Yes No Are you finding yourself harsher than you meant to be when disciplining your child?

17. Yes No Are you having more physical problems than usual?

18. Yes No Are you feeling more impatient with your child and finding yourself wishing that he/she would just "snap out of it!"?

(cont'd.)

Scoring

Count the number of times you circled Yes to get your "Trouble with Depression" score.

<u>Severe trouble: time to seek help</u>

18 to 13   You and your relationship with your child are definitely affected by his/her depression. You are experiencing many of the classic secondary effects of depression and are at risk for depression yourself. Your relationship is also suffering significantly from your child's depression and the negative interactions between the two of you may result in a worsening of his/her depression. Your relationship may be at risk for several severe problems such as increased hostility, communication breakdowns, and isolation from one another. You should definitely gather more information on depression's effects on loved ones and relationships. You should also consult with a mental health professional for both yourself and your relationship.

<u>Moderate trouble: time to be concerned</u>

12 to 7   You and your relationship are affected by your child's depression. You may be feeling overburdened, resentful, stressed, and/or distant from your child. The two of you may be arguing more frequently and intensely. You should gather more information about depression and its secondary effects. You may also want to consult with a mental health professional for the sake of both yourself and your relationship. If you act now you can neutralize depression's toxic effects on you and your relationship before you reach the Severe trouble stage.

<u>Little or no trouble: keep your eyes open</u>

6 or less   Although you and your relationship may be experiencing some difficulties, depression is no more likely than other factors to have caused the trouble. However, because depression is so common and its effects on loved ones and relationships are so pervasive, it is always a good idea to keep your eyes open to the warning signs described in this questionaire.

Psychotherapy Treatments

Individual psychotherapy is the most common type of treatment for depressed children and teenagers. Children under eight or nine years old often have trouble talking openly about their experiences or feelings and tend to express themselves nonverbally through play. Therapists use play therapy with younger children, encouraging them to use dolls, puppets, blocks, and other games to express their feelings and conflicts. Children over the age of nine or ten are usually more verbal and can handle talking therapy, along with play therapy. In talking psychotherapy, your child will be encouraged to share his thoughts and feelings with the therapist. In both play and talking therapy, the goal is to understand what the child is thinking and feeling and then to modify the maladaptive thoughts and emotions.

For children and adolescents, group therapy can also be useful because the social acceptance that comes from revealing problems to peers can be powerful. The groups serve to protect against the isolation and feelings of alienation that depressed adolescents are especially vulnerable to. In addition, teenagers are more likely to accept solutions from peers than from a doctor, whom they see as a distant expert. The group therapist facilitates discussion among the children and acts more as a coach than as an authority figure.

Family therapy is often recommended, for two reasons. First, family therapists believe that a family member's depression may be a reflection of family stress or relationship difficulties and that by resolving such conflicts, the depression will be alleviated. And second, although the depressed family member may be the identified patient, the depression affects every member of the family, and family therapy helps all of them to cope with the depression more effectively. From our perspective, there is no doubt that the entire family can benefit from family therapy, especially when a child is the depressed family member. Having a depressed child stirs up particularly strong feelings of guilt, anger, and frustration in both parents and siblings. In family therapy, the depressed child gains the sense that his family cares about him and that his behavior affects others. Other family members gain insight into how their reactions to the depressed child affect him and learn how to problem-solve with each other, as well as cope more effectively with their own feelings.

Pharmacological Treatments

Although psychotherapy is usually the first line of treatment for depression in children, medication is sometimes used with depressions that seem to linger or are very severe. Contradictory research results have been reported about the efficacy of antidepressants for children before puberty. In addition, because most of the medications have been used only for the past ten to fifteen years, the data on effectiveness or side effects are scant. More study of antidepressant medications in children is clearly needed. Many physicians (both pediatricians and psychiatrists) continue to be cautious about prescribing medication for children who are still growing and developing. Although antidepressant medications seem to be safe, the long-term effects on growth and development remain unknown. Nevertheless, depression itself can have devastating and lifelong effects on a child's emotional and intellectual growth and can even lead to suicide. Given the dangers of childhood depression, you must weigh the potential risks and benefits before deciding on medication for your child and discuss the possibility of medication carefully with your child's doctor. If you are considering medication for your child, it will also be useful to read Chapter 13 for more information about pharmacological treatments for depression.

What You Can Do When Your Child Is Depressed

Having a depressed child can be difficult and frightening. Many parents feel at a loss about what to do. They feel alone, worried, and guilty for their child's depression. As we have stressed in our discussions of the SAD, the first step is to notice the trouble in your relationship with your child. Then pay attention to your own reactions and begin to learn all that you can about the depression. By learning more about depression and its effects on relationships, you have already moved into the Information-Gathering stage.

Once you know that your child is depressed and understand something about depression, what can you do? The following guidelines offer some specific advice about how to move through the SAD more effectively. We guide you through the Reaction and Information-Gathering phases and help you to reach the Problem-Solving stage with your child. Although these guidelines are the same ones we have already introduced, here they are geared specifically to the unique issues of coping with your child's depression. Keep in mind that although having support from parents can help a depressed child, research has indicated that having a stressful, argumentative relationship with family members can actually be worse than having no support at all. Relationships that are tense can contribute to a child's depression rather than help to alleviate it. Although you may be well meaning in your attempts to help, sometimes giving your child space may be the best way to help him.

Learn all you can. Be alert for sudden or dramatic changes that might indicate that your child is depressed. Using the eleven warning signs of depression we have discussed, pay attention to the trouble in your relationship. Many parents make excuses for changes in their child's behavior. Do not waste valuable time arguing with your spouse, trying to ignore the changes you observe, or letting well-meaning friends or relatives talk you out of your concerns. If your son has always been a cautious and careful person, you should be concerned if he is suddenly taking risks such as shoplifting or cutting school. If depression is diagnosed by a mental health professional or your child's pediatrician and you are still unsure, learn more about depression and get a second opinion. The more educated you are about depression and its treatments, the more effective you will be in helping your child.

Have realistic expectations. Do not expect your child to be his "old self" right away. Like Brian, he might not be interested in his usual activities or may not want to join in on a family outing. Respect your child's limitations when he is depressed. Using your new knowledge about depression, be realistic about what you can and cannot expect. Many parents assume that if their child is in treatment, he should automatically be "cured." However, depression is a complicated illness that can take time to recover from. In addition, do not expect to be able to make all of your child's pain go away. In the past, you may have been able to allay his fears or anxieties with a hug or a smile, but depression does not lift so readily. Keep your expectations realistic, for both you and your child.

Offer unqualified support. Let your child know that he is not alone and that if he feels he cannot handle something, he can seek help from you or other family members. Children who are depressed tend to feel isolated and separate from others. Brian felt that he was "alone in a sea of sadness" and had no one to turn to. When he and his parents discussed his feelings of wanting to die, he realized for the first time how much his parents cared about him. Throughout his treatment, it was important for both Mr. and Mrs. Walker to let Brian know that they were there for him. Brian reported, "Just knowing I could call my dad at his office when I felt down really helped me get through some hard days."

One of the best ways to offer unqualified support is to listen. It can be hard to get a depressed child to start talking. We recommend using passive listening to encourage your child to talk to you. In other words, just listen and say nothing or make simple comments such as, "Hmm, I'd like to hear more about that." Or if he tells you about something that was clearly difficult for him, you could reply, "That must have been hard." A calm, even-tempered manner works best. Another strategy is to plan for private times with him. If you and your child have uninterrupted time together, chances are that he will begin to open up to you. Do not demand that he tell you things. Instead, be nonjudgmental and give him the opportunity to express himself. Do not badger him and do not feel you always have to solve all of his problems. Many parents (even if they promised themselves that they would *never* sound like their own parents) end up lecturing or ordering their children to do things. Try to sit back a bit, and give your child nonverbal acceptance.

Another way to offer unqualified support is to help your child to develop and maintain a positive self-image. Encourage him to become involved in school and community activities. Getting active can decrease depression, just as sitting alone can make a child feel isolated and sad. Yet do not push your child to do more than he wants. Try not to put down or label your child as the "sad sack" in the family. For example, if you constantly call your son "the mopey one" when he does not feel up to doing things, he will begin to think of himself as incapable and sad. Instead, try to let your child know what you especially like about him. You might tell your son that you understand that he does not feel like going swimming today, but that you were really impressed with how he played soccer yesterday. You could tell him how you wish you were able to be as athletic as he is. Try to build on the positive things that your child does well rather than only commenting on how the depression has affected him.

Maintain your routine as much as possible. When your child is depressed, it can be hard to keep to a regular schedule, but having set mealtimes, bedtimes, and activities can help both you and your depressed child. You may have to give up some of your usual activities, as Mr. Walker had to give up his Saturday golf game when Brian was depressed, but try to keep most of your regular routine intact. The Walkers continued to have dinner at the usual time, visit Mrs. Walker's mother on Sunday afternoons, and go to the movies regularly. It was especially important for Brian's two younger sisters that the whole family routine did not change when Brian was depressed. Remind yourself to keep things as regular as possible.

Share your feelings. Having a depressed child is bound to elicit strong feelings and reactions: worry, frustration, shame, and anger. You may experience these feelings one after another or even simultaneously. We will try to help ease your feelings as we guide you through the SAD, but you must also learn to cope with negative feelings toward yourself and your child. Unfortunately, those negative feelings are part of how depression affects families. Reading this book and following the guidelines should help lessen them but will not eliminate them. Part of coping with the depression is learning to tolerate those strong feelings. One of the best ways to do that is to acknowledge how you feel. Talking about your feelings with someone you trust helps make them less shameful and less painful. When your depressed loved one is a child, it can be hard to share your feelings about his depression directly. With a young child especially, it may be unfair or inappropriate to tell him the details about how you are feeling. However, you can let him know that you are concerned about him and want to help him feel better. You can express your more adult feelings to yourself, your partner, or a close friend. Talking through your experiences is an effective way to begin to tolerate your feelings.

It's not your fault. Many concerned and well-meaning parents take their child's diagnosis of depression personally. Common feelings when your child is diagnosed with depression are denial, anger, shame and guilt, and a sense of responsibility for your child's unhappiness. It is true that some things that you do, such as divorcing your spouse, can trigger a depression in your child. But depression is an illness and is not your fault. It can happen to anyone. Your child may have a genetic vulnerability to be depressed that came from your mother's side two generations back and has nothing to do with the kind of parent you have been. One of the best ways not to take the depression personally is to learn more about it. If you are familiar with the facts about depression, you will be able to be more objective and less self-blaming. One mother of a depressed child was convinced that her child's depression meant that she was a terrible mother and that her work schedule had "made" her son depressed. Only after learning more about depression did she begin to understand that her schedule had not caused her son's depression. Once she stopped blaming herself, she was able to get past her feelings of shame and begin to take responsibility for the things she had some control over. She cut back on some of her hours for awhile to help her son through the depression but then returned to her regular schedule without her previous feelings of guilt.

Ask for help. Many parents, especially those who see themselves as capable and self-sufficient like Mr. Walker, do not want to seek outside help. They prefer to keep it a family matter and bear with whatever is going on. When your child is depressed, however, you need to ask for help, for both your sake and the sake of your child. Too many families suffer needlessly by keeping their problems and concerns to themselves. You certainly do not need to broadcast your child's difficulties to the entire PTA, but you do need to seek appropriate and sensitive help.

First, communicate with your child's teachers who have the opportunity to see your child interact with his peers, as well as notice any acting-out behaviors. Teachers are often able to observe aspects of how children behave that parents miss, and their observations are very helpful. If the teachers are aware of your child's difficulties, they may be able to give him extra time to complete assignments and more support. The Walkers met with Brian's math teacher to explain that Brian was experiencing a depression and under a psychologist's care. As a result, the teacher was able to keep an eye on Brian's behavior at school and not penalize him for incomplete homework assignments. Instead, she was understanding and helped him make up some of the work that he missed due to his absences. In addition, she communicated directly with the Walkers when she overheard Brian telling one of his friends that he "would be better off dead" so that they could inform his therapist.

Second, seek professional help. This is an extremely important step. You should be sure to get regular health care for your child. If you are worried that your child might be depressed, see your pediatrician so he or she can rule out other potentially serious health problems that can mimic the signs of depression, such as mononucleosis, diabetes, an eating disorder, or even (in very rare cases) a brain tumor. If the doctor does not discover any medical basis for the changes, seek help from a mental health professional. Remember that no matter how much you love your child, you cannot fight the depression all alone. If your child is a teenager, it may be even more difficult for you to get him to agree to see someone. Teenagers are notoriously rebellious and may resist following your orders to see a professional, but you must insist that he "at least get checked out." Chapter 14 gives specific advice about getting a loved one into treatment, particularly when he or she is resistant to seeking help.

Consider individual therapy for your child. Most children are not able to express their feelings as directly as adults can. A depressed child can have a particularly hard time talking about how he is feeling. Individual therapy can help him begin to express himself. If your child is in therapy, do not expect him to talk to you about what goes on in his therapy sessions. It is important for your child to feel confidence in telling his therapist his feelings. The therapist will tell him that his confidences will be broken only if the therapist thinks he is in danger, either by hurting himself or others or by being hurt by someone else. However, always communicate any concerns you have about dangerous or reckless behavior to your child's therapist.

Think about family therapy to help the whole family cope with the depression and to understand what communication or relationship difficulties might have contributed to your child's depression. We believe that family therapy can be a very effective treatment for depression, particularly in the case of a depressed child. In many cases, family therapy is used in addition to individual therapy.

Brian was seen in weekly individual therapy, and the Walker family was seen in family therapy once every two weeks. In the family sessions, the Walkers learned how to work as a team against the depression rather than as adversaries working at odds with one another. They learned that some of their communication patterns might have contributed to Brian's depression. When they disagreed, Mr. and Mrs. Walker tended not to talk out their differences but withdrew and held in their resentment. In their sessions, they learned how to communicate more constructively and express their feelings more directly. The whole family practiced problem solving together and learned how to ask for help from one another. Instead of blaming each other for having caused Brian's depression, Mr. and Mrs. Walker were able to support each other during a difficult time for their family. Brian's sisters were able to express their feelings more constructively. Rather than picking fights with Brian, they talked about how Brian's depression made them feel sad and ignored by their parents. The Walkers agreed that family therapy was very important in helping all of them cope with Brian's depression.

Work as a team with your child and other family members. To combat the depression, you need to work as a team with your child and other family members. Even if you decide not to pursue family therapy, there are many things you can do at home on your own to increase the teamwork in your family. One of the most important steps in working collaboratively is to devote time and attention to your child so that he feels special. Setting aside this time is particularly important when you have several children or many other responsibilities that take you away from your child. Be sure to demonstrate affection for your child. Respect that there are times when a child or teenager does not want to be hugged or kissed, but let him know you are there if he wants closeness. We often recommend that parents try to put aside even five to ten minutes a day that they spend with just the depressed child to let him know that he is loved. Take a walk, go for a ride in the car, or set the table together. It does not matter what you do as long as the two of you are alone together.

Mr. and Mrs. Walker both tried to spend some individual time with Brian when he was depressed. Mrs. Walker joined Brian on his after-school walks with the dog, and Mr. Walker took Brian with him on his Saturday morning errands. After several weeks, both reported feeling closer to Brian than they had in years, and Brian seemed more able to open up to them about his feelings. A little quality time goes a long way when your child is depressed. Try to take time in your lives to switch the focus from striving toward something to just being together.

When you spend time with your child, try to teach him how to handle stress and disappointment. Set a good example in how you manage stress. Tell your child how you have handled difficult situations in your own life. If your child sees you keeping your feelings inside and moping around, chances are he will learn to do the same thing when he is under stress. Let your child see you handle difficult situations by talking through them and trying to problem-solve. Children are natural imitators and will follow your lead in dealing with problems. Encourage him to exercise, talk through his problems, and ask for help. By discussing problems with him, you let him know that there are ways to solve things together by looking at alternatives and trying to foresee the consequences of different options. For example, if your son is disappointed about not making the baseball team at school, discuss other after-school activities he could do. He might find that he enjoys playing the guitar or being part of the student government. Point out the many other options that he has not considered.

To increase the spirit of collaboration in your family, have family meetings, either formally or over a meal, at a regular time each week. Family meetings should give everyone a chance to learn more about depression, reducing the embarrassment and misunderstanding that often arise. Allow time for discussion of fears or worries and time to solve problems together. Family meetings also let the depressed child know that his behavior affects the rest of the family, and they give everyone a sense of camaraderie and family unity. In these meetings, everyone should have a turn to speak, but a parent or both parents should run the meeting and have the right to veto any decisions.

A good plan for a family meeting is to introduce it as "a time for us to all get together to talk about how we're doing and try to solve any problems." The beginning of the meeting should be a "go-around," in which each family member has the floor for anywhere from three to five minutes to speak about what he or she sees as the biggest problem in the family. During each person's go-around time, the rest of the family should not interrupt by asking questions or making comments. After everyone has had a chance to speak, the parent or parents should make a list of all the problems mentioned and pick one (generally the most pressing or upsetting one) to work on during that meeting. Then all family members should come up with suggestions or possible solutions for that problem. You can list them on a piece of paper and then read them back to everyone. Family members should evaluate the various solutions and then pick one or two to try that week. At the next family meeting, family members can report back on how helpful or not helpful the solutions were during the previous week. This kind of family meeting can be an effective strategy for problem solving during the last stage of your family's adaptation to the depression.

To protect your depressed child from danger, collaborate with other family members to keep alcohol, drugs, and other potentially dangerous objects (guns, knives, etc.) away from your depressed child. In children especially, suicide attempts are often an impulsive response to depression or disappointment. Because the finality of death is a difficult concept for children under age twelve, help your child to realize that death is permanent. If he is talking about suicide, suggest putting off such a long-term permanent decision about life and trying some alternative solutions instead. Chapter 11 will go into more detail about suicide. If your child is voicing suicidal thoughts or has made a suicide attempt, put this book down and get immediate professional help.

If your child is depressed, keep these guidelines in mind as you interact with him. Remember that the goal is to move from the Trouble and Reaction phases to the Information-Gathering and Problem-Solving phases of the SAD. Through the Walkers' family therapy and Brian's individual therapy, the Walkers were able to move through the SAD without major difficulties. Mr. and Mrs. Walker learned not to blame themselves, to communicate more directly with each other and their children, and to keep their routine despite their strong negative feelings about Brian's being depressed. Brian's younger sisters learned what depression is and how to get their needs met even when Brian was depressed. And Brian learned how to communicate his feelings more effectively and how to ask for help from his family. As a family, they developed good problem-solving skills and were able to work together as a team against the depression rather than against each other.

In the chapters to come, we will first turn to relationships with depressed parents and depressed friends, but then return to problems that are common to all relationships with a depressed person, regardless of age. As you read on, remember that your tasks at this point are to gather information about depression and then begin to problem-solve more effectively with your loved one.

5

When Your Parent Is Depressed

Albert was seventy-two years old. In recent months he had been complaining about feeling nauseous, telling his daughter, Diana, and his seventeen-year-old grandson Jeff that he had never experienced anything quite like it before. The nausea, he explained, was waking him up two hours earlier than usual and kept him from going back to sleep. He also complained of a general malaise. Diana noticed that her father was looking ill. He no longer took daily walks, was unsteady on his feet, and appeared frailer than she had ever seen him. Three years ago, Albert had had a heart attack, and although he had recovered quickly, he now seemed as weak as he did in the weeks after it first happened. Worried that something was again wrong with his heart, Diana offered to take him to his cardiologist for a checkup.

The cardiologist reported good news about Albert's heart but was also concerned about the daily nausea and weakness. Consequently, she referred Albert to a gastroenterologist for a checkup. The gastroenterologist prescribed an antacid and told him to call back in a week if there was no improvement. Relieved that there appeared to be a reason and remedy for his complaints, Albert followed the doctor's directions. But his nausea continued, and he grew increasingly anxious and hopeless. Jeff began to spend more and more time with his grandfather, his concern growing with the frequency of Albert's complaints. Albert and his grandson had always been close, making it all the more difficult for Jeff to see him so unhappy.

As time passed, Diana became irritated with her father's complaints. She was particularly impatient with his negative attitude about his chances for recovery. She found herself agreeing with a friend who told her that Albert sounded like a "typical old man" preoccupied with aches and pains. Nonetheless, at Jeff's urging, Diana took her father back to the gastroenterologist. Because Albert felt too unstable to drive himself, she had to take a day off from work, once again, to drive him to the appointment.

This time another medication was prescribed, and it helped the nausea a bit Albert said, but he was still being woken up by it in the early morning. He was feeling weaker and becoming increasingly anxious and hopeless. Feeling frustrated, his new doctor recommended an extensive battery of tests. Despite several diagnostic procedures, including an upper GI series, nothing was found. Diana missed more days at work, and Jeff had to take days off from school to drive Albert to several of these tests. The doctor, Diana, Jeff, and Albert were all becoming frustrated and worried. In the six weeks during which he had been seeing the gastroenterologist, he had lost fifteen pounds. Befuddled, the physician suggested that he be hospitalized for even more extensive tests, including a CAT scan of his digestive tract.

In Chapter 1, we told you about Gail and her mother. Gail knew early on that her mother was depressed, but many children of depressed people do not recognize depression in their parents. Diana mistook symptoms of depression for physical ailments and for behaviors she thought were typical of older people. Because Albert did not complain of feeling sad, Diana, Jeff, Albert's physicians, and Albert himself did not consider the possibility that a major depression was at the root of his suffering. Diana and Jeff were gathering the wrong kind of information. They did not consider the possibility that depression was causing the trouble in their relationships with Albert. Instead, they wondered whether his ailments, his personality, or his advanced age were causing the trouble. They were stuck between the Reaction and Information-Gathering SAD. If you believe you may have a parent who is depressed, then you have successfully negotiated the Trouble and Reaction phases of the SAD and are now attempting to gather the information you will need to know how to problem-solve constructively.

In this chapter, we will describe the common problems that can arise when a parent is depressed. Whether you are an adult like Diana, or an adolescent, like Jeff, you will benefit from understanding the special circumstances that arise when your parent or grandparent is depressed. Particular issues that can come up include misunderstandings created by the generation gap between you and your parent, a greater tendency to try and go it alone, the impulse to become a parent to your parent, and the importance of finding the right kind of professional help if your parent is elderly.

Depression in the Elderly

Recent research shows that depression among men and women age sixty-five and older nearly triples the risk of a stroke. A study of more than 10,000 elderly men and women with diagnosed hypertension found that over a three-year period, those with symptoms of depression suffered strokes at up to 2.7 times the rate of those being treated for hypertension but without depression. This research underscores the need to treat depression in the elderly—not just to raise their spirits but also to protect their physical health.

Other studies have found that elderly people with depression fared worse in recovering from heart attack, hip fracture, and severe infections like pneumonia, and they had more difficulty regaining functions like walking after being stricken by diseases of all kinds. Some research even suggests that prolonged depression interferes with the functioning of the immune system. Moreover, slowed recovery from all of these medical problems can worsen the depression. In short, untreated depression in the elderly results in much more than emotional suffering.

One of the difficulties of diagnosing depression is that many medications can mimic some of the symptoms of depression. Dysphoric mood, sleep disturbances, changes in appetite, weight loss, and fatigue are all possible side effects of many medications used to treat various disorders in older people. In addition, certain diseases can mimic some of the signs of depression.

The best response to the question of whether your elderly parent has depression or medication side effects, or another illness, is to ensure that your parent's health care is coordinated by a physician who is truly knowledgeable about all aspects of your parent's health care. Many health maintenance organizations require a primary physician, in order to coordinate multiple health care providers better. However, this can happen only if your parent's primary physician is aware of all the medications and tests your parent has received, not just the ones he or she has prescribed. Ask your parent's primary physician about the possible interactions of various medications and ensure that he or she is up to date on all the treatment your parent is receiving. A physician who is aware of an elderly person's medications, recent diagnostic tests, and history will be better equipped to rule out the various other problems that can mimic depression. As well meaning and expert as Albert's doctors were, no one was coordinating his care, and no one was specifically trained in identifying depression. Certainly in this time of increasing specialization, it is difficult to be well versed in all areas, and recently several medical centers and health maintenance organizations have developed training programs for helping primary care physicians identify depression. Albert would have been diagnosed with depression much earlier had one of his physicians participated in such a program.

Finally, if you suspect depression, be sure that your parent sees a psychologist or psychiatrist who is knowledgeable about mental disorders in the elderly. Never hesitate to question a practitioner's area of expertise. If a health care provider is offended by such a question, you are probably better off not having him or her care for your loved one. It is a reasonable and intelligent question to ask.

The Generation Gap and Depression

A revolution has occurred in the mental health field in the past twenty years as medications and psychotherapies specifically designed to alleviate depression have been refined and tested scientifically. Treatments for depression are readily available that are almost always effective. What is doubtful, however, is whether a person with depression will seek treatment. In fact, estimates of untreated depressions in this country range in the millions. Many of these people suffer through it and come out the other side completely recovered after the depression has run its course. Nevertheless, these people suffer needlessly for months or even years, and some never recover. The risks of untreated depression include compromised health care and suicide. In short, quick identification and treatment of clinical depression can save your parent unnecessary suffering and even death.

If you have read the first several chapters, you probably have a good grasp on how to identify depression, but the generation gap between you and your parent can cloud both your own and your parent's ability to identify the disorder quickly. And once it is identified, generational differences can make it difficult to convince your parent to seek professional help.

Because of the relatively recent revolution in treatments for depression, more people than ever are in psychotherapy or taking antidepressant medications, or both. You probably know someone in treatment, but it is much less likely that your parent does. As recently as the 1970s, there was much stigma attached to seeking treatment for emotional problems. Such people were labeled "psycho" or described as having had "a nervous breakdown." Stigma still exists, but the degree of ignorance and intolerance has lessened substantially.

Many of us have received the message that our moods are a private affair that should be handled alone or within the family unit. Advice such as "cheer up," "it will pass with time," "you just need a drink," or "look on the bright side" are old-fashioned ideas about how to handle a depression. Stoic silence is yet another outdated way to deal with depression. If your parent is responding to his depression in this way, you may be inclined to follow along. A parent who is not close to someone who has received psychological or psychiatric help or is unaware of recent advances in the treatment of depression will be likely to lean more on conventional wisdom than on modern science.

Diana's father felt that he had "a right" to be depressed. He was seventy-two years old, widowed, and unable to do many of the activities he used to enjoy. He was correct that sadness and even clinical depression often follow the death of a spouse and decreased mobility. However, it is *not* natural for the depression to persist, with little or no relief. No one should suffer for so long.

Albert felt ashamed about relying so much on Diana and Jeff. They drove him everywhere now, which felt humiliating to him. Seeking professional help would have felt like even more of a failure, and he did not need to feel even more incompetent than he already did. He was proud of his daughter and her son and said that he found it easier to rely on them for emotional support than to "admit defeat and speak to a stranger." What he did not realize was that his feeling that he was a failure was actually a symptom of the depression, not a fact about his character. He was stuck in the Reaction phase of the SAD, jumping to conclusions about what was the matter rather than gathering the information that would have helped to heal the rifts developing in his relationships with his daughter and grandson.

Diana and Jeff had their work cut out for them. Not only were they battling the depression that had taken hold of Albert's personality and physical health, but they also had to contend with his fragile self-esteem and ignorance about what it meant to seek professional help. In school and on television, Jeff had learned that "normal" people have sought counseling. Even Bruce Springsteen, one of his favorite rock stars, was quoted in *Rolling Stone* magazine as saying "therapy was the best thing I ever did." Bruce was certainly successful. But Jeff knew of his grandfather's tenuous self-esteem and attitudes about such help, so he put off talking to him about therapy and instead tried to fix the problem himself. He spent more time with Albert in the evenings, often listening to his grandfather's despair about life. Albert praised Jeff repeatedly, saying, "I don't know what I would do without you" and "You are so mature for your age!" Hearing these comments felt good to Jeff, but he was also becoming resentful. Not aware of his anger, Jeff would unknowingly let slip little comments revealing his irritation at not being able to spend time with his friends. Albert would feel worse and reply, "I feel terrible that I am burdening you so much—you should be out with your friends," indicating that he clearly understood the burden his depression was placing on Jeff. But Diana had taught Jeff that families stick together in times of need, and he believed that this was the right thing to do; he would feel guilty for wanting to see his friends instead of his grandfather. Afterward, he would silently resolve never to complain again. For these reasons and because there was something intrinsically gratifying about being needed by his grandfather, Jeff buried his anger. The result was that he became more irritable, dysphoric, and socially isolated. Jeff, Diana, and Albert were all stuck in the vicious cycle of depression, unable to extricate themselves, much less begin to help each other.

Jeff had frequent blowups with his mother about not doing his chores around the house, he neglected his studies, and he became more mopey around the house. Because of the frequent fights and Jeff's academic problems, Diana reluctantly brought her son in for a family consultation.

What became clear over the course of our meeting was that Jeff was angry with Albert for being so needy. He was stalled in the Reaction phase of the SAD and not learning how to engage in effective problem solving with Albert and Diana. As he became unstuck, he revealed, though hesitantly, that he had very different ideas than his mother did about what to do when he felt sad. He said that he would talk with a counselor. Diana, also immersed in her own reactions to Albert's depression, replied that she did not think Albert's problems were due to a mental illness. We pointed out that she was able to see her son's emotional problems as important enough to seek help and wondered why she thought her father's emotional problems were not "big enough." In the ensuing conversation, we focused on getting her to challenge her views on depression and how it should be handled. We shared our views, similar to Jeff's as it turned out, that seeking professional help was actually a sign of strength, not weakness. Her initial response was, "What else are you going to say? Your business relies on it!" Over the next several meetings, however, she began to feel differently. Our using the example of an alcoholic who does not seek treatment because of his sense of pride, and his children who do not insist he get help because of a sense of family loyalty, seemed to hit home. Diana could see the psychological problem as severe enough to warrant outside help. It was also easy for her to see how old-fashioned ideas, such as "I would feel like a failure if I went to a therapist," could lead to unnecessary suffering. And she came to realize how Albert's overreliance on her son and herself was truly making matters worse for everyone in the family.

Ironically, Jeff did not immediately accept his mother's suggestion that he not visit with Albert that coming weekend. Her decision to speak to her father about getting psychological help troubled Jeff, who was stuck in the depressive cycle. He felt guilty and protective of his grandfather, worrying that Albert would feel humiliated and get more depressed if he went to a therapist. With reassurance from his mother that she now believed that Albert needed the kind of help that the family could not provide, Jeff began to understand that his mother had changed her perspective on seeking outside help. She had come to see that not all emotional problems can be solved within the family.

Armed with these new insights, Diana sat down with her father to encourage him to see a therapist. Although he was quite resistant to the idea at first, he agreed to give it a try since nothing else seemed to be working. The generation gap, at least with regard to getting professional help for emotional problems, had been narrowed. Albert and his loved ones had successfully reached the Problem-Solving stage of the SAD.

Have Realistic Expectations

A common reaction for an offspring of a depressed person is to try to trade places with the parent, to think that they can solve the problem themselves. Whether you are a child, an adolescent, or an adult, the impulse to do for your parent, as they have done for you, can be overwhelming. This brings us back to the first two guidelines we introduced in Chapter 1: learning all that you can about depression and having realistic expectations about what you can do for your loved one.

You cannot cure someone's depression through kindness or support. Depression can be cured with medication or psychotherapy administered by a trained professional. When you were a child and had a high fever for more than several days, did your parents continue to give you only kindness, support, and aspirin? Probably not. Your parents understood that they had certain limitations and called the pediatrician.

Diana and Jeff did all they could do to help Albert feel better. They knew that a visit, a good conversation, simply time spent together was uplifting for Albert, but like a fever that persists, so did Albert's depression. Their initial reaction was to try to care for him in the way they had been cared for whenever they felt blue, but they were in over their heads and did not know it.

Ask for Help

It is especially important that you do not fall prey to the it's-a-family-problem syndrome when your parent is depressed. One of the symptoms of depression is social isolation. However, it is harder for a depressed person to avoid family members than it is to withdraw from friends. Your depressed parent may be living with you or you may call and visit frequently. If you are waiting for him to come out of the bathroom down the hall, it can be hard for your depressed parent to avoid you. While in some instances a depressed parent may withdraw from his family as well, what can and often does happen is that the family as a unit becomes socially isolated.

In the early stages of Albert's depression, during the Trouble and Reaction stages, Diana and Jeff had stopped spending time with their friends as their time was increasingly taken up by Albert. Because of their sense of family loyalty, they did not talk much with their friends about what was happening, yet the kind of loyalty they had been expressing was not working for any of them. Albert got worse, Jeff developed problems, and Diana felt very stressed. Diana and Jeff had been confusing isolation with loyalty.

Consider the following scenario. Your father has a serious drinking problem, so serious that his license has been suspended due to a conviction of driving while intoxicated. In fact, he totaled his car during his most recent drunk-driving accident. He asks to borrow your car to attend a wedding, but you need it that day so you do not have to deal with confronting the problem directly. Subsequently you hear that he has borrowed his neighbor's car. His neighbor knows nothing of your father's drinking problem. You know that he is an excellent driver when he is not drinking, but you doubt his reassurance that he will not drink at the wedding reception and drive because he has been unable to control his drinking in the past. Where do your loyalties lie? Do you tell his neighbor about his drinking problem and suspended license, or do you keep the problem within the family as your father has demanded? If you are a loyal son, you probably would do whatever you had to to ensure that he did not drive without a license in a situation where there will be pressure to drink.

In this scenario, the question of where your loyalties lie is not as complicated as when your parent is depressed. Your loyalties lie with your father, his safety, and the safety of other people. Because of increased public awareness, most people today believe that driving an automobile while intoxicated is self-destructive and dangerous to others. Thirty years ago, it would have been much more difficult to cross family lines because the prevailing wisdom about drinking and driving was quite different. Characters in films played by Cary Grant, W. C. Fields, and many others were funny and even endearing when drunk. They were certainly not self-destructive or dangerous. This is an example of how the right kind of information can lead to effective problem solving. With education about the effects of alcohol on one's capacity to operate a motor vehicle comes an increased willingness to challenge the self-destructive wishes of people we care about, even if it means speaking out.

If Diana and Jeff had been more educated about the dangers and problems stemming from untreated depression, it would have been easier for them to express their loyalty to Albert in a different way. Not seeking treatment for clinical depression is self-destructive and dangerous. Complying with a depressed relative's wish to continue along as if nothing were wrong is misplaced loyalty.

Find the Right Doctor

Older people present a unique set of challenges for physicians. That is why there are geriatric specialties in medicine, psychology, and social work. Nevertheless, many well-meaning doctors make the same mistake Diana did with Albert, confusing depressive symptoms in the elderly with symptoms they believe to be typical of older people. Let us illustrate how easy it is for anyone to generalize about older people. Most people believe that it is natural for older people to become senile. Is senility a common part of growing old? No. Only about 1 percent of people over age sixty-five ever develop symptoms of senility.

Physicians and therapists are not immune to such generalizations. If you have concern about the physical health of an elderly parent, be sure to seek a consultation with a physician who specializes in geriatric medicine. If you think that the problem might be related to depression, seek the help of a psychologist or psychiatrist who specializes in geriatric patients. Physicians unfamiliar with mood disorders and the elderly may easily miss making the correct diagnosis of depression. (In Chapter 14 we provide specific advice on where to find help for elderly people with depression.)

Epidemiological research shows that of the 32 million Americans age sixty-five and older, about 6 million suffer from some type of clinical depression. Estimates are that over 75 percent of these cases are undiagnosed and go untreated. Instead, a large proportion are routinely treated for other illnesses by doctors who fail to recognize that their patients are depressed. One reason that depression is not diagnosed is that doctors do not ask. In addition, older people do not divulge it unless they are asked directly, in part because of their generation's proclivity to stigmatize psychiatric problems.

If you are still unsure whether your parent's depression has caused trouble for you and your relationship, take the quiz shown. It was designed to help you determine the extent to which you and your relationship with your parent may be suffering from the secondary effects of his or her depression. Once again, remember to use your own reactions and feelings as a guide to answering the questions.

What You Can Do When Your Parent Is Depressed

In this chapter, we highlighted many of the common problems that arise when a parent is depressed. The guidelines set out in previous chapters hold here too:

Have realistic expectations. If what normally works is no longer lifting your parent's spirits, it is time to readjust your expectations about the help that you can provide.

Keep your routine. At first, your normal routine will suffer as you strive to help your parent, a natural and usually effective response when someone we love is hurting. If the problem is depression, however, it will persist for weeks or longer. In this case, returning to your normal routine will help you and your depressed parent.

Give unqualified support. Do not hesitate to let your depressed parent know that you care about what is going on with him. You do not have to visit him in person to communicate this. An elderly parent may be particularly susceptible to feeling isolated and alone. Many of his friends may be deceased or unable to offer support as they used to. Let

How Much Trouble Has Your Parent's Depression Caused You and Your Relationship?

To determine the extent to which you and your relationship with your parent may be suffering from the secondary effects of his/her depression, answer each question by circling "Yes" or "No."

1. Yes No   Do you feel especially unappreciated or disliked by your depressed parent?

2. Yes No   Are you feeling less interested in spending time with him/her?

3. Yes No   Do you feel frustrated because your attempts to help are being pushed away?

4. Yes No   Do you find yourself spending so much time with your parent that you no longer have time for other people and activities?

5. Yes No   Are you experiencing any signs of depression yourself such as feeling down, less interested in your usual activities, taking less pleasure in life, trouble with sleep, weight, appetite, concentration, energy level, and/or feelings of worthlessness?

6. Yes No   Are you and your parent arguing more intensely and/or more often?

7. Yes No   Are you "picking up the slack" so much that you feel overburdened ?

8. Yes No   Are you feeling more stress at work or school?

9. Yes No   Are you feeling isolated or more lonely than usual?

10. Yes No   Do you feel more tense and anxious since your parent has been depressed?

11. Yes No   Have you been spending more and more time handling matters for your parent that he/she used to take care of alone?

12. Yes No   Have you been drinking or using drugs more than usual?

13. Yes No   Have you missed a significant amount of work, since your parent's depression started?

14. Yes No   Do you worry that your parent no longer has the will to live?

15. Yes No   Are you and your parent having communication problems such as frequently interrupting each other, putting each other down, and not listening to each other?

16. Yes No   Are you finding yourself harsher than you meant to be when angry with your parent?

17. Yes No   Are you having more physical problems than usual?

18. Yes No   Have you been spending more time than usual helping your parent to get medical care for physical problems?

(cont'd.)

How Much Trouble (con't.)

19. Yes   No   Are you feeling more impatient with your parent and finding yourself thinking that he/she should "just snap out of it!"?

Scoring
Count the number of times you circled Yes to get your "Trouble with Depression" score.

19 to 13	Severe trouble: time to seek help

Severe trouble: time to seek help

19 to 13   You and your relationship with your parent are definitely affected by his/her depression. You are experiencing many of the classic secondary effects of depression and are at risk for depression yourself. Your relationship is also suffering significantly from your parent's depression and the negative interactions between the two of you may result in a worsening of his/her depression. Your relationship may be at risk for several severe problems such as increased hostility, communication breakdowns, and isolation from one another. You and your loved one should definitely gather more information on depression's effects on loved ones and relationships. You should also consult with a mental health professional for both yourself and your relationship.

Moderate trouble: time to be concerned

12 to 7   You and your relationship are affected by your parent's depression. You may be feeling overburdened, resentful, stressed, and/or distant from your parent. The two of you may be arguing more frequently and intensely. You should gather more information about depression and its secondary effects. You may also want to consult with a mental health professional for the sake of both yourself and your relationship. If you act now you can neutralize depression's toxic effects on you and your relationship before you reach the Severe trouble stage.

Little or no trouble: keep your eyes open

6 or less   Although you and your relationship may be experiencing some difficulties, depression is no more likely than other factors to have caused the trouble. However, because depression is so common and its effects on loved ones and relationships are so pervasive, it is always a good idea to keep your eyes open to the warning signs described in this questionaire.

him know that although you arè busy with your own life, you are available if he needs you.

Don't take it personally. Children grow up thinking they have a lot of influence over their parent's mood, and you may be holding on to this childhood myth. Just because your parent is unable to "snap out of it" does not mean you are at fault.

Share your feelings. If you can do it constructively, it is almost always valuable to share what you are feeling with your depressed parent. Diana told her father, "I've been feeling worried and frustrated that we haven't figured out what is wrong yet. Although I usually would take your side on something like this, I've been getting annoyed with you for not agreeing to see a psychologist. It would make me feel a lot better if you could do this for me."

Ask for help. Depression is an illness with biological and environmental causes. It requires treatment that you cannot provide. If your parent is resistant to seeking outside help, try to help him understand that seeking professional help for emotional problems is a sign of courage. It is rarely an easy thing for anyone to do. It is also an indication of being educated about these disorders.

Find the right doctor. If you and your parent have decided to get some help, read the last chapter of this book carefully. If your parent is elderly, make certain that the psychologist or psychiatrist working with him is knowledgeable about geriatric psychiatry.

Work as a team. Remember that the main problem is the illness, not you or your parent. Do not try to strong-arm your parent into treatment if he is reluctant. Try to understand his fears, and work to allay them. You will first have to convey a genuine understanding of what he fears in order to open a constructive line of communication. (In Chapter 14 we supply specific strategies to talk to your parent about getting help.) When problems arise in your relationship with your depressed parent, remember to work on the trouble together rather than ascribing responsibility to only yourself or to your parent. You are in it together. By working together, you stand a better chance of not letting the depression hurt you and your relationship with your parent in the process.

By following these guidelines, you will have a better chance of moving quickly to an effective Problem-Solving stage. The first step, however, as always, is to gather the information you will need to help your parent and yourself respond effectively to the challenges raised by a depression.

6

Friendships and Depression

Chris was getting really angry at his friend David. For the fifth time this month, he had canceled their plans at the last minute, leaving Chris hanging with nothing to do. He tried to talk to David about it but felt terrible afterward because David was so down on himself for canceling capriciously. In fact, they both felt guilty after that conversation—David for being "undependable" and "wishy-washy" and Chris for getting mad when it was clear that his friend was feeling really bad about himself. David was aware that he was depressed but kept telling himself that he would snap out of it. He wanted to talk to Chris about it but had no idea as to what he would say. He was feeling very lonely and that his life had no meaning and no purpose. He thought, "I sure as hell am not going to say that!" He was getting more and more angry with himself and kept telling himself to "get over it."

Chris, meanwhile, felt helpless and confused about what he should do. He realized that David was feeling down and should probably get some help, but he did not know how to broach the topic with him. Chris had seen David down in the dumps before and knew that he was very stoic and did not like to talk about his moods. He hoped that over time he would come out of it but was beginning to worry that it was taking too long. He didn't want to say anything because he thought David would get offended. Besides, David always said that therapy was for "whacked-out" people and that he never understood the need for it.

Maria walked over to where Peggy was sitting. They had both been invited to the wedding of a mutual friend who knew of their current estrangement, so they had not been seated together at the reception. Maria was nervous and not sure about what she would say. Although they had been close friends for over fifteen years, they had not spoken once during the last two years. Maria had been clinically depressed during much of that time. At first she was not sure what was wrong. The only thing she was sure of was that she did not want to talk on the telephone with anyone and wanted to be left alone. When she did answer the telephone, she found herself being increasingly quiet and uninterested in the conversation. This continued for many months during which Peggy was also going through an extremely difficult period. Peggy and her husband had separated a year prior, and the divorce and custody battle was proving to be very painful. Peggy's response to her crisis was to reach out to her friends and to ask for support. But after Maria had not returned several of Peggy's calls and after the last several conversations during which Maria seemed aloof and disinterested, Peggy began to feel that perhaps their friendship was one-sided.

Maria was unaware of her friend's reaction. Even if she had been aware, there was little she could have done about it because she was naive to the fact that she was depressed. When she finally learned that she was clinically depressed, she hesitated to tell Peggy. She felt terribly guilty and ashamed for having been such a poor friend in Peggy's time of need. By the time she sought treatment and was showing improvement, the damage had already been done. Now Peggy was not returning Maria's calls.

When a friend is depressed, a special set of problems arises. Generally it is not uncommon for someone to show less of her unattractive side to a friend than to a relative. Similarly, friends are often less likely to confront one another with "failings" than are people who are related to one another. The reason is that friendships tend to be more fragile than blood relationships. (Hence, the sayings, "Blood is thicker than water" and "Friends may come and go but your brother will always be your brother.") Friendships can end, even marriages can end, but family is always family. These relationships, even estranged ones, are permanent. This is not to say that family relationships are necessarily more stable or close, only that when it comes to relatives, you almost always can make attempts to mend any rift in the relationship. The problem with the relative impermanence of friendships is that friends are less willing to expose themselves. With less openness, misunderstandings are more common when a friend becomes depressed. In this context, two particular problems are common during the Information-Gathering and Problem-Solving phases of the SAD: faulty explanations or assumptions about the cause of the trouble and destructive conversations about the trouble.

The first problem results from an increased tendency for incorrect attributions or explanations for the trouble in the relationship. This leads to a focus on the wrong information during the Information-Gathering phase of the SAD. This was the case with Peggy. Mutual friends, who typically had less contact with Maria, told Peggy that as far as they knew, Maria seemed to be doing well. So Peggy attributed Maria's withdrawal to a character flaw (selfishness) and decided to end the friendship because she felt abandoned in her time of need.

A second problem can develop even when the trouble is correctly recognized as depression. The question of when and how to respond, or whether to say anything at all, can be extremely difficult even if friends have arrived at the Problem-Solving stage with good information about what has been causing the trouble. Meanwhile, for the depressed person the question of whether to tell friends just how badly he is feeling can be particularly difficult. Both Chris and David guessed that David was depressed, but because neither of them could talk about it—Chris because he felt guilty and David due to his shame—the friendship suffered. Both consequently missed out on each other's company, support, and collaboration in resolving the problem. Moreover, David ended up losing social support that could have been critical to his recovery from the depression. (Social support is essential to any prescription for relief from depression. Ironically, depression often results in a loss of social support.)

Our description of the problem of faulty assumptions about the cause of the trouble emphasizes the crucial importance of quickly identifying the cause of the trouble in the friendship as depression. If you refer back to Chapters 1 and 2, you will be aware of the early warning signs and diagnostic criteria for depression, though it may be difficult to use this information effectively if you do not typically see your friend every day. Nonetheless, if a friendship is to survive the depression of one of its members and move through the SAD effectively, quick and accurate identification of the problem is essential. The solution to the problem of infrequent contact is to open a line of communication about depression with your friend. Once the two of you are talking about the possibility that your friend is depressed, you can rely on her observations on how she is doing during the time you are not together. But in order to get to the point where you can talk about depression, the trouble in the relationship needs to be put in the proper context. The tension in the friendship needs to be understood by both members as a consequence of depression rather than solely the result of each other's actions.

Your feelings and reactions to your loved one can be important early warning signs that you can use to talk about your feelings constructively, initiating a discussion about the depression and ultimately an effective passage through the Information-Gathering and Problem-Solving stages. If there is trouble in the relationship resulting in bad feelings and knee-jerk reactions (e.g., Peggy's disappointment and subsequent withdrawal from Maria), and both members work on the problem in isolation from one another, focusing on the wrong information, misunderstandings flourish and effective problem solving becomes nearly impossible. If Peggy had considered depression as a cause for Maria's behavior, she would have been able to talk about her feelings of disappointment and anger more openly and empathically. She might have said, "I felt really hurt when we talked last. After we hung up, I was left with the feeling that you had no interest in what was going on with me. It made me angry, but it also made me wonder what was going on with you. I usually feel as if you care a lot about me. Are you OK?" Had she been able to do this early on, the deep rift in their friendship that developed would probably not have occurred at all.

This brings us to the second common problem: how to talk about feelings and reactions constructively. Later in this chapter we describe ways in which this problem can be identified and remedied. We teach you how to express your feelings in a manner that will minimize your friend's defensiveness and optimize her openness, advise on how to discuss your feelings and the trouble in the relationship in a manner that leads to collaboration rather than to isolation, and show you how to broach the topic of depression with a friend who seems unaware that she is depressed. For the friend who is aware of being depressed but uses it as an excuse to treat you poorly, we will show you how to confront her in a manner that leads to relief for both of you.

Prior to giving you these guidelines, we tell you about recent research on the effects of depression on friendships in order to increase your ability to identify the early warning signs of depression by paying attention to your feelings about the friendship. Another goal is to convince you of the critical importance of working together on the problem rather than allowing the depression to split you and your friend apart. As you will learn, without effective social support, depressed people only get worse, and their friends lose out as well.

Research on Friendships and Depression

In research efforts to understand the effects of depression on friendships and even on casual acquaintances, two key findings have emerged: Interacting with a depressed friend can leave *you* feeling depressed and angry, and there are specific types of interactions, easily identified, that can increase your friend's depression. If they are not corrected, depressive interactions can dismantle social support, which is particularly damaging to the depressed person.

One common feature of depressed persons' interactions with others is that due to the distress they communicate, people are quickly engaged and left feeling responsible. The first few times David told Chris about how badly he was feeling about himself, Chris listened attentively and tried to reassure him. David talked about feeling disorganized at work: "I am really in a bad mood. I am such an idiot. I procrastinate constantly and never do what I am supposed to do. I am the biggest screw-up. I wait until the last minute, then rush around like a chicken with his head cut off. I should be so lucky as to have my head cut off!" Chris's natural reaction was to listen attentively and try to reassure David that he was not "an idiot or a screw-up." Chris thought his friend was talking about himself this way because he needed reassurance and wanted to make Chris feel better about their relationship. With increased interest and a sense of responsibility, the burden of the interaction shifts onto the nondepressed person. In this context, the depressed person's distress can be aversive and guilt inducing. If this happens repeatedly, offers of support to the depressed person are fewer and less heartfelt. This is one of the essential characteristics of the depressive dance we told you about. For example, you may attempt to hide your aversive reactions by outwardly providing the support being asked for, but you may still communicate your impatience, hostility, and rejection even if you are not describing these feelings explicitly. The subtle hostility and rejection that the depressed person gets confirms her sense of worthlessness and leads to more expressions of distress; the pattern of alienation continues.

If you are involved in such a pattern, it is easy to see how you could become depressed and hostile when you spend time with your depressed friend. You may feel overly responsible for how she is feeling because you feel as if you are being asked for help, but nothing you do seems to offer relief. You end up feeling as if you are failing your friend in a time of need because your attempts to help do nothing to lift her spirits. Making matters worse for the relationship, you feel guilty that your desire to spend time with your friend is rapidly waning. You feel angry about having to carry so much guilt and burden, and you feel increasingly helpless to do anything about the depression or your reactions to it. In Chapter 9 we give you specific instructions to cope with your help being turned away.

The Vicious Cycle

Some researchers have proposed a model of depression that views depressive symptoms, in part, as a consequence of a dysfunctional relationship(s). In the downward depressive spiral, the depressed person's complaints and self-derogating and help-seeking behaviors alienate the people closest to her. In particular, symptoms of depression can arouse guilt in others and thereby inhibit any direct expressions of anger. For example, as a sympathetic friend, you may initially react with concern about a depressed friend's feelings. You may go to great lengths to reassure her that you care and that she is not as worthless as she believes. If your friend's symptoms persist (e.g., repeated complaints about feeling hopeless and comments reflecting poor self-esteem) and particularly if she rejects your offers of support, you may understandably feel irritated or even angry. You may be genuinely trying to offer support and reassurance, but you undoubtedly also convey resentment and hostility. These aversive interactions with your friend can lead to your responding more negatively and to avoiding her altogether. In such cases, the depressive syndrome worsens as the depressed person responds to the discrepancy between reassuring words that are spoken aloud and the anger and rejection that are communicated silently. As the depressed person becomes more aware of the implicit communications, she displays more symptoms of distress in an attempt to regain the support she got initially, further stimulating the depressive social process and leading to an escalation of symptoms.

At this point you might be thinking: "This makes some sense, but I know I wouldn't let my friend know I was tired of hearing her complain about how badly she feels. I know how to hide such feelings. After all, she's feeling lousy and doesn't need to hear me complain about her!" If you are thinking this or something like it, you have fallen right into the depressive-spiral trap! People are generally not as good at hiding their negative feelings as they might think. The belief that you can hide such feelings will prevent you from satisfying your needs in the relationship, thereby worsening the negative feelings. The more intense they get, the harder they are to hide.

Let us look at David and Chris. Chris initially "cut David some slack" after he canceled the first time, thinking, "I know he feels bad and he can't talk about it. I'll just forget about it." After the second time, however, when the two of them were making plans to get together, Chris was reluctant to commit, saying, "Why don't you call me on Thursday in the afternoon? I should know by then if I've done enough work that I can take the night off." David later revealed that he felt Chris did not want to see him at all because he had always been eager to make plans well in advance. Work had never been an issue before. Now David felt worse about himself and less supported. He wanted to say something, but he thought that if Chris was feeling fed up with him, then it would only make matters worse. Nevertheless, he felt ambivalent about calling Chris that Thursday afternoon; although he wanted to get together, he felt Chris really did not want to see him while he was feeling so blue. He went back and forth, unsure if he should call, and hoping Chris would call so that he could feel reassured that Chris really wanted to see him. In the end, confused and more depressed, he "forgot" to call. By 6:00 P.M. Chris called him, feeling rejected and angry but once again deciding not to talk about his feelings.

Did Chris hide his negative feelings? At one level, yes. He did not say he was hurt or angry. All he did was play a little "hard to get" and ask David to call him. The first problem is that Chris asked for this because he was feeling rejected and angry, not because he had too much work to do. Ironically, the fact that it was not about work was easy for David to figure out because of another effect of depression: A depressed person's interpretation of himself and of the world around him becomes very negative. Researchers refer to these negative perceptions and beliefs as *cognitive distortions*. In other words, depressed people are constantly looking for evidence that will support their negative view of themselves and of life. Trying to hide your negative feelings from a depressed person is impossible. One way or another, consciously or subconsciously, she will know that you are feeling negatively about her.

As we promised at the outset of this chapter, we will show you how to express such negative feelings constructively in order to problem-solve effectively. But first we will briefly describe the research on social support and how it relates to our recommendation that you interrupt the downward depressive spiral by communicating together more constructively.

The Importance of Social Support

Social support can work as a vaccine against coming down with depression. Research studies have shown that people with fewer close relationships, a smaller social network, and less supportive relationships are more likely to become depressed. People who report less social support are thirteen times more likely to meet criteria for major depression than persons who report higher levels of social support. There has also been a suggestion that the quality of one's closest relationships is most crucial; support from other relationships does not make up for deficiencies in intimate relationships. You might be asking yourself what the cause and the effect are here. Do depressed people have fewer good relationships? Or is it that they had fewer good relationships to begin with and that is part of the reason they were vulnerable to depression?

The answer to both questions is yes. Some studies have shown that even before they became depressed, depressed people had less social support than nondepressed people did. The point is that social support can serve as both a vaccine and a medicine for depression.

Social support can be very helpful in the fight against depression. The problem is that people with depression can be difficult to spend any time with, especially quality time. Their distress leads to difficult interpersonal relations over time. Studies even show that the concern and good intentions of family members can be stressful. Some researchers have proposed that having social support may be more a matter of freedom from conflict and negative interactions than anything else. They suggest that coping with a stressful life event in the context of a conflictual relationship may be more difficult than not having a relationship at all.

Given the connection between social support and depression, you can see how important it is to establish a constructive, trouble-free (or nearly so) relationship with your depressed friend. In the next section, we will show you ways to avoid the vicious cycle of depression and how to optimize your ability to give the social support your friend will need to fight effectively against the depression.

Giving Social Support

The depression of a friend can have a big impact on your own mood. How you feel and react can also have an effect on your ability to help your friend. Your own anger, sadness, or worry will have a negative impact on your reactions, and then your friend may respond in a way that only perpetuates the depressive dance.

Peggy had been feeling hurt by Maria's distance on the telephone. Several times she had asked Maria, "Are you still listening? Although Maria would invariably answer yes, Peggy knew it didn't feel as if she was listening. Rather than push the issue, she began to call less often and to disclose less about what was going on in her life when they did speak. She found herself chatting aimlessly to fill up the space left by their withdrawal from one another. Maria sensed Peggy's pulling back and guessed correctly that it was because of her inattention to what Peggy said. Now she felt even worse about herself; she had honestly tried to listen attentively when Peggy had been talking with her about her problems, but she just could not do it. She was too preoccupied with her negative thoughts about herself and her life. She had wanted to say something to this effect, to let Peggy in on how she was feeling and to explain that her lack of attention was not because she didn't care about her. However, she couldn't bring herself to do this because she worried that Peggy would get tired of hearing about her problems and resent having to deal with them again at a time when Peggy had her divorce to deal with.

These friends were experiencing the depressive dance. As a result, both of them were hurt, and Maria's depression worsened. However, all is not lost. Just as there are lessons for dance, there are lessons for constructive communication with a depressed person.

When communicating negative feelings, there are several ways to increase the odds that the discussion will result in a constructive outcome. First, consider the costs and benefits of talking about how you are feeling. Ask yourself whether *not* talking about your feelings is making you less interested in spending time with her. If the answer is yes, then given everything we have talked about up to this point, the next step should be obvious: You need to talk with your friend about how her depression has affected you and your relationship with her. Here are some guidelines to keep in mind when you talk about your negative feelings:

Wait to talk about how you are feeling. The first time you realize you are angry, say to yourself, "I can always tell him later. I don't have to do it right now." Give yourself the time to sort through what you are feeling and to think about how you want to talk about it. Give yourself and your friend the benefit of the doubt. If you have not yet established a pattern of constructive communication about negative feelings, then try *not* to talk about your negative feelings the moment you identify them. Trust that you can always talk about it tomorrow. Unlike Scarlett O'Hara in *Gone with the Wind,* "tomorrow is another day" is not an indication of avoidance or repression of negative feelings. In this instance, it gives you the time to plan how to talk about your feelings constructively (more on this in Chapter 7) and the time you will need to turn the depressive dance into a productive dance.

Reassure your friend. Explain that you are telling her about your negative feelings because you want to feel good about the time you spend together and because you want to help her. One of the major symptoms of depression is an increased sense of worthlessness. Someone who is depressed is prone to interpret the opinions of others negatively. Consequently, when talking about how her depression makes you feel, you need to reassure her that you value your friendship with her. You are speaking up because you feel she is worth the trouble. The first time Chris talked to David about his anger at being stood up, the conversation ended in David's feeling worse about himself and Chris's feeling guilty for saying anything. Chris described his experience of the conversation in this way: "Now I know what people mean when they say that you shouldn't kick a dog when it's down." The problem was that Chris began the talk by saying, "Your canceling our plans at the last minute is really rude. If you say you're going to do something, then you should do it!" David quickly agreed and added, "I know I am being a jerk. I don't know what to tell you. If you don't want to hang out next Thursday, I would understand." The conversation continued in this vein until Chris ended it abruptly, feeling not only guilty but also angrier. If Chris had instead prefaced his remarks by reassuring David and telling him that he missed the time they spent together, it would have made it more difficult for David to interpret Chris's feelings the way he did. David's reply revealed that he was quick to feel that no one would want to spend time with him while he was feeling so low.

Separate the depression from your friend. Depression can be a tricky illness. Unlike other illnesses, where the symptoms are clearly separate from your impression of the person's personality, such as sneezing and watery eyes during allergy season, depressive symptoms can easily be mistaken for personality traits. Peggy felt that Maria's lack of interest in her was due to an overly narcissistic personality. She came to the conclusion that Maria was incapable of caring for her friends when they needed help. Had Peggy been more educated about the syndrome of depression, she would have recognized that Maria was plagued by anhedonia and poor concentration, two commonly misunderstood symptoms of depression. A pervasive lack of interest in people and activities that usually give pleasure is often interpreted as something personal by people unfamiliar with the symptom of anhedonia. Hence, Peggy thought, "She doesn't care about me," which ultimately led to her confusing a symptom of depression with a personality trait.

Don't play the blaming game. Invite your friend to see the depression as the cause of the trouble in your friendship rather than as you or he being at fault. Whenever we feel badly, our natural reflex is to try to determine who or what is to blame. After all, something must be making you, or your friend, feel blue, irritable, or guilty. Someone must be at fault. David was quick to blame himself for the trouble in his relationship with Chris. Peggy was quick to blame Maria. The blaming game is probably one of the most insidious problems that arises during the early phases of the SAD.

There are two problems with blaming one person for the way another one feels. One is that it puts people on the defensive and usually results in increased distance and less collaboration. The second is that blaming one person for a problem in a relationship is usually a gross oversimplification of what is really going on.

The remedy to the first problem is simple: Don't blame yourself or the other person. Blame only breeds defensiveness and guilt, and neither will help matters. Human emotions and interactions are amazingly complex. To jump to the conclusion, as Peggy did, that you feel angry solely because your depressed friend ignored your needs is too simplistic. Some people are quick to feel angry in situations like the one Peggy found herself in with Maria, while others would never feel anything more than mild frustration. The reasons for this variability are many. Your individual sensitivity to being ignored, the quality of the previous interactions with your friend, and the degree of patience you possess can all affect how you feel. Try to say to yourself, "I know what I am feeling and what triggered it, but there may be more here than meets the eye." Give yourself the time and space to explore the possibilities. You may be surprised by what you learn about why you are feeling the way you do.

The solution to the second problem involves distinguishing blame from responsibility. Because Peggy was so consumed by her own problems and had a sensitivity to being ignored, she could not easily see that Maria was seriously depressed. That oversight was her contribution to the trouble in their relationship. Maria's contribution to the trouble stemmed from the anhedonia, low energy, and poor concentration caused by the depression. In addition, her sense of shame hampered her ability to communicate effectively how incapacitated she really was. The depression, personal sensitivities, life circumstances, and shame were all partly to blame for what happened to Maria and Peggy's friend-ship. If both Maria and Peggy had taken responsibility for their personal contribution to the trouble, then a productive resolution would have become possible. If at the time, as she did much later, Peggy had thought about the intensity of her anger rather than just reacting to it by withdrawing, she would have come to the realization that it had as much to do with a raw nerve for her as it had to do with what Maria was doing. Peggy knew from experience that having a friend pull back was a particularly sore subject for her and that one of the reasons she had become good friends with Maria in the first place was that she was typically attentive and interested in what Peggy had to say. When Peggy came to realize that she was as deeply angry as she was because of this raw nerve, she took responsibility for the intensity of her feelings. She was more willing and able to talk with Maria about what happened.

Use "I" rather than "you." For example, say, "I feel angry," rather than, "You make me angry." This wording helps to minimize your friend's de-fensiveness and keeps the focus on solving the problem as a team rather than suggesting that it is entirely your friend's responsibility to fix it. This is an especially important guideline; it conveys that you are not out to blame your friend for how you are feeling. Using *I* rather than *you* implies that you have not jumped to any conclusions, that you are open to exploring the possibilities for why you feel the way you do, and that you want to resolve the trouble *with* your friend. When Chris told David, "Canceling our plans at the last minute is really rude," David felt blamed for the way Chris was feeling. He felt that it was all his fault. Later, after talking it over in therapy, Chris changed his tactics and said, "I felt hurt and angry last week when you canceled at the last minute." At first David still felt blamed, but Chris reminded him that he wanted him to know how he was feeling so that they could try and fix the problem. He told David he was not saying he was a jerk, but that something he was doing was hurtful to him and that he wanted to talk about it. By continuing to focus on how he was feeling ("*I* felt hurt and angry when you did . . .") rather than making negative generalizations about David's manners ("*You* were rude . . ."), he was able to involve David in some effective problem solving. They ultimately concluded that if David could be more up-front about how he was feeling, then it would be easier for Chris not to take his abrupt cancellations personally. In addition, they discovered that David felt he could have gone out with Chris if they had done something that did not require a lot of effort. A few weeks later, Chris reported that he had recently received a cancellation call from David an hour before they were going to get together. At first, it was the same old dynamic, with David sounding guilty and abrupt, but this time Chris encouraged David to talk about what was going on. With some prompting, David revealed that he was feeling badly and would like to see Chris but did not think he would be good company. Chris suggested that they go to a movie because in a dark theater David would not have to "put on a happy face" if he did not feel up. He also told David that he would understand if he did not feel like going. Feeling less pressured, David agreed to go to a movie. Although they did not talk much that evening, Chris was glad to see David, and despite his depression, David told Chris that he appreciated the company and the chance to get out of his apartment.

Up to now, we have focused on particular types of relationships and their adaptation to depression. Next, we show you ways in which you can work together with your depressed loved one to begin to solve the problems raised by the depression.

7

Constructive Communication

Audrey complained bitterly about her younger sister, Sheila. She asked, "Why is she so incredibly difficult? Why does every conversation we have end either in an angry silence or a shouting match?" Audrey explained that they had always been somewhat competitive but that they had maintained a fairly good relationship through college and the early years of their marriages. They talked on the telephone weekly and visited each other's homes frequently. Now Audrey felt distant and angry at Sheila, and she was beginning to think that Sheila felt the same way about her.

Whenever they spoke on the telephone, the conversation would start off fine but then disintegrate into accusations and name calling. Audrey knew that Sheila had been having a tough time with her career and was feeling that she had not lived up to her potential, but that was no excuse to be so curt and uninterested. Audrey wondered if Sheila was depressed but did not understand why Sheila did not just say so. She reasoned "If Sheila is really that down on her life, then maybe I could help her," but when she tried to talk to Sheila about her bad moods, Sheila would get furious at her for being a "bossy older sister," and the conversation would end abruptly. Audrey began to resent Sheila's constant complaining about her life but not doing anything about it and accused her of "enjoying her misery." Each time Audrey tried to communicate with Sheila, she found herself getting more and more frustrated. Finally Audrey backed off and stopped calling Sheila.

When Sheila finally called Audrey several weeks later, she blamed her for not caring, and they had a heated argument about who called whom more often.

Communication Breakdowns in Depression

Audrey and Sheila are having a communication breakdown. They are angry at each other and the more they try to talk about what is bothering them, the more their communication seems to break down. If someone you care about is depressed, you may have had some of the same experiences as Audrey. You may feel that no matter what you do, the depressed person will "bite your head off" and make it impossible to discuss anything in a rational way. Communication breakdowns are not unusual. We all go to school to learn how to read and write, but no one ever teaches us the basics of how to communicate constructively in relationships.

Communication problems abound in all relationships, with parents, other relatives, friends, and even coworkers. Being unable to talk in a clear and constructive way is not uncommon. In fact, one of the primary complaints of all couples who seek marital counseling is that "we don't communicate." In general, women tend to complain that men do not open up enough, and men complain that women do not say what they really mean. The popularity of such best-selling books as *You Just Don't Understand* by Deborah Tannen and *Women Are from Venus and Men Are from Mars* by John Gray reflects that communication problems hit home for most people and that gender differences account for many kinds of communication difficulties. We all know what it is like to feel misunderstood or as if we are speaking a different language from someone we care about.

When someone you love is depressed, communication problems are even more intense. In fact, they are at the crux of how depression can affect relationships. The depressive dance, which leads to worsening depression and relationship difficulties, usually begins with a communication breakdown. Depression, as you know by now, is a complicated and multifaceted illness that affects every aspect of a person's functioning, from mood, to sleep and appetite, and even to how one thinks and responds to other people. Researchers interested in how depressed people think have found that they have cognitive distortions about themselves and others, seeing things in a negative light. For example, if a get-together is canceled because the host is feeling ill, a depressed man may assume that he was not really wanted at the party anyway. If a project at work is temporarily put on hold because of budget cuts, a woman who is depressed may jump to the assumption that the project will never get off the ground and blame herself for it.

These kinds of negative attributions are typical in depression and can affect communication with your loved one. It is hard to enter the Problem-Solving phase of the SAD if you are having difficulty talking with your loved you. The depressed person's distorted interpretation of what you say can cloud what you mean. When you tell your friend, "I can't meet you tonight for dinner because I have this project to get done," she may infer that she is not enjoyable to be with. When you're communicating with a depressed person, you need to be especially careful to ensure that there are no misunderstandings. Improving your ability to communicate will make it more difficult for the depressed person to distort or misinterpret your intentions and will prevent the depressive dance from becoming the routine way you interact.

Another related problem is that your own reactions and feelings can be obstacles to communicating clearly. It is not always what you say but how you say it. If you have strong feelings of resentment or anger toward the depressed person, those feelings may be conveyed in indirect and possibly destructive ways. For example, Audrey resented the fact that she was always the one to call Sheila; when Sheila answered the phone, Audrey would say, "Well, hello stranger. I thought you must have left the country," a comment that would make Sheila feel both guilty that she had not called Audrey and annoyed that Audrey expected so much from her. This kind of scenario lays the groundwork for further breakdowns in communication.

If you don't tell a loved one your true feelings about something because you do not want to add to her misery, it can also result in communication problems. Imagine that you would rather stay home and relax this weekend than see your in-laws, but you worry that canceling the plans will upset your wife, who is already depressed, so you go along with the plan but feel resentful. As a result, the way you relate to your wife during the weekend will be affected. Instead of rolling with the punches when your nieces and nephews are running around the house, you take her aside and complain, "All this noise is giving me a headache! Is this what I needed on a day off?" In turn, your wife may get angry and say, "Don't blame me. You wanted to see my family. I didn't!" By this time, any kind of rational discussion about what the two of you need and want is virtually impossible. If you had been able to be honest and direct about your feelings from the beginning, this kind of communication breakdown could probably have been avoided.

Practice Makes Perfect

A strong desire to improve the communication in your relationship is a good first step, but change requires a lot of effort and practice, and many of us picked up bad communication habits along the way. How do you unlearn bad communication habits learned over a lifetime of relating to others?

Asking for help is an essential first step as you move into the Information-Gathering phase of the SAD. You need to learn more about good communication skills. Psychologists, social workers, and other mental health professionals have been trained to help individuals learn how to communicate better. Family therapy, in particular, focuses on helping family members to work together to solve problems through talking about them. You may want to consider seeing a professional who can help you learn how to communicate more effectively. Chapter 14 will give you advice about how to find help.

Most people, however, can vastly improve their communication skills on their own. By understanding what makes for good and bad communication and practicing the skills in daily conversations, you can see dramatic changes in your relationships. Once you learn the skills, practice, practice, and more practice is the best way to change habits. When you are ready to practice what you have learned, you will be moving into the Problem-Solving phase of the SAD, where you and your loved one can begin to work together to combat the depression.

How to Communicate Constructively

Communicating constructively is crucial if you are to navigate the Problem-Solving phase of the SAD with your depressed loved one. You need to be able to talk to one another in order to collaborate and come up with solutions to your problems. In the sections that follow, we guide you step by step through the general guidelines for constructive communication and then through the specific Do's and Don't of Constructive Communication. And finally, given the gender differences in how we communicate, we give you Five Effective Ways To Communicate With A Depressed Man and Five Effective Ways To Communicate With A Depressed Woman. Following the specific strategies in this chapter will enable you to break the vicious cycle of the depressive dance and move on to the productive dance of working together to solve problems in your relationship.

Communication can be destructive, resulting in more misunderstanding, distance, and increased negative emotions in a relationship, or constructive, functioning to increase the understanding, closeness, and positive emotions in a relationship. At various times and in different situations, we all take part in both destructive and constructive communication, but when someone you love is depressed, communicating constructively as much as you can is vital.

The first step is to pay attention to your own role in conversation. If asked to recall a recent conversation, most people will remember most clearly what the other person said and did. It is much harder to notice one's own contribution to the flow of conversation. We tend to see other people's comments as steering the course of communication, rather than our own. In fact, however, it takes two to communicate. What you say and do has a big influence on how your communication goes with other people. Try to notice whether you communicate differently with the depressed person than you do with other people. Chances are that you do. You might be less patient, bossier, or less direct about how you feel because you do not want to upset her. Keep the following communication guidelines in mind as you enter the Problem-Solving phase of the SAD with the depressed person close to you, and remember the guidelines you have already learned in earlier chapters. Don't expect to be able to use all of these guidelines all of the time and immediately. You will need time and practice to make changes in how you communicate.

General Guidelines for Constructive Communication

Make time for communication. The most important ingredient of good communication is having the time to talk. If you live with the depressed person, try to set aside a regular time to discuss the day's events and share your experiences. If you do not live with the depressed person, try to have regular telephone conversations or make frequent visits to keep in touch. Make the time to communicate separate from other activities. Too many of us eat dinner in front of the television set or try to catch up with a family member while simultaneously opening the mail and thinking about the next task. Make communication a priority in your relationship.

It was helpful for Audrey and Sheila to make regular times to talk on the telephone. Once they knew that Sunday mornings at eleven o'clock was their time, they were much less likely to spend their conversations arguing about who called whom last. Instead, they could focus on catching up with one another and trying to communicate their feelings constructively.

Pay attention to nonverbal behavior. Body language is important in all communication but especially when communicating with a depressed person, who is prone to interpret things negatively. If you are averting your eyes or fidgeting in your seat, the depressed person is likely to think you are uninterested in what he has to say. Maintain eye contact. Sit still, and lean forward to show that you are involved in the conversation. Your facial expression and vocal inflection are also important. If you are verbally expressing sympathy but using a flat, uninterested tone or rolling your eyes, the effect can be the opposite of what you think you are conveying. Quite a few depressed patients have told us that they got "bad vibes" from family members who seemed to be saying one thing but acted as if they felt a different way. Be aware of what your nonverbal body language communicates.

Audrey discovered that if she changed her tone when talking to

Sheila from accusatory to warm, they were able to communicate more effectively. But if she started off a conversation with an edge in her voice, chances were that they would have a difficult and unpleasant conversation. Once she noticed this phenomenon, Audrey made a conscious effort to keep a positive and open tone rather than convey annoyance and anger. This was not easy for her, but the first few times she tried it, she noticed that the conversation went much better. Because the reward was so immediate, it became easier and easier for her to change her tone.

Be sure to listen. The art of listening is often overlooked. Most of us are much better at communicating our own thoughts than really absorbing what other people say. When there are silences in conversation, we often chat just to fill them. When you are communicating with a depressed person, it is especially likely that there may be such lulls because depressed people are often reluctant to open up. As a result, you may find yourself chattering about anything just to make conversation. Instead, try to tolerate the silence and listen. Chances are that the depressed person will feel more able to open up if she is given both the space and an interested listener. In addition, you might find yourself giving advice and not listening carefully. The impulse to give advice, make suggestions, and alleviate pain are natural reactions to a loved one's depression. But often the best choice is to start by listening to her and then respond to what she says.

One of the most effective ways to convey that you want to listen is to reflect back what was said and make a guess at the feeling underneath the spoken words. For example, you could say, "It sounds as if you feel annoyed about that. Is that because you expected it to be different?" Active listening invites the speaker to communicate more.

Audrey had trouble actively listening to what Sheila had to say. As soon as Sheila began to complain about her job, Audrey tended to jump in with a host of suggestions. Sheila, in turn, became frustrated at not being able to express her feelings before Audrey responded. If Audrey had stopped and listened, Sheila would probably have felt more understood and closer to Audrey. Try to catch yourself if you are doing more than your share of the talking in your conversations with the depressed person. Sit back, listen, and see what unfolds.

Speak calmly, clearly, and slowly. A depressed person's thoughts and ability to comprehend what is being said are often slowed down. She can feel easily overwhelmed and unable to pay attention. The experience of being depressed is often described as "like I'm in a slow-motion movie while everyone else is in double speed." Normal conversation can sound too fast and too loud. It can be particularly hard for the person to keep up with conversation that jumps from one idea to another. When you speak to your depressed loved one, be calm, clear, and slow. The tone of your voice should be composed and as mellow as possible. This is not to say that you cannot convey anger or negative feelings, but even then try to keep the tone calm. Being clear is also important. For example, you might say, "I felt angry when you didn't return my call" rather than, "Why didn't you call me back? I don't know what's wrong with you. I feel as if I can't count on you for anything." Remember that people who are depressed can have cognitive distortions and interpret whatever you say negatively. To avoid misunderstandings, be clear; spell out what you mean, and do not leave any ambiguities that might be misinterpreted. Speak slowly so that you can be understood. Try to imagine what it must be like to try to think clearly when you feel as if you are thinking in slow motion.

After several sessions of individual therapy to help her cope with her sister's depression, Audrey commented, "I think I come on too fast for Sheila." She explained that she had not realized how Sheila's depression had slowed her down, but now that she knew more about how depression affects people, she realized that she spoke very quickly and often in abstract terms. She tended to be vague with Sheila and say, "Just pull yourself up by your bootstraps," instead of being specific and clear about what she meant. In the weeks that followed, Audrey made a concerted effort to slow her pace and speak more clearly. In turn, Sheila responded by spending more time on the phone with Audrey and seemingly paying more attention to what she said.

Don't talk down. While you do want to speak calmly, clearly, and slowly, you should not speak in a condescending manner to the depressed person. Just because someone is depressed does not mean that she is less intelligent or less able to have opinions. If the depressed person senses that you are talking down to her, she may get angry and lose patience with you. Such conflict certainly will not help your communication.

When Audrey told Sheila what to do, Sheila felt insulted that Audrey treated her like a "three year old." As a result, Sheila withdrew from Audrey, and the distance between them grew. Do not treat the depressed person like a child, and do not assume that you know what is best for her. If the depressed person you are talking to is a child, continue to talk to her in the same manner as you would to a nondepressed child of the same age. Remember to speak to the depressed person with the same respect that you would with anyone else close to you.

Don't come on too strong. When someone you care about is depressed, you may feel the urge to give advice. If you see someone moping around, it's natural to want to help her feel better. But be aware of coming on too strong. One of the hallmarks of being depressed is a sense of hopelessness. When you bombard a depressed person with one suggestion after another, she may feel as if you do not understand her situation. She feels as if there is no hope, but here you are giving her advice and expecting her to feel 100 percent better. Convey that you understand how hopeless she feels. Then offer advice, but try to limit it to one suggestion at a time. What matters more than the actual suggestion is that you convey respect and an understanding of what she feels she is up against. Sometimes it is most helpful to encourage your loved one to get out of the house and stay active; at other times, it may be better to suggest that she take some time to be alone. To figure out the best advice to give, you need to consult with your loved one about what she thinks would be most helpful.

Through the course of her own individual therapy, Audrey recognized what she termed her "tendency to assault Sheila with one piece of advice after another." Instead of offering eight suggestions about how Sheila could stand up to her boss, Audrey tried making just one suggestion at a time, but only after asking Sheila about what she thought might be helpful. In turn, Sheila was able to hear that one piece of advice clearly and evaluate whether it was worth trying. As a result, the sisters spent much less of their conversations arguing about who was "more bossy" and were able to begin to share deeper feelings about their lives.

Express your feelings directly. Your thoughts and feelings are important. Although we have emphasized that you need to listen and be aware of how you talk to the depressed person, you still need to share your feelings. Open, honest communication is possible only if both members in a relationship are able to express themselves. Try to become aware of what you are feeling, and then communicate it to the depressed person in a direct way. Probably, you worry that expressing your negative feelings will be hurtful to someone who is depressed. However, we believe that you can communicate your feelings directly to the depressed person (given that she is not a young child) if you follow certain rules about communicating constructively. If your depressed loved one is a child, it may be more appropriate for you to share your feelings with another adult. (Turn to Chapter 4 for more specific advice about how to share your feelings when your child is depressed.)

The first step in communicating constructively is to reassure the depressed person that you are letting her know how you feel because the relationship with her is important to you. Tell her that you do not want to attack her or blame her for anything. Rather, you want to express how you are feeling because you want to improve your relationship with her. The next step is to practice speaking directly and calmly about your feelings. Tell her clearly how you feel in the particular situation that you are discussing. Make sure that she understands what you are saying and does not get too defensive. If she begins to get defensive, back off a bit and try to rephrase what you are saying.

It took Audrey a bit of practice to talk directly to her sister about how she was feeling. She was used to attacking her or keeping her concerns inside. Expressing herself directly felt awkward and clumsy at first. Audrey began the conversation by saying, "I want to talk to you about something that's been on my mind. But I don't want you to feel that I'm nagging or being your bossy older sister. I just want you to understand some of the things I've been feeling about our relationship. I'm only bringing it up because I love you and I miss the closeness that we used to have." Although Sheila was initially defensive, she was better able to hear what Audrey had to say in this conversation. Rather than rushing off the phone as she had in the past few conversations, Sheila answered, "What are you talking about?"

"Mostly that I miss being close to you."

"Why, what did I do?" Sheila asked.

"It's not what you did as much as how I'm feeling about the fact that it seems as if you have been having a hard time returning my calls. It's annoying, but it's also confusing to me."

"I miss you too. I guess I'm not really sure about why we've been so distant."

This conversation opened up a dialogue in which there was room for Audrey's feelings. These two sisters had successfully entered the Problem-Solving phase of the SAD. Their communication breakdown had begun to be repaired.

The Do's and Don'ts of Constructive Communication

Based on the communication guidelines we have already discussed, the following do's and don'ts are designed to start you on your way to communicating more effectively. Using these rules, you can begin to express your feelings more directly to your loved one and work together to solve the problems in your relationship.

Do's

Acknowledge what you have heard. Let the other person know that you have understood what she has said. One of the best ways to do this is to reflect back what you have just heard. If someone tells you about a difficult situation at work, you might respond by saying, "It sure sounds as if you're having a tough time." Be as specific as you can about what you have heard.

Show empathy. All people, depressed or not, want empathy from others. When someone is depressed and feeling isolated, empathy is even more important. Convey to the depressed person that you are trying to imagine what it is like to be in her shoes. For example, if your friend is complaining about her sister, you might say, "That must make you mad. I know that I would be angry as hell if I were you."

Be direct. The foundation of good communication is honesty. Be sincere and straightforward in conversation. Rather than sugar-coating or beating around the bush, present difficult topics openly and plainly. For example, don't say, "I'm busy" when you mean, "I'm sorry, but I can't always be available when you want me to be." Most people, even if they are depressed, appreciate hearing the truth. Let the depressed person know how you feel.

Take your share of the responsibility. All communication takes two people. Acknowledge that you play a role in what happens between you and the person you care about. Take responsibility for what has gone wrong in your relationship, but also encourage the depressed person to think about her contribution to the trouble.

Use humor. Laughing together is one of the best ways to defuse tension in a relationship. Despite what you might think, depressed people do not usually lose their sense of humor. Point out the absurdity or humor in a stressful situation. Show the depressed person that you can laugh at yourself. But be especially careful not to be sarcastic and make the depressed person the butt of your jokes. Humor should not be hurtful. Use it to lighten the mood, not darken it.

Dont's

Don't talk behind the person's back. It is much better to talk directly to the person you want to communicate with than to involve a third party. Talking to someone else, who may or may not talk to yet another person, quickly leads to the kind of misunderstandings that happen in a game of telephone. The risk of communication problems increases as the number of intermediaries between you and the depressed person increases. If you have something to say, talk to her directly.

Don't name-call. If you are angry at someone, let her know it without calling her names. This is a hard habit to break because we all learned how to name-call as children. But labeling someone as "selfish" or a "couch potato" will not help your communication. In fact, it will probably just offend your listener and make it hard for her to hear the rest of what you are saying.

Don't generalize. If you are upset about something, be specific when you discuss it. Don't use words like *always* and *never* unless they apply to the situation. For example, saying, "I'm upset because you didn't take the garbage out last night" is very different from saying, "You never take out the garbage." Do not speak in absolutes. Be as specific as you can so your listener does not get defensive and can understand exactly what you are talking about.

Don't "kitchen sink." Couples' therapists use the term *kitchen sinking* to describe a tactic couples often use when they fight: They throw everything into the argument, including the kitchen sink. For example, if you and your partner are fighting about saving money, do not bring up other conflicts, such as how often you see your in-laws or who does more of the housework. Keep the conversation on a particular topic, and try to keep the kitchen sink out of it.

Don't yell or shout. Keep cool, calm, and collected. It's hard to listen to someone who is yelling or shouting. Sometimes we feel as if we have to raise our voices to be heard, but it is usually not true. In fact, the opposite often works quite well. Lower your voice to a whisper, and the other person has to listen carefully to hear you. The calmer you can be, the less likely it is that your communication will escalate to a point where you have a communication breakdown.

Gender Differences and Communication

There are gender differences in how people experience and express depression. There is evidence that women are more likely to experience depression during their lifetimes and report being depressed more frequently than men. And although men may get depressed at close to the rate of women, they are more likely to mask their depression through drugs, alcohol, and even workaholism. Many depressed men withdraw from those around them and do not seek support from their significant others. Depressed women, on other hand, tend to verbalize their feelings and are more likely to turn to their significant others for support.

The popular press has been paying increasing attention to the differences in conversational style between men and women. It is not uncommon for a couple to come for couples therapy and report, "We speak different languages. I can't understand her, and she can't understand me." The notion that men and women have different ways of expressing themselves has been ingrained into our collective psyches. According to Deborah Tannen, author of the best-selling book *You Just Don't Understand,* the definition of conversation differs for men and women. For men, "conversations are negotiations . . . to preserve independence and avoid failure," while for women "conversations are negotiations for closeness . . . to preserve intimacy and avoid isolation." Because of these different basic definitions of the function of conversation, men and women are unable to understand each other. Only through learning what the other gender means when he or she says something can we learn to communicate effectively across gender lines.

When someone you love is depressed, gender can play an even more important role in how you communicate. Research has shown that men tend to cope with problems by engaging in problem solving; they make suggestions, give advice, and try to find solutions. Women, on the other hand, tend to cope with problems by empathizing. They make sympathetic comments, inquire about how the person is doing, and spend more time listening than suggesting. When people are depressed, they tend to want the kind of support that they would naturally give. Thus, a depressed man may want concrete and specific advice from his wife about how to cope with problems at his job and get frustrated when she just sympathizes with his anxiety. A depressed woman, however, may prefer to have her husband just listen to her complaints than try to solve her dilemma.

Clearly problems can arise when you and your depressed loved one are members of the opposite sex. So what can you do if you are a man married to a depressed woman? Or a sister of a depressed man? The following guidelines were developed to help you communicate more constructively with a depressed person of the opposite sex. Keep in mind that these guidelines are based on gender stereotypes and will not be true for every relationship, and even if your depressed loved one is a member of the same sex as you are, some of these guidelines may prove helpful in your interactions.

Five Effective Ways to Communicate with a Depressed Woman

1. *Try to shift your thinking away from solving her problems and more toward understanding them.* Women do not think in terms of problem solving as much as men do. If you start to imagine all sorts of scenarios that will resolve everything, push them out of your mind. You need to concentrate on her experience of the depression, not the goal of ridding her of the depression. For example, instead of responding to her description of a problem with, "Well, you know what you could do . . .," try to say, "I can see why you felt that way."

2. *Ask about her experience of depression.* What are her theories about why she feels this way? Has she ever felt this way before? What does it feel like? Is this the worst she ever felt? Show that you are curious and want to learn more about what she is going through.

3. *Sympathize with her pain.* Make an effort to understand how she is feeling. Try to put yourself in her shoes and really feel what she feels. When she tells you about an upsetting incident, listen carefully and then repeat back what you have heard. Ask her if she thinks you understood what she just said. For example, one man asked his girlfriend, "It seems that you feel as if no one likes you anymore. Is that right?" She answered, "Yes. I feel that everyone is sick of hearing me complain." He was then able to sympathize and said, "Now I think I understand how vulnerable you must feel."

4. *Tell her about a time when you felt down in the dumps.* Women often do this with each other as a way of feeling close and connected. Sharing your own experiences with her will help her feel more connected to you. You could say, "You know, I once felt really down and as if I had no one to turn to. It's an awful way to feel." But be sure not to launch into a treatise on how you solved your problem. Just let her know that you know how it feels to be sad.

5. *Don't offer her advice or suggestions right away.* Women feel as if they are not being heard if they are bombarded with a host of suggestions. Let her know that if she wants concrete help dealing with a situation, you are willing to give it to her, but don't start off with specific advice. Instead, tell her, "I'm sure you don't want advice right now, but if you do, I'd be glad to try to help you with this situation."

Five Effective Ways to Communicate with a Depressed Man

1. *Don't expect a depressed man to talk readily about what is bothering him.* He may tend to keep his feelings inside and try to solve the problem by drinking or using drugs. Don't push him to talk to you. Instead, let him know that you are there if he wants to talk about what is on his mind. You could say, "I'm concerned about you, but I don't want you to feel any pressure to talk about what's bothering you. I just want you to know that I'm here to listen if you need me." Don't ask question after question about his experience if he is slow to reveal it.

2. *Be sensitive to his male ego and how important it is for him to feel self-sufficient.* Remember that men are socialized to be independent. Just because he is depressed does not mean that he will be comfortable accepting your help. Respect his independence and do not continually check in with him about how he's doing. Most important, do not baby him. You might say, "I know how hard it is for you not to be able to do everything you usually do. If there's anything I can do, let me know."

3. *If he can't talk easily about his feelings, you might give him multiple choices to describe how he feels*—for example, "Are you feeling angry, sad, or worried right now?" Most men will be able to pick one of the feelings or come up with his own description of how he feels. Talking about the feeling may then open up a whole dialogue about his experience of being depressed. Sometimes it is hard for a man to begin to open up, but if you provide the opportunity, he may seize the chance to share his feelings.

4. *Share your experiences.* It can be difficult to empathize with a man. When trying to do so, be mindful of how he is responding to your sharing your own similar experiences. Independence and self-sufficiency are very important to men. He may be reluctant to equate his feelings with yours because he experiences it as a sign of weakness. Or he may feel as if he should clam up about his own depression and focus instead on your experiences. Alternatively, he may feel competitive about whose problems are worse. This is not to say that you cannot draw on your own experiences in empathizing with a depressed man, but remain watchful of his reactions.

5. *Try to engage in some active problem solving.* If you talk about how he can reach his goals, you will be speaking a language most men readily understand. Ask him about his own ideas for solving his problems. Working together, offer other possible solutions he may not have considered, and discuss the pros and cons of them with him. However, do not come on too strong, and do not problem-solve to the exclusion of understanding and sympathizing with his experience.

Change Is Possible

Now that you are armed with the knowledge of how to communicate more effectively, you are ready to battle the communication breakdowns in your relationship with the depressed person. Practice the guidelines that were introduced in this chapter and remind yourself of the Do's and Don'ts of Constructive Communication, as well as Five Effective Ways to Communicate with a Depressed Woman and Five Effective Ways to Communicate with a Depressed Man. Think about how you communicate with the depressed person, and try to make changes in how you speak to her. If you can, teach the depressed person what you have learned so that she can take her share in the responsibility of communicating constructively. You may even invite the depressed person to read this chapter. Communicating about the communication process can be very helpful. If one of you can say "Hey, we're kitchen-sinking again!" it can put a stop to the vicious cycle of communication difficulties. Try to keep an open dialogue with your loved one about how the two of you communicate. You can even use humor to point out how absurd some of your communication problems are.

Do not be discouraged if you see some improvement but then continue to have some of the same communication problems. In relationships, particularly long-term ones, established patterns of interaction are hard to shift. When you start to respond differently to the depressed person, she may still respond in her old ways. And even if she responds in new ways, both of you may fall back into your old habits, especially when discussions get heated. But if you practice communicating more effectively, you will probably start to notice some real changes in how both of you communicate with each other. What's wonderful about relationships is that they are constantly changing and have the ability to grow and develop.

It took a great deal of effort and practice before Audrey and Sheila's communication improved. Audrey initially came to therapy to discuss her concerns about her relationship with Sheila. She complained that Sheila was difficult and that they had lost the closeness they once had. Clearly Audrey viewed Sheila as the problem. It took a great deal of discussion about how the sisters communicated before Audrey could see her contribution to the problems. She eventually recognized that she did not really listen to what Sheila said and that she came on much too strong. She also acknowledged that she talked down to Sheila and tended to "kitchen sink" every time they disagreed. It was hard for Audrey to share her feelings and let Sheila know how she felt about the changes in their relationship. With our support and her new knowledge about how to communicate more effectively, Audrey began to change how she interacted with Sheila. She listened more, offered empathy for Sheila's difficult job situation, and told Sheila how helpless she felt that she could no longer protect her younger sister from unhappiness.

As Audrey improved her communication skills, her relationship with Sheila began to change as well. Sheila revealed more about what she was going through and even confided that she was seeing a therapist to help her with her depression. They spoke on the telephone more frequently, and the conversations were much more natural and friendly. The sisters even planned a family reunion so that their children could get to spend more time together. Although they continued to have disagreements and moments of tension in their relationship, the communication breakdown was virtually repaired.

If you have had communication breakdowns with a depressed person whom you care about, there is hope. Try to use the guidelines in this chapter to improve your communication skills. Be aware of what you bring to the conversations. Practice listening and talking directly. And remember that no one is ever formally taught how to communicate. It takes knowledge and effort.

The next two chapters focus on specific problems that often come up in communication with a depressed loved one: the tendency to feel as if it is not appropriate or possible to ask for what you want or need when someone you love is depressed and coping with the depressed person's rejection of our offers of support or advice.

8

Is it Fair to Ask for What *You* Need?

One Sunday, Joe wanted to take the hour-long drive to his daughter's home to visit with her and her family. He was particularly eager to see his grandchildren, who had called him and his wife, Helen, the previous day, begging them both to visit. Joe knew that Helen was once again deeply depressed. Whenever she was that down, she wanted nothing more than to stay in their bedroom watching television. Experience had taught them both that if Helen forced herself to go out when she was depressed, she felt even more engulfed in the depression. She described feeling as if she was fighting through layers and layers of cotton just to follow a simple conversation. When she felt this way, she did not want to be around her daughter, her son-in-law, or her grandchildren. Helen and Joe both knew that if she agreed to go, she would feel more miserable and useless than she already did.

Joe had a dilemma about what *he* wanted to do. He did not think he should leave Helen alone because he knew that his being at home was comforting to her, even if they were not interacting much, but he wanted to see his grandchildren. Joe struggled with the only options he could see: forget the whole idea and stay home with Helen, go alone and feel guilty, or push her into coming with him.

Helen had struggled with multiple episodes of major depression for the past decade. She had tried many different antidepressant medications, but none seemed to help much. More recently, she had begun psychotherapy in the hope that this form of treatment could help her in ways that the medications had not. In recent weeks, she felt that there had been some improvement. She was feeling less hopeless about the future, sleeping through the night again, and beginning to believe that the depression would not go on forever. However, she was still feeling extremely dysphoric and unable to concentrate. She felt worse when Joe was at work, and she looked forward to the weekends when he was at home with her because she felt less anxious and depressed then.

Helen was aware that her depressions took a toll on Joe as well. She was particularly aware of Joe's dilemma about seeing their grandchildren, a struggle she had seen him deal with before. As much as she wanted to help him with it, she found herself feeling as helpless and confused as Joe did. She tried to reassure him that it would be all right with her if he went to their daughter's home, but she knew that her sadness at the prospect of being left alone was showing through her reassuring smiles.

Joe did see through his wife's reassurances, and he felt terribly guilty—and a little resentful. He felt that going alone would be selfish. How could he go knowing that his wife was suffering alone at home? How could he leave her when he knew that she would feel better if he stayed with her? But how could he not see his grandchildren whom he loved dearly and hadn't seen for several months? Joe decided that the only solution was to try to pressure Helen into going with him.

When Does Taking Care of Your Needs Become Selfish?

Many people equate selfishness with narcissism. They see taking care of their own needs as a character flaw. But just as too much selflessness becomes masochism in the person who lets others abuse him, too little narcissism is a recipe for disaster in relationships. Narcissism is healthy; too little or too much is not. Early television sitcoms gave us characters like the brow-beaten, frail-looking Henry, whose main retort during any interaction with his wife was, "Yes, dear," and the silver-haired, nose-high anchorman Ted Baxter, who had trouble understanding that every conversation between his coworkers was not about him. Henry suffered from having too little narcissism; Ted's coworkers suffered from his having too much. No book or person can tell you what the right amount should be. This is something you have to work out with yourself and the people in your life.

Finding a balance between healthy narcissism and selfishness can be especially difficult when you are dealing with someone who is depressed. Joe wanted to see his grandchildren but feared being selfish. He knew that if he stayed at home because of Helen, he would be angry with her. He had been feeling lonely and bored around Helen during the past several months. Her depression had clearly gotten the best of her. He used to enjoy her companionship, but now she was depressing to be around. Joe badly needed the uplifting affection and sweet voices of his grandchildren as Helen's depression was becoming contagious.

One way of understanding Joe's desire to see his grandchildren is to speak of it as a healthy narcissistic need. He was hungry for the adoration he knew he would get from them and for the feeling of being effective. His simply appearing at the threshold of their home would lift their spirits, causing them to tumble into the room, shouting, "Poppy's here!" He felt ineffective with Helen and yearned for some interaction where he could have an obviously positive impact. He also craved sharing an emotion with someone else who was feeling as he was. Joe knew he would feel joy when he saw his grandchildren and that they would be happy to see him too. Since her most recent bout with depression, Helen had been unable to share such experiences with him. Her feelings never seemed to match his in the way they used to. This was probably one of the hardest things for Joe to handle during the Trouble stage of their relationship's adaptation to the depression. Helen had almost always been able to empathize with him, and this was probably the most important ingredient to the closeness he felt with her. He was used to feeling understood by her. However, during the Trouble stage, this ingredient to what had been a successful relationship was missing.

Healthy Narcissism

Narcissism is an aspect of personality that is defined by relationships, or lack of them. The *Oxford American Dictionary* (1980) defines narcissism as "a tendency to self-worship, excessive . . . interest in one's own personal features, inordinate fascination with oneself." That does not sound very healthy, does it? When we talk about *healthy narcissism,* we mean a sound sense of one's self as worthy, as effective in the world, as loved and appreciated, and as someone who is not unlike the people around him. These characteristics of healthy narcissism develop over a lifetime and require constant nourishment to be sustained. Joe always felt effective in his ability to lift people's spirits. He loved to make people laugh, and this ability was an important source of his self-esteem. Joe had a wonderful sense of humor and could usually cheer Helen up. In fact, his attempts at trying to make her smile were his natural reaction to the early part of the Trouble stage, but they did not work because she was depressed. For several months, he had been spending nearly all of his free time with her, unable to lift her spirits appreciably and feeling more and more ineffective. Being able to make others smile was an integral part of his sense of himself. Without the nourishment such interactions usually provided for him, he was beginning to feel ineffective and worthless rather than effective and capable. He knew that Helen appreciated him, but that was different from having the experience that he could make a real difference in how she felt.

Healthy narcissism is usually constructive for relationships; it can bring people closer together. In order for it to be positive, you must understand, accept, and communicate your needs. Because Joe misunderstood the importance of his own basic needs, he was unable to communicate with Helen in a manner that was constructive for both of them.

Unaware that his decision to try to force Helen to go with him was based more on his needs than on hers, Joe argued his case in a subtle yet critical manner. Believing he had her best interests in mind, Joe told Helen, "You have to get out because the more you stay in the house, the worse *you're* making things for yourself. Sometimes you just have to pick yourself by your bootstraps and tough it out." He said nothing about his desire to see their grandchildren or about his dilemma about the trip to their daughter's home. Since Helen was still depressed and suffering from the cognitive distortions of depression, she amplified the implicit criticism and heard Joe's pep talk as, "Get off your butt and stop feeling sorry for yourself! If you just tried, you wouldn't feel so bad, and you wouldn't be depriving me of seeing my grandchildren!" As a result, Helen felt even less inclined to go and angrily told Joe to go alone. Joe's dilemma was unresolved.

Joe felt angry at Helen for making him feel guilty. Why couldn't she just agree to go with him? Helen felt guilty and angry at Joe for making her feel even greater responsibility than she already did, for both her depression and the burden it placed on her husband. The discussion quickly deteriorated into a fight that left them both feeling guilty and attacked by the other. If Joe had understood the fact that he, like everyone else, has basic narcissistic needs that are as important to his emotional well-being as air is to his physical well-being, he might have tried to resolve his dilemma in a more constructive way. During Joe and Helen's passage through the Information-Gathering stage of the SAD, they had not learned why Joe should have been more mindful of his own needs.

At one time or another, you have probably been given the advice that only after you love yourself can you love someone else. Although you may be inclined to dismiss this axiom of pop psychology as simplistic and uninformative, it rests on a tenet that is based on both common sense and scientific fact. We all have basic emotional needs that must be met before we can muster the resources to give to others. This is particularly important when it comes to narcissistic needs when we are in a relationship with a depressed person. Before describing the guidelines that will help you to strike a healthy balance between your needs and those of your depressed loved one, you need to be familiar with three particularly salient narcissistic needs that we all have—mirroring, idealizing, and twinship needs—so you can identify them more easily in yourself and be less likely to mistake them for "selfishness," as Joe did.

Relational Psychology and the Self

Among the many different orientations or ways of thinking about personality functioning, one that focuses on the healthy development of the self in its relationships with others is called *relational psychology*. One of the central themes of this school of thought is described best by Stephen Mitchell in his book, *Relational Concepts in Psychoanalysis*: "Human beings did not evolve and then enter into social and cultural interactions; the human mind is, in its very origins and nature, a social product" (p.18). Because we are born into relationships, develop in them, and spend our whole lives in them, they are an integral part of how we experience ourselves as persons. Relationships that give us experiences of self-worth, effectiveness, identification, and closeness with others are essential to sustaining a healthy self. How people develop a cohesive, stable, healthy sense of self has been the subject of much study. Although different theorists have different ideas about the process, they all agree that it begins at birth and continues throughout one's lifetime.

Three Important Needs

Three needs stand out as especially important to the development and maintenance of a healthy sense of self. Mirroring, idealizing, and twinship needs are first met by one's parents or other caregivers early in life; then progressively, they are met by others outside the family, and finally more and more by oneself. To differing degrees, at different times in our lives, our sense of self is shored up by both experiences with others and activities that give us experiences that meet these needs.

The need to feel mirrored. In order to develop and maintain a healthy sense of self, we need to feel *mirrored,* or empathized with. The intensity of mirroring needs varies for different people at different stages of life, and it must be age appropriate to have the desired effect. For example, clapping your hands and praising a twelve year old when he rides a bicycle would have less positive impact, and perhaps some negative consequences, than would doing the same thing when a four year old rides a bicycle. Empathy requires that you understand another's experience from that person's unique perspective and communicate that understanding to him. This is not the same as feeling what you would feel if you were in their place. Rather, mirroring requires being finely tuned to another's experience and being able to communicate the empathy you feel in a manner that is heard. As such, it is not always easy to give or to receive. The mother who smiles back at her infant who is grinning up at her, the friend whose eyes well up with tears when you tell him of a deep sadness you are feeling, or the supervisor who communicates a feeling of genuine pride in an employee who has just mastered a difficult task that had previously eluded him are all instances of mirroring. In the past, Helen would become excited too whenever Joe talked excitedly about a successful deal at work.

The need to idealize. Everybody has had the experience of idealizing another person. Early in life, we idealized our parents. Later in life, we may idealize a spouse, a coworker, a friend, a politician, or even a celebrity. Healthy and strongly held ideals and values are derived from relationships in which we idealize others to some extent. During infancy and childhood, idealization may involve a parent or older sibling whom we think is perfect and whom we aspire to be like. We adopt their values because of how much we look up to them. In adulthood, these needs are more internalized as we develop our own values, but we still find ourselves idealizing others. In fact, this is probably the most recognizable aspect of falling in love. We say that love is blind to describe the way in which someone who has fallen in love views the object of their love. No blemish or flaw is noticed when we idealize someone else.

The twinship need. We all have the need to feel a *twinship* with others— a sense of sameness, or of not feeling alienated, that develops from relationships in which we feel this connection with others. If you think back on your own life, you will probably be able to think of someone whom you experienced, or experience today, as very much like yourself. These kinds of relationships give us the experience of belonging, or of being part of the larger community of people. They help us to identify who we are in relation to other people and to guard against feelings of alienation. Joe had always experienced Helen as very much like himself in several key ways. Their similarities made him feel less alone in the world.

How Our Needs Are Met

In infancy, the three narcissistic needs are intense and must be met by our parents or some other central caregiver. In childhood, we develop tolerance for distance from our parents as our narcissistic needs begin to be met by others and as we develop our own inner resources. In adolescence, the peer group becomes a particularly important source of fulfillment of these needs. Finally, throughout adulthood, our partner, friends, and vocation become the main source of fulfillment from the outside world. In addition to broadening the possibilities of who and what may serve as sources of fulfillment, the healthy individual develops reliable inner resources that assume many of the functions provided by these relationships. She can calm herself when anxious, reassure herself when she feels alienated, and remind herself of her successes when she feels like a failure.

We are driven to preserve a sense of continuity to our connections to other people because, among other reasons, we define who we are by these connections. When a loved one becomes depressed, the connection is altered and usually weakened. Your depressed loved one may no longer be able to meet the narcissistic needs that he previously met.

Joe had always counted on Helen for mirroring and for experiences of twinship. When not depressed, she was finely tuned to his moods and empathized about his experiences. She also shared his values and his sense of humor, and they enjoyed many of the same activities. When he first met her years before, he was drawn to how similar they were. Among other things, he felt understood and less alienated when they were together. Now that she was depressed, his mirroring and twinship needs were not being met adequately. As a result, he craved having someone to share his experiences with. He wanted to see his grandchildren because he loved them and missed them, but he also was drawn to them because they were keenly tuned into his mood and because they were like him in many ways. The joy he felt when he saw them was mirrored in the joy they experienced when he walked through the front door. When he watched them playing with one another, he saw himself in their mannerisms, their humor, and their vitality.

There were other important narcissistic needs that Helen's depression had made it more difficult for Joe to get met. Increased anxiety, a sense of alienation, and depression can occur when we do not get sufficient narcissistic supplies. Joe admitted that he was feeling increasingly lonely and anxious. A brief visit with his grandchildren would have helped to shore up his sense of himself as connected to people and as someone who was effective in the world. Joe knew he wanted to spend time with his grandchildren, but because he was still stuck in the Reaction phase of the SAD he did not know how helpful it would have been for him to be with them for an afternoon. Because he was unaware of the extent of his own needs and did not pay attention to the bigger picture with respect to Helen's needs, he ended up feeling guilty and confused about the intensity of his desire to see his grandchildren. He worried that he was trying to get away from Helen. He wondered if his desire to go, despite Helen's depression, meant he was an unsupportive husband.

How to Strike a Healthy Balance

Here are some guidelines that can help you find the right balance between your basic needs and the needs of your depressed loved one.

Don't be quick to judge your needs. If you immediately assume that what you want is selfish, unreasonable, and unfair to your depressed loved one, you will lose an important opportunity to sort out the possibility of getting your needs met in a way that is healthy for you, your loved one, and the relationship. If you have the thought, "This is selfish," do not assume it is necessarily a bad thing for you and your loved one. Your own needs may be every bit as worthy as the needs of your loved one. The trick is not to dismiss your needs outright. Give yourself the time to determine whether they can be met constructively within the confines of the relationship.

Talk about your needs constructively. Try to bring up what it is you want in a noncritical, collaborative manner. Ask for your loved one's help in resolving your dilemma, but do not place the entire burden of resolving the problem on her. Tell her you have not figured out what you want to do about what you want yet but want her input. Convey that you want to resolve your dilemma together.

Look for ways in which your loved one can help you. Just because someone is depressed does not mean that she is unable to give to you. In fact, the more your depressed loved one can feel that she is useful and less of a burden, the better off she will feel. If Joe had thanked Helen for allowing him to go without her though he could see it was a difficult thing for her to offer, he would have given her an opportunity to feel less like a burden and more like a partner in their relationship. Maybe he could have asked for her help with his dilemma.

Don't be afraid to disappoint your loved one occasionally. No one is capable of meeting every need another person has. Although this observation may sound obvious, you may be surprised as to how often we can forget this indisputable fact when we feel guilty about disappointing a loved one. Joe was truly frightened of disappointing Helen. He was worried about the change that had come over her and felt that she was more frail emotionally than he had ever seen her. If he let her down, perhaps she would withdraw even further. He did not think she was strong enough to bounce back. Looking at his situation from the opposite angle, we could describe him as believing that he could, and should, satisfy her every need. But he couldn't possibly do that. No matter how hard we try, we all disappoint those close to us at times.

Keep an eye on the big picture. It is common to feel conflicting feelings. Joe wanted to go, and he wanted to stay. Helen wanted him to go, and she wanted him to stay. Ambivalence is a central aspect of human nature. However, sometimes people are not aware that they are feeling ambivalent or conflicted about something, and when they are depressed, their defenses are down, making it much harder to hide their mixed feelings. The difficulty about mixed feelings is that they can be misinterpreted and acted upon if not brought out into the open.

Joe thought that Helen's sadness about the possibility that he would go without her meant that she was not sincere when she said, "It's okay to go without me." However, Joe was mistaken. She was simply too depressed to hide her ambivalence, which is why her sadness showed through her reassurances. If Joe had kept his eye on the big picture, he would have understood that her reassurances were genuine and that his going away would have been good for both of them, despite the fact that she would have felt lonely. The problem was not that she did not truly want him to go alone. The problem was she had mixed feelings about it.

Work as a team. You probably thought you had heard the last of this guideline. We keep repeating it not only because it is so important but also because teamwork can take many forms. In asking for what you want, it is important that you frame the issue as something that you want both of you to work on. Reassure your depressed loved one that you are aware that you might be asking for something that is difficult for her to give. Let her know of your dilemma, and give her the opportunity to give to you.

Because Joe and Helen never got together to work on the problem, each assumed what the best resolution would be in isolation and missed several other possible solutions—for example, that Joe could have shortened the trip, or Helen's best friend and confidante might have been able to spend the day with her.

Weigh your needs carefully against those of your loved one. Paying attention to your own needs does not mean you have to ignore your depressed loved one's needs. You also don't want to ignore the fact that the depression is putting her in a more vulnerable position than she normally would be when not depressed. The best way to strike a healthy balance is to be open. The balance can be tipped abruptly if you unintentionally let the depressed person add a weighty sense of guilt. Both you and your loved one should try to put everything out on the table, within reason, so that you can balance the scales together, weighing each of your needs one by one.

After learning these guidelines, Joe understood that he had been feeling guilty and that the guilt had been motivating him to ignore his own needs. The more guilt he felt, the more he ignored his needs, and the angrier he got. He decided to talk with Helen about his feelings and the interaction we described at the outset of this chapter. He said, "I am sorry for pushing you so hard to go with me that Sunday. I know you try, and I didn't mean to accuse you of being lazy. I realized I really wanted to see the kids and just felt so guilty about leaving you. The more I thought about it, you really weren't telling me to stay; I kept thinking that's what you wanted because you looked so disappointed when I told you I wanted to go, but that's not what you said. Was that what you wanted? Did you want me to stay despite the fact that you told me to go?"

"Not really," answered Helen. "You're right that I was feeling really low and didn't want to be alone. But I also felt that I wanted you to have this. I wanted you to go and enjoy yourself. You stay by my side so much as it is. I felt it wasn't fair to you or to the kids. I just felt like I couldn't go with you. I wanted to give you that."

Joe had realized that his needs could not be ignored and that he had not been listening carefully to Helen. He had not been keeping an eye on the bigger picture. After the conversation, Joe saw that Helen would have truly valued an experience of giving something back to him by encouraging him to go but that she needed reassurance that he was not angry with her for not wanting to go herself. Helen learned that Joe was not angry with her for not wanting to go. Instead, they both came to see that his implicit anger and criticism were reactions to his guilt. He was telling her to go because he felt guilty, and *this* is what made him angry, not the fact that she did not want to go with him.

After learning more about what each was feeling, all of the facts could be weighed in purposefully and consciously. Joe and Helen were able to work together as a team. Joe realized that it was not only okay with Helen if he disappointed her sometimes but that it might actually give her an opportunity to feel effective herself. Certainly if he had gone, she would have still missed him, and perhaps even felt somewhat sadder in the short run, but he believed her reassurances that it would also have given her a small sense of accomplishment. Once Helen came to believe that Joe was not blaming her for the depression, because he had learned that depression was not a willful act but an illness, she was able to communicate her reassurances to him more convincingly. The next time Joe had one of his dilemmas, they quickly came to a solution that involved Joe's going his separate way for the day but telephoning Helen to touch base several times. They also came to a general agreement that neither would assume what the other was feeling. Instead, they would check with the other to be sure. They came to understand that ambivalence was unavoidable sometimes, but ambivalence did not mean that sincerity was impossible. Helen was ambivalent about Joe leaving her that Sunday but sincere in her desire for him to visit their grandchildren without her.

While learning to weigh the relative importance of each other's needs, they came to another agreement: If they were still at an impasse even after talking about what each of them wanted and after checking in with each other to be sure that they both felt understood, they would implement what they called the *tie-breaker rule*. They would mentally take a step back, stop talking about the particulars (e.g., Joe's visit to see their grandchildren) and about what was "fair," and instead try to identify who felt more strongly about what he or she wanted. Who would have felt worse if the other got his or her way? Regardless of whether it seemed fair, they agreed that in the event of an impasse, the person who would feel worse would make the decision. Whether you agree with their particular strategy, the point here was that Helen and Joe were able to work as a team.

By working together, you and your loved one can leave room for both of your needs to be met. However, one of the pitfalls common to teamwork with a depressed person is the tendency of depressed people to turn away help. This does not mean they do not want their needs met. Rather, you must learn how to give them what they need in a way in which they can accept it. In the next chapter, we give you specific advice about how to do this, while still paying attention to your own needs as well.

9

When Your Help Is Turned Away

Josh and Donna had been married for about ten years when she became depressed. She stopped eating, could not sleep, and spent most of her time staring out the window, complaining of feeling blue. She lost all interest in their two children and could barely drag herself out of bed to go to work. Concerned about Donna, Josh insisted that she get professional help. Donna was initially reluctant but then agreed. After an evaluation, she was diagnosed with depression and began psychotherapy, as well as a course of antidepressant medication.

During Donna's depression, Josh tried to help her. He said, "I know you feel overwhelmed and miserable. Let me do more of the errands and help around the house." In the past, Donna had always been a high-energy person who worked full time and took care of most of the household responsibilities. When she first became depressed, she responded to his offers of help by allowing him to do the laundry, which had always been her domain. But as her depression continued, Josh noticed that every time he offered to help out, by taking the children to school or making dinner for the family, Donna would snap, "Stop babying me. I'm not completely disabled, you know!" Then she would break down in tears and complain that he could not begin to understand how terrible she felt. She told him, "Nothing you could do would help anyway because my problems at work are so huge! Your offers to make dinner are just a drop in the bucket." Josh attempted to offer her advice about work, but Donna accused him of always giving advice when she would have preferred for him to just listen. Josh then tried just to listen and sympathize with how awful she felt, but she cut him off: "Just leave me alone, okay?"

At this point, Josh felt frustrated and shut out. Donna made it seem as if he was intruding or butting in whenever he tried to help. He complained to his best friend that Donna did not appreciate his concern and found fault with all of his suggestions. His friend suggested that in order to avoid her strong reactions, Josh should stop trying to help. "Back off," he said. "Let her see how it feels when you're not concerned." So Josh stopped making suggestions and didn't offer to do as much around the house. But instead of Donna's appreciating how much he had tried to help before, she now complained, "You never lift a finger to help me around here anymore, and you obviously don't care." Josh felt completely frustrated about their relationship and noticed that Donna seemed even more depressed than ever.

Donna did appreciate Josh's help but had difficulty accepting his support. His offers to drive the children or wash the dishes made her feel as if she was a "basket case." His advice about work made her feel as if she must be totally incompetent to need that kind of hand holding. She felt guilty that she was rejecting his offers of support but hopeless that he could help at all anyway. When Josh switched tactics, she felt alone and unsupported. She acknowledged that Josh was in a difficult position but was unable to talk to him about it. She knew that she was turning him away but could not figure out how to stop it.

Do Depressed People Turn Away Help?

Josh and Donna's experience is not unique. Many of us have experienced similar kinds of communication breakdowns when we try to offer help to a depressed loved one. Family members and friends often find that one of the hardest parts of being close to a depressed person is that nothing seems to help. In our practices, we have heard time and time again from family members who complain that the depressed person turns away all offers of support, both advice and emotional reassurance. Given the depressed person's experience of feeling bad, relatives are perplexed that the depressed person often rejects support that might help her feel better.

Research has shown that depressed people do reject support more often and more consistently than nondepressed people. They are more likely to tell someone close to them that their advice will not help or that the other person does not understand what they are going through. In contrast, nondepressed individuals are more likely to tell someone close to them that their suggestions are really helpful or that they are grateful for that person's emotional support. There seems to be something inherent in being depressed that leads people to turn away help, yet the research does not suggest that depressed people do not want help. In fact, the evidence is strong that depressed people seek help more frequently than nondepressed people.

Josh reported that one of the most frustrating aspects of Donna's depression was that she seemed to want his help initially but then turned it away. She complained about not being able to keep up at work, told him how overwhelmed she felt with all of her responsibilities, and even cried on his shoulder most evenings. Wasn't she asking for help?

Depressed people do seek help from those close to them, but in indirect ways, so what they want is not always clear. Donna sought Josh's support indirectly by complaining about how she felt so overwhelmed, but she never told him what kind of specific help she wanted. Research has shown that depressed individuals are more likely to engage in indirect support seeking, such as withdrawing, sulking, or picking a fight with their partner in order to get support. In contrast, nondepressed individuals are more likely to engage in direct support seeking, such as telling their partner that they need help with something specific or asking their partner's opinion about a particular thing.

Why would depressed people seek help more indirectly and then turn away support? If the person feels bad, why would she reject offers of help? Researchers have proffered a number of hypotheses. First, it may be that depressed people deny, to themselves and others, their need for help by rejecting the support offered to them. Accepting help from someone makes them feel like a failure because it implies that they are unable to deal with their own problems. This tendency is particularly evident with people like Donna, who were self-sufficient and responsible until the depression struck. If you have always been able to handle things on your own, it's hard to ask for and accept help from others. It can make you feel vulnerable, inadequate, and worse than you already do. In fact, researchers have found that when depressed people notice the supportive efforts of others, they report feeling bad about themselves and question their own self-sufficiency. If they are not aware that others are helping them even when they are, depressed people do not have the same reactions and are more likely to accept the help.

A second explanation for why depressed people turn away help is that they experience others' attempts to help as intrusive and useless because of cognitive distortions. Recall that one of the symptoms of depression is the tendency to interpret things negatively. As a result, the depressed person may be pessimistic and believe that her problems are too all-encompassing to be helped by anyone. She thinks that nothing can alleviate her distress, so why bother listening to someone else's advice? The hopelessness and pessimism associated with depression make seeking support from others seem futile. Many depressed people have told us that they appreciate the support from their friends or family but believe that it is not going to help them feel better. They are locked into thinking that nothing will help.

Another possible explanation for why depressed people turn away help is that accepting support from someone close to them would change the structure of their relationship and disturb the status quo. Donna had always been the more responsible one. She organized the household, clothed and fed the children, and handled all of their social plans. Josh's offer to help changed the structure of their relationship. Donna was no longer the main caregiver but instead the recipient of Josh's care. She had difficulty accepting his help because doing so would change the whole dynamic of their marriage. She may not have been completely aware of it at the time she was depressed, but Donna was able to say in retrospect that if she readily accepted help from Josh, it would have put her in a one-down position to him. She would lose her defining role in their marriage as the responsible one. Such a change may have exacerbated her already low self-esteem and made her feel even more vulnerable, so she rejected his offers of help rather than change the structure of their relationship. Her reaction was her initial knee-jerk response and probably not even conscious. Many couples and families have reported similar stories when someone who has always been capable gets depressed. It is hard for them to accept changes in the relationship.

This indirect style of support seeking may help to explain why it is hard to offer help to a depressed person. If your loved one seeks support from you in an indirect way, you may not know how best to help. Josh knew that Donna wanted and needed his help, but he could not figure out what to offer. Unsure as to what the depressed person wants from you, you may feel burdened by her seemingly unending need for support. If she then rejects your offers of support, you feel helpless, frustrated, and angry. At this point, you and your loved one are doing the depressive dance, which serves only to worsen the depression. Each step that you take affects her next step, and each step that she takes affects your next step. The more Josh tried to help, the more Donna rejected his offers of help. When he backed off, she felt alone and more depressed. But before you can learn how to break this dance step and begin a more productive dance with your loved one, you need more information about the dilemmas of helping.

The Dilemmas of Helping

The tendency of depressed people to seek help indirectly and reject offered support can be very hard on the people close to them. How do you cope with your support being rejected? How do you know when you should continue to give support and when to back off? And how do you know what is helpful and what is harmful to the depressed person? It can be hard to reach an effective Problem-Solving phase of the SAD when you are coping with the dilemmas of helping.

If you continually offer support and it is repeatedly rejected, you will probably feel angry, hostile, and resentful—and helpless, frustrated, and worried. You may even feel like never offering help in the future. Most likely, you will feel a combination of all of these feelings. As the pattern of trying to help and having your help rejected is repeated, you will probably feel unable to help the depressed person in any meaningful way.

These feelings are part of the dilemmas of helping someone who is depressed. In a study of couples coping with either a heart attack or depression in one member of the couple, researchers identified a number of difficulties of helping in a close relationship whether someone is depressed or physically ill. By virtue of being in a close relationship, one's own well-being is directly and indirectly affected when something happens to one's loved one. Getting help, attempting to give help, and letting your loved one get by without help pose complex decisions for you. There are times when it is better not to push and times when it is better to insist that the depressed person do something. But how do you know what to do when your loved one may not be clear about what she wants from you and then may reject your offers of support? When you are so busy and preoccupied with helping the depressed person, you may lose your ability to focus on yourself and what needs to be done in your own life. As Josh tried to help Donna, he fell behind at work and stopped talking to his friends. It's hard to continue to help someone when you can't take care of your own needs.

Another dilemma of helping is related to the idea of *contagious depression*—that being around a depressed person can increase the likelihood of being depressed oneself. The theory is that the negative outlook, self-devaluation, and low energy level of the depressed person have a strong impact on our own worldviews. Depression becomes particularly contagious when the depressed person rejects your offers of support. If you are continually trying to help the depressed person feel better and she is repeatedly turning away your help, you are likely to feel ineffective, frustrated, and sad. In other words, you may begin to feel depressed. We have seen numerous family members of depressed people who report feeling "burned out," "blue," or "down in the dumps" when they are not able to alleviate the depression. In fact, a large impetus for writing this book was to help family members inoculate themselves against their loved one's depression. Learning to help your loved one while simultaneously not falling prey to depression is a dilemma of helping a depressed person.

The last dilemma in helping is related to gender differences. Recall that men tend to problem-solve by offering advice, while women tend to offer emotional support rather than advice. The dilemma in helping comes about when a person of one gender tries to offer help to a depressed person of the other gender. Most people tend to want the kind of help that they would naturally give to someone. For example, Josh tried to help Donna with her problems at work by suggesting how to deal with her boss because that is how he would approach his own problems at work. Donna would have preferred emotional reassurance and accused him of not listening to her. She blamed him for "always jumping the gun" with advice. The reverse can happen as well. A depressed man may want concrete advice from his wife and feel frustrated when she reassures him but doesn't offer specific guidance. When you are offering support to a depressed person, it's important to think about the differences in how you and he think about help. Refer to Five Effective Ways to Communicate with a Depressed Woman and Five Effective Ways to Communicate with a Depressed Man in Chapter 7.

The dilemmas of helping are complicated and considerable, and feeling overwhelmed when trying to help the depressed person is common. Before we offer step-by-step solutions to coping, you need to learn more about the importance of your support for the depressed person.

Social Support and Depression

Social support is usually defined as the various forms of aid and assistance supplied by family members, friends, neighbors, and others. Having people on whom we can rely and who let us know that they care about, value, and love us helps us cope with stress. Researchers have found that social support is indeed a buffer against many illnesses, ranging from peptic ulcer to heart disease. Having more social support is also related to psychological well-being and a lower probability of mental illness. Studies of social networks have shown that those with a larger network of friends and family members are less likely to experience psychological distress, particularly depression.

Based on the previous research about support and depression, one of us (Laura Epstein Rosen) recently examined the support process in the intimate relationships of couples. Previous studies had looked at depressed people's relationships in general, not specifically relationships with significant others. The results indicated that both members of the couple are affected when one member is depressed. Those couples tended to argue more and feel more frustrated about both helping one another and accepting help from one another. The depressed individuals in the study reported seeking support from their spouses more indirectly and were more likely to reject the support offered to them. Additionally, the partners of the depressed subjects had strong reactions to their mates. They reported being less willing to offer support because their offers of help tended to be rejected and they reported feeling frustrated, angry, and hopeless about being able to make a difference in the depressed person's life. These results confirm our notion of the depressive dance. Both members of the relationship get locked into taking steps that affect the other, worsen the depression, and increase the risk of contagious depression.

These findings are not just related to the fact that depressed people tend to isolate themselves once they become depressed. In fact, research has found that having fewer close friends, a smaller social network, and less supportive relationships usually predates the first depressive episode. The results of these studies are striking. For example, people who report low levels of social support are thirteen times more likely to go on to suffer from a major depression in their lifetimes, and women who lack a confiding relationship with an intimate are three times more likely to become depressed when faced with a stressful life event.

Based on the initial findings that social support protects against depression, researchers have tried to figure out what it is about support that protects us from getting depressed. Is it the quantity of people in one's life or the quality of those relationships? The results have suggested that quantity is important but that quality of relationships is even more important in preventing and treating depression. To be protected from depression, you need to have at least one close relationship, and the benefits of social support increase with the number of people close to you, up to about five people. But the type of relationship you have is even more important in protecting against depression. A relationship that is free from conflict and low in negative interactions is best. Good communication, ability to confide in one another, and trust are all indicators of a relationship that can buffer against depression. A relationship that is difficult, with high levels of conflict and misunderstandings, does not protect against depression and may increase the risk of getting depressed. Coping with a stressful life event, such as a work crisis or a loss of a loved one, in the context of a conflictual relationship may be even more difficult than not having a close relationship at all.

When Donna got depressed, Josh experienced many of these feelings. You may also have had similar feelings when your offers of support have been turned away. If your advice or reassurance is not accepted, you may begin to feel angry and resentful, as well as helpless in your desire to help your depressed loved one. Or it may be that the hopelessness and pessimism about the situation's ever getting better may be contagious. If the depressed person does not seem to benefit when you try to help, investing time and energy in continuing to offer support may feel useless. However, all people, whether they are depressed or not, need support from those around them.

What Can You Do When Your Help Is Turned Away?

Finding ways to be supportive when your help is rejected is difficult but possible. First, acknowledge that your depressed loved one turns away your offers of support. Many of us know that we are not getting along with the depressed person in our lives but find it difficult to identify what is wrong. We do not recognize the problems in the support process. Think back to the last interaction you had with the depressed person and recall whether she spurned your offers of support. Chances are that she did or that she has done so on other recent occasions. If not, then you have been lucky. Nevertheless, continue reading because given the natural tendency of depressed people to have trouble accepting support, this problem is bound to come up in your relationship. You cannot begin to cope with your help being turned away until you admit that it is a problem in your relationship.

The next step is to think about how you feel when your help is turned away. Frustrated? Angry? Resentful? Sad? Or perhaps some combination of these feelings? Know how the rejection makes you feel so that you can begin to cope with those feelings and figure out what action you want to take in the future. Try to put your reaction into words, even if you say it aloud only to yourself, so you can think more clearly about the dynamics of your relationship with the depressed person. Josh had difficulty acknowledging that Donna was rejecting his offers of help because he felt as if *he* was being rejected. He was already consumed with guilt about her depression and his inability to "make it go away," and each time she turned away his help, Josh felt more alone and guilty. He also felt as if he could not share his pain with Donna because she "had enough of her own troubles."

Once you have identified your feelings, be optimistic about making changes. There is hope for you and the depressed person in your life. Follow the guidelines in the next section to improve the support process in your relationship.

Guidelines for the Support Process

By now, these guidelines probably look very familiar. They are the same ones we have highlighted throughout the book to help you and your loved one move through the SAD. However, we are not just repeating them here. Although the general guidelines may be the same, the details are not. These specifically apply to the support process with your depressed loved one.

Have realistic expectations. You naturally want to help your depressed loved one, but do not expect to solve all of her problems. No one can do that. Remember that you do not always have to have an answer or a solution for every difficulty your depressed loved one has. At times, you may convey more interest and receptiveness by paying attention and listening but not suggesting anything. Most important, do not expect the depressed person to embrace all of your suggestions joyfully. Given her mood and cognitive distortions, she may be pessimistic that anything can help her feel better. Expect that, and be pleasantly surprised if she accepts your help. It took some time until Josh recognized that he had to have more realistic expectations about what he could and could not do for Donna. He could certainly help out by doing more chores around the house but he could not make her depression go away. Another important realization was that it was unrealistic to expect Donna to accept all offers of help. He had to understand that there would be times that she would turn down his support. Having realistic expectations helped Josh prevent Donna's depression from becoming contagious.

Offer unqualified support. Continuing to offer unqualified support is particularly difficult when you do not get the reaction that you want. If you feel annoyed or resentful that your support is not accepted by your loved one, you might feel like giving up. But given what we know about how support buffers against and alleviates depression, continue to offer support, even if it is not accepted immediately or at all. Be patient. Sometimes the depressed person may initially turn down your help but then gradually accept it. Just let her know that you are there for her, when and if she wants your help. Josh made a concerted effort to continue to let Donna know that he was there for her and would do anything that would be helpful. Sometimes she continued to push him away, but sometimes she was grateful for his help. He learned that it was better for their relationship if he could be consistent in his support, although he admitted that "it can be hard when you feel frustrated that you can do no right. Sometimes I wonder why I even bother." Learning to tolerate the negative feelings and still offer unqualified support was a large part of Josh's adjustment to Donna's depression.

Maintain your routine as much as possible. Although you may need to adjust your work schedule or other routines to accommodate helping your depressed loved one, try to keep your life as regular as possible. Don't drop out of all your usual activities or cut yourself off from your social network. Helping someone who is depressed can be difficult. Her turning down your offers of support can make you feel ineffective and frustrated. If, in addition to helping her, you are not doing anything in your life for yourself, you are bound to feel resentful and frustrated. These negative feelings will come out, in subtle or not-so-subtle ways, when you interact with your depressed loved one, resulting in a communication breakdown.

Because Josh was trying to help out, he gave up his morning jog so that he could drive the children to school. Over time, he began to resent that he was not able to do something that he liked to do, but he promised himself that he would not make Donna feel bad by "throwing it up in her face." Then Donna commented that his pants seemed a bit tight across the middle, and Josh snapped, "Well, don't blame me. It's not my fault that I don't jog anymore these days." Donna then felt guilty that Josh was giving up his exercise and angry at him for doing something that "I didn't ask him to do anyway." A communication breakdown then ensued, with the result that they felt angry and distant from each other. This kind of difficulty could have been prevented if Josh had tried to maintain some semblance of his regular routine. He could have offered to drive the children most mornings but not every morning, or exercised in the evenings instead of the morning. Many of us who care about a depressed person make the same kind of mistake as Josh did in our effort to be helpful. Then when we feel angry and frustrated, the chances of getting depressed ourselves also increase. In most cases, you can be more helpful if you also feel that you are taking care of yourself. Offer support to your loved one, but try keep your routine as regular as possible.

Share your feelings. When your support is rejected, tell the depressed person how you feel. She may not realize how it is for you when she does not immediately accept your help. Don't feel guilty. It is important for both you and your relationship to share your feelings. Talk to your loved one in a calm and nonaccusatory way, explaining how your ways of asking for and giving help to one another can have an effect on your relationship. This kind of conversation can prevent the kind of built-up resentments that Josh experienced when Donna turned down his offers of support. It can also prevent the depression from catching, like the flu.

In this kind of discussion, it helps to ask the depressed person what specific kind of support would be best. For example, if your wife wants you just to listen to her description of her awful day and empathize rather than try to solve her difficulties with specific suggestions, it would be important to know that. You could just listen to her and let her know you hear and understand. She will feel more supported than if you offer suggestions that she did not want anyway.

Here is an important caveat in sharing your thoughts and feelings with the depressed person: *Don't come on too strong.* People who are depressed are particularly sensitive to criticism and feel easily overwhelmed. Tell her how you feel when she turns down your help, but do not attack her and blame her for being depressed. If you want to help by offering advice, limit it to one suggestion at a time, and don't insist that the depressed person follow your advice. Donna did not know that her rejection of Josh's help was making him feel so frustrated and alone. It would have been helpful for him to explain to her how he felt when she did not accept his offers of support. Donna may have been able to tell him more specifically what she needed, as well as be more aware in the future of how her behavior affected him. It may feel awkward and difficult at first, but try to be honest with your loved one about your feelings. Let her know how you feel about the support process between you.

Try not to take it personally. Remind yourself that both research and anecdotal evidence indicate that depressed people reject help more often than nondepressed people do. This fact is part of the depression, not your fault. If your loved one had a heart condition and you wanted her to exercise according to the doctor's orders, chances are that you would not take it personally if she refused to exercise one day because she felt short of breath. You would not think she was rejecting your offer to go running with her because she did not want to go with you. You would try to understand that it was part of her illness and not take the rejection personally.

Although the kind of rejection of your support that can come up when a loved one is depressed is more frequent and feels more personal than turning down an offer to go running, try to think about it in the same way. Her rejection is not of you; rather, it reflects that she is depressed and has difficulty accepting help. As was the case with Josh, part of adjusting to a loved one's depression is learning to tolerate some of the feelings that come up. There are going to be times when you feel angry that your loved one turns down your offers of help, but if you can remind yourself that it is the depression and not something that the depressed person is "doing" to you, you will have an easier time coping with those feelings and are much less likely to get depressed yourself. A wife of a depressed man who came to treatment with us found that it helped her to carry a piece of paper in her wallet with the motto, "It's the depression, not me." When nothing seemed to satisfy her husband, she would take the paper out of her wallet and remind herself that he was not purposely doing this to her and it was not her fault.

Ask for help. The task of trying to help a depressed loved one can be difficult and unsettling. Be sure to ask for help from other family members, friends, and professional colleagues. A relaxing dinner out with a close friend may go a long way in helping you cope with a depressed loved one at home. Take care of yourself, and do not hesitate to lean on other people when you are trying to help a depressed person. Do not feel guilty about needing extra help. Feel that you have a right to ask for help. After all, you cannot do it alone and should not have to. Other people may be able to relieve some of your burden of helping the depressed person alone. A sibling might be able to take up some of the slack in looking after your elderly depressed mother, or an adult child may be able to help your depressed wife get to her doctor's appointment when you have to be at work. Whatever the case, feel comfortable asking for help.

It may also be enlightening to discuss the problem with someone trained in relationship issues—a family or couples therapist to meet with you and your depressed loved one together to try to improve the communication and support process in your relationship, or individual psychotherapy to help you cope with the feelings and reactions that come up when your loved one rejects your support.

Work as a team with your depressed loved one. You need to collaborate to improve the communication and increase the intimacy in your relationship. This guideline is never more important than when you are trying to improve the support process in your relationship. You must work together to feel comfortable in seeking and providing support to one another. If your relationship is anything like Josh and Donna's, with one of you being more the giver and the other more the recipient of support, you need to develop a more symmetrical method of support seeking and offering. Rather than having one person in the relationship always feel responsible for offering support to the other, try reversing roles and being the one to seek support from your depressed loved one. For example, if you are always the helper, you might say to your loved one, "You know, I'm usually the one to help you out of jams, but I have a real problem that I was wondering if you could help me with. Would you be willing to talk to me about it?" You may be very surprised to see that your loved one can help you too, even when he is depressed. In fact, depressed people have told us that it makes them feel better to "be needed" or "be useful" when they are depressed. In these kinds of conversations, let your loved one know what you are thinking and feeling. Remember that you both are on the same team and need to work together to solve the problems in your relationship.

A Time of Change

During the course of Donna's treatment for depression, her psychologist suggested that Josh attend several sessions. The therapist was concerned that they were having conflicts over providing and accepting support from one another. In the first session, the therapist helped Josh to articulate his feelings of anger, resentment, and hopelessness when Donna turned away his help. Initially, he had difficulty focusing on his own feelings because he was so attuned to helping Donna. He tended to say things like, "I feel . . . well, you are so down that I want to be able to help you." With practice and coaching from the therapist, however, he was able to begin to let Donna know how he felt. He told her, "When you push away my offers of support, like you did last night when you didn't want me to do the dishes, it makes me feel so helpless, like I can't make anything better for you." In turn, Donna was able to recognize for the first time how hard her depression had really been on Josh. She could see how she had been difficult to give help to. With the therapist's help, she began to talk about feeling weak and incompetent for accepting his help. She explained, "If I let you do the dishes, it would make me feel like I was really a basket case. I guess I just have to keep up the illusion that I'm okay." Josh had never considered before how Donna felt about her depending on him.

In the week following this discussion, Donna asked Josh for specific help with preparing meals and even asked for a hug on several occasions. Josh asked Donna what kind of help would be the most useful before he jumped into action to help her. As they continued to talk about the problem, Josh realized he had been taking her rejections of his help personally, and he developed more realistic expectations of how much he could help. He came to understand that he could not cure her depression but that he could work with her to give her the support she wanted and needed. Donna also realized how hard it was for Josh when she rejected his support, and she tried to take his feelings into account when he tried to help her. As time went on, Josh and Donna were able to work as a team rather than individual opponents in the fight against depression. An important part of traveling through the SAD for them was understanding and talking about the support process in their relationship. Through the course of Donna's therapy, they journeyed from the initial trouble in their relationship to effective collaboration and problem solving.

In the following two chapters, we turn to two other aspects of depression that can affect relationships: the problem of alcohol and drugs and the very real risk of suicide.

10

Alcohol and Drugs

Juan was not looking forward to the holiday. He was planning to spend it with his parents at his brother George's house. George and Juan had been close growing up but had drifted apart over the past two years. While packing for the trip to George's house, Juan told his girlfriend, Becca, "I can't believe I agreed to this. I know that you want to meet my parents but I wish we could do it without George being there. The last time I spent a week at George's house, he drank wine every night until he fell asleep. That wouldn't be so bad except he's a pain in the ass when he's drinking! He starts off happy, then gets irritable until every other word is a criticism."

Becca replied, "Why don't you say something to him this time? I know how much it hurts you to see him this way. After all, you've always told me that you guys were best friends your whole life."

"I've tried, but he doesn't listen. He accused me of calling him an alcoholic. That was the biggest fight we ever had."

"What do your parents say?" Becca asked.

"Not much. I think they're angry with him too, but we don't really talk about it. I mean, we talk about the fact that he's become grumpy in his old age. But if this is what he's like at forty, I hate to see what he's going to be like at sixty!"

Juan had once tried to talk with George about his drinking, but George told him that he did not know what he was talking about and to mind his own business. Juan laughed and called George a hypocrite.

Ironically, several years earlier, George had mobilized the family to confront their father about *his* drinking problem. Nonetheless, in the heat of the argument with Juan, George heard only the insult and not his brother's concern about him.

Substance abuse often goes hand in hand with clinical depression. Research on families indicates that addictive disorders and clinical depression are closely tied to one another. Several studies have found that approximately half of all diagnosed alcoholics suffer from clinical depression. Juan and George's father suffered from alcohol dependency. After intensive family intervention, the two brothers had convinced their father to get treatment. Unfortunately for Juan and George, they never learned about the genetic and psychological effects of having a parent who is an alcoholic. As a consequence, Juan was easily misled into thinking that his brother's only problem was his alcohol abuse. He was unaware of the fact that George had been depressed since his divorce nearly two years ago and that he was unconsciously trying to medicate the depression by drinking. Ironically, excessive drinking can actually cause depression. In this chapter, we will teach you about the relationship between substance abuse and depression. You will be taught how to identify whether someone you love is using substances to medicate a depression. The Trouble phase of the SAD is a time during which you can assess whether depression is at the root of your loved one's abuse of substances. We will give you tactics you can use to talk to your loved one about his substance use and to convince him to get professional help.

Substance Abuse and Depression

The idea that depressed people may turn to substances to help them to feel better is intuitive. In our clinical practice, experience has taught us that when a patient presents with a substance abuse disorder, one of the first things we need to evaluate is whether there is a depression as well. Substances like alcohol can temporarily improve mood and other symptoms of depression like loss of energy, appetite, and sleep. Research provides data that corroborate our clinical experience. A recent study of the Amish, who virtually never use alcohol, found that men and women have the same rate of major depression and bipolar depression. Taken together with other research on the incidence of depression in men, this finding suggests that many (non-Amish) men may drink to cope with depression, thereby masking the more obvious symptoms. Specifically, studies of the general population, in which drinking is common, have found depression to be approximately twice as common in women than in men. A popular explanation for the equal rates found in the Amish is that it may reflect the true rate of depressive disorders in men, while the findings in the general population underestimate the incidence of depression in men because of increased alcohol use. In other words, men may be disguising their depression, from themselves and others, by drinking excessively. Other studies that support this idea have found that over 50 percent of alcoholics are also clinically depressed.

Alternatively, some instances of depression are caused by rather than at the root of substance abuse. George's drinking was both an attempt to feel better and, ironically, the cause of the depression's worsening. Alcohol, cocaine, amphetamines, some prescription drugs, and other substances can trigger a depression. Like alcohol, cocaine and amphetamines can temporarily improve mood; however, the after-effects can cause a physiologically based depression. The difference is that this type of depression is usually short-lived or self-limiting because it is associated with use or recent discontinuation of the substance. For these reasons, when we see a patient in our practice who is abusing substances and complaining of depression, we first treat the substance abuse. In many cases, once the substance abuse is stopped, the depression lifts.

When Does Substance Use Become Abuse?

Substance abuse is not something you can easily define. Depending on your background, you may be very comfortable with a lot of drinking or very uncomfortable with even a little. Often the alcoholic's family, friends, and employer may all agree that he has a drinking problem, while the alcoholic does not. This denial is a useful way to think about the stark differences in opinion that are so common between the drinker and the people in his life.

For the depressed person who is drinking, the relief it provides, even if temporary, far outweighs the imagined alternative. (We will use the word *drinking* for simplicity. For the purposes of this chapter, drinking refers to all forms of substance use—alcohol, cocaine, marijuana, food—and means of delivery of the substance into the body—e.g., smoking, ingesting, intravenous—unless explicitly stated otherwise.) For that person, drinking provides a respite from despair, self-recriminations, pessimism, and sadness and a reprieve from the torment of the depression. For the depressed substance abuser, the only definition of abuse he will accept is one that offers some hope. He needs to believe that the alternative to drinking will not be worse than the drinking. By talking with him about his depression and teaching him about the treatments for it, you can help him to understand that the drinking is making things far worse, not better. You can give him hope that only by stopping drinking can he get the help he needs to make him feel better.

So when does drinking become abusive and detrimental to recovery from depression? There is consensus in the mental health field regarding the key symptoms of abuse. Telltale signs of substance abuse are persistence in using the substance despite the fact that it causes problems or exacerbates preexisting problems (e.g., drinks despite having an ulcer, repeated family arguments about the substance use, uses it at work or school) and using the substance in situations that are hazardous (e.g., while driving). Severe abuse can lead to physiological and/or psychological dependence. The person with a substance dependency disorder will show some or all of the following signs:

- Failed attempts to cut down or stop using the substance.
- Taking the substance in larger amounts than originally intended.
- Using the substance over a longer period than intended.
- Continuing to use the substance despite voicing a persistent desire to stop.
- Spending a lot of time in activities necessary to get the substance, to take it, or recovering from its use.
- Not going to work or school because of being high or hung over.
- Persisting in using the substance despite significant negative consequences (e.g., driving while intoxicated, health problems, family arguments about the substance use, use at work).

- Giving up usual activities to use the substance.
- Developing withdrawal symptoms when not using the substance.
- Developing a tolerance (it takes more of the substance to reach the desired effect).
- Some of these signs have lasted for at least a month or have occurred repeatedly over a longer period of time.

If you have determined that your loved one is abusing a substance and have decided to intervene, then it will be important for you to understand some of the reasons behind the abuse. Is he drinking to medicate a depression? If he is, it will alter the way in which you encourage him to get help. Once Juan realized that George was drinking to feel less depressed, he knew that confronting him about the drinking was going to be especially difficult. In the next section, we provide you with information to help you determine if the substance abuse is associated with a depression.

Is the Substance Medicating or Causing a Depression?

When you first notice difficulty in your relationship with someone that is related to his use of substances, consider the possibility that the person may be depressed. The substance abuse may be a consequence of the depression, meaning that your loved one is drinking in an attempt to feel better. Or the substance abuse may be causing the depression or worsening a preexisting mood disorder. Regardless, when substance abuse is a component of the Trouble phase of the SAD, depression is often missed. The reason for this oversight is that the substance abuse rather than the mood disorder is what gets focused on in interactions. If your loved one is abusing substances, you should be suspicious that depression is either at the root of the substance abuse or a result of it. To determine if your substance-abusing loved one is depressed, you should look for:

- *Depressed mood or anhedonia.* The difficulty in assessing mood in someone abusing substances is that many substances have a short-term effect on mood. Ironically, alcohol, cocaine, and other substances can make you feel good, even euphoric, in the short run, but cause dysphoria many hours later. Look for depressed mood or anhedonia, particularly when your loved one is not taking the substance. For example, do you see a pattern of dysphoria or disinterest in usual activities on the mornings after use of the substance? Although Juan did not see it, George revealed later that he was even more depressed on mornings following a night of drinking.

• *Excessive self-criticism and feelings of worthlessness.* Depressive thinking includes excessive self-criticism and feelings of worthlessness. Is your loved one especially hard on himself?

• *Excessive criticism of others.* Although criticism of others is not a formal part of the criteria for major depression, we believe that it can sometimes be related to self-criticism and feelings of worthlessness. It may come as no surprise to you that people sometimes act toward others in the way that they feel about themselves. The self-critical person may project his experience outward, resulting in seeing others in the way that he unconsciously or consciously sees himself. If your loved one is critical of you, scrutinizes your behavior, and labels it negatively (e.g., "you're stupid," "don't be a fool," "can't you do anything right?"), ask yourself whether he may be feeling the same things about himself.

• *Suicidal thoughts.* Suicidal thoughts are a major clue that your loved one may be depressed. They are also an important warning sign because the combination of substance abuse and suicidality is particularly lethal. Drugs and alcohol lower inhibitions, making it easier to engage in risky behavior, including attempting suicide. If a substance-abusing loved one is also suicidal, he must get help immediately. Refer to Chapter 11 on suicide to learn how to assess whether your loved one is having suicidal thoughts, what the risk factors for suicide are, and what you can do about it.

• *Problems with sleep.* An important symptom of depression involves disturbances of sleep. Has your loved one had trouble falling asleep? Is he waking up in the middle of the night or waking up earlier than usual? Is he sleeping much more than usual? If the answer to any of these questions is yes, you must consider depression.

• *Weight gain or loss.* Has your loved one lost or gained a noticeable amount of weight when he was not actively dieting? If so, then depression should be considered. Turn to Chapter 2 to determine whether the change in weight is clinically significant.

How You and Your Relationship Can Be Affected

If your loved one has been medicating a depression by drinking, then chances are that your relationship with him has been affected in ways that support his misuse of the substance. On the face of it, this may seem counterintuitive. The last thing you would want to do is encourage someone you care about to abuse a substance. However, it is not so surprising when you consider that the drinking often provides immediate relief, for both you and your loved one, from his very painful feelings.

George became depressed shortly after his divorce. Juan and he would talk frequently and get together for dinner every couple of weeks. During these dinners, Juan noticed that George was drinking more heavily than usual but also saw that it helped him to feel better. At the start of the evening, George would be flat, despondent, and anxious about his future. By the second glass of wine, his sense of humor had returned, and by the fourth he was displaying a laissez-faire attitude about his future. Juan was almost always relieved to see his brother's anxiety lessen and buoyant personality return. In the early months of George's depression, Juan found himself encouraging George to have another glass of wine. On special occasions, he bought him bottles of wine. He even began to make a habit of picking George up and driving him home whenever they got together so he would not have to worry about George's driving intoxicated.

As time went on and George's alcohol use worsened his depression, he became more irritable when he drank. Juan found that he began to drink much more when he was with George. They were both reacting to the depression, stalled in the Reaction phase of the SAD, because they did not have the information they needed regarding the link between drinking and depression. There was pressure from George to join him, and drinking made his irritability a lot easier for Juan to handle. Juan knew from experience that he was not good at limiting his drinking when he got started. One morning, he awoke to the realization that the night before he had been driving while drunk, something he swore he would never do. Juan was angry with himself and renewed his vow to drink moderately or not at all. He knew enough about alcoholism to understand that if his father had a problem with it and George seemed to have a problem with it, then chances were high that he would as well. As a consequence, he began to avoid George. He interrupted their routine of dinners out together and began to avoid any situation where he might get pressure from George to drink.

You may also experience something similar. At first, you might unconsciously encourage your loved one to drink. There are many ways to do this, including joining in with the drinking. If you are close to someone who is abusing a substance, it is worth asking yourself: "What about my substance use? Has it increased? Has my mood been affected? Is it inadvertently supporting my loved one's abuse of the substance?"

If you come to the conclusion that you are drinking more than you want to, you may also withdraw from your loved one who is drinking. With your withdrawal may come an increase of trouble and tension in the relationship, furthering the distance between the two of you. This type of withdrawal, without explanation and without support of your loved one, can be hurtful to everyone involved. You may end up feeling guilty, and your loved one may feel hurt and rejected. The depression may worsen as the social support you provided drops. Your loved one's drinking may worsen as well. The key to not getting swept into the substance abuse and the depression of a loved one is to confront both problems directly.

How to Encourage Your Loved One to Get Help

If you have arrived at the conclusion that your loved one is self-medicating depression, or perhaps causing depression by abusing a substance, then you have successfully navigated the Trouble, Reaction, and Information-gathering phases of the SAD. You are now ready to tackle the Problem-Solving stage.

The first step is to test the defensive waters with your loved one. In other words, you need to know how defensive he is about talking about his substance use. Start by telling your loved one that you had been thinking about his drinking (eating, smoking, etc.) and wanted to know if he was willing to hear your thoughts on the subject. Initially, Juan had not done this. He simply told George that he though he was drinking too much. After consulting with us, he tried a different approach.

He began, "I've been thinking about how you drink wine at night. It's been troubling me. I would really like to talk with you about it if you're willing. Can we talk about it?"

George's answer—"Don't be stupid. OK? There's nothing to talk about!"—indicated that he was still very defensive about it, so Juan backed off: "I don't want to argue, George. I just wanted to talk about how I was feeling about it. If you don't want to, that's OK." He then changed the topic.

Juan had realized that George was still very defensive and that talking about it would get them both nowhere fast. He realized this in part because he felt a surge of anger when George dismissed his concern so quickly. In particular, he felt dismissed and criticized. He had come to learn that his anger was sometimes a mirror for what someone else was feeling. Consequently, when he felt angered by George's quick-tempered response, he thought to himself, "This anger is probably what he's feeling. Don't take it personally and back off." Juan also felt that something positive was accomplished in that he did not get into a fight with George. Rather, he left him with his own defensive words echoing in his ears instead of Juan's recriminations.

As it turned out, Juan was right on both counts. George was clearly feeling too defensive to hear what his brother had to say; nonetheless, he was in fact left with, "Don't be stupid . . . there's nothing to talk about!" replaying loudly in his ears. In particular, he realized that Juan really had no interest in criticizing him. He wanted to talk about how he was feeling. Obviously, Juan felt there was something to talk about, and George wondered whether he was being unnecessarily defensive by refusing to discuss it. Although he did not have the wherewithal to tell Juan this at the time, he did begin to question his own response.

The second step is to keep testing the defensive waters. If they are too deep, get out fast as Juan did. If you do it with respect and with emphasis on how you are feeling, rather than what your loved one is doing, you will eventually help him to lower his defenses.

What if his defensive waters are at flood level, with no abatement in sight? If your loved one continues not to give you any openings to discuss your concerns, then it is time to involve other people who are close to him. If they too confront him with their concerns, he may be more likely to listen. In addition, if your loved one has children, impress on him how important it will be for them to know whether their parent has depression or a substance abuse disorder. If they grow up unaware that these disorders exist, ignorant of their presence in their genetic makeup, they will be much more at risk for succumbing to these disorders in the future. Had Juan and George's parents been knowledgeable about depression and alcoholism, the family would have been more watchful for signs of these disorders. Had Juan and George been told that their father had a drinking problem and was depressed, things would have gone differently. George may never have resorted to drinking to medicate his depression, making matters worse for himself. In short, if your substance-abusing loved one is a parent, appeal to his love for his children if he continues to be defensive. Ask him to listen for their sake, if not his own. Tell him you might be wrong about what you think is the matter, or he may be right and there is no problem, but for his children's sake, he should find out for sure. He should get the opinion of a professional.

The third step requires that your loved one's defenses have dropped enough for you to have a conversation about your worries. George's defenses began to drop within a week of Juan's using the tactics just described. Juan told George that he would still like to talk with him about how he was feeling about his drinking and hoped that he would listen. George answered, "You're probably feeling I am drinking too much. Right?"

"No, that's not right," answered Juan. "That's a judgment you have to make for yourself. I can't tell you what's too much or not for you. What I am feeling is worried. I wonder if your drinking habit is a symptom of something serious, but I don't know for sure. I guess I just wanted to tell you what I've been learning about it and see what you think. Maybe you can allay my fears."

"What are you talking about?" George asked.

Juan proceeded to tell George about what he had learned about the co-occurrence of depression and alcohol abuse in families. They discussed their father's struggles with alcohol, and George admitted that their family history was consistent with what Juan was telling him. Juan also emphasized the fact that when people are depressed, they often feel criticized or self-denigrated. He explained that he thought that George had been doing that. George admitted that he was getting into more fights with his new girlfriend and that he felt very criticized by her, despite her constant reassurance that criticism was not her intention.

By paying attention to his own feelings as an indicator, Juan was able to help his brother see how defensive he had been. Juan also refrained from acting on his anger and further entangling himself in George's depressive communications. He stayed focused on his worry for his brother, which enabled him not to get drawn into an argument. Juan stayed focused on how he was feeling (worried) rather than on what George was doing (drinking).

The fourth step is to tell your loved one that you believe that he needs to get professional help to determine if he is depressed. In many cases, this can be easier than trying to convince someone to get help for a substance abuse problem. Substance abusers who do not see their substance use as a problem are probably relying heavily on the substance and are not inclined to give it up. By contrast, the depressed substance abuser is more likely, and often eager, to seek help for the depression. He feels down and is open to getting help for his mood. The good news is that regardless of whether treatment for the depression or the substance abuse is the catalyst for seeking professional help, both problems will invariably become a focus of the treatment. As we do in our practice, most mental health professionals will assess both depression and substance abuse. Often, substance abuse will be evident, and the initial focus of treatment will be on substance abuse, with treatment for depression to follow if still necessary. The four steps to encouraging your loved one to get help can be summarized as follows:

1. *Test the defensive waters.* Is your loved one unable to talk with you about your concerns? If so, tell him you are concerned, then drop the subject for the time being. Do not raise your concerns when he is drinking or during an argument. Be aware of how open your loved one is feeling before you raise the issue.

2. *Keep testing to look for an opening.* Stay aware of how open your loved one is to talking, and look for ways to bring the topic up. If he is

complaining of feeling blue, you can use this as a vehicle for raising the bigger issues. If he is complaining, he may genuinely welcome feedback if he thinks that the recommendation you are making will offer him some relief from the depression.

3. *Have a constructive conversation.* Refer to Chapter 7 to learn more about the essential elements of constructive communication. Remember that you are powerless to make your loved one get help (unless, of course, he is your child). A destructive argument about it will only make it harder to bring up the next time. Follow the advice we gave you in Chapter 7. In particular, pick a time to talk when both of you are calm. Use "I" statements and focus on how you are feeling. Respect your loved one's point of view, even if you disagree with it. It is far better to agree to disagree than to try to sell your point of view to an uninterested and angry adversary.

4. *Recommend professional help.* Remember to have realistic expectations. You did not cause the depression or substance abuse, and you cannot fix it. Don't be afraid to ask for help. Once you have accepted the necessity of getting outside help, recommend this to your loved one. But try not to jump to this step prematurely. Your loved one will need to conceptualize the problem in the way that you have before he can consider getting outside help. Give him time to think about what you said your concerns are. Tell him about your own feelings of powerlessness in the face of his depression and substance use. Suggest treatment for the depression rather than for substance abuse if he persists in thinking the drinking is not a problem.

Juan and George had several conversations about depression, and although George would not admit that he had a drinking problem, he became convinced that he was depressed and probably had been for the past year. A lot of what Juan told him about depression fit with his experience. He had been having trouble falling asleep at night, he was gaining weight, he felt blue most of the day until his first glass of wine in the evening, and he felt guilty for his angry outbursts. He decided that Juan's advice to get help made sense.

George saw a psychologist who quickly confirmed that he was suffering from both major depression and alcohol dependency. Although

George was initially skeptical about the diagnosis, he was willing to continue in therapy because he wanted relief from the depression. After several weeks, during which George developed a trusting relationship with his therapist and began to question whether his drinking could be related to the depression, he agreed to try to abstain from drinking. Although he continued to think that he did not have a drinking problem, he accepted his therapist's advice that they could not cure the depression while he was drinking.

Although the treatment of alcohol dependency is beyond the scope of this book, it is worth noting that a major focus of treatment of George's depression was his drinking problem. In the Recommended Readings section at the end of this book, we provide you with sources that focus on substance abuse. George tried to abstain from drinking but found himself unable to go more than a week. He tried several times but kept failing. Only after he saw that he was truly unable to stop drinking did he accept the fact that it was problematic, and he agreed to get help for his drinking problem.

If you are anything like Juan, you may have tried to protect your loved one from his self-destructive actions. You may find yourself trying to compensate for him or frequently explaining his behavior to others in an effort to smooth things over. Alternatively, you may have withdrawn from your loved one because you do not want to be around him when he is abusing substances. You may not like who he becomes when he is drunk or high. Both types of feelings and reactions are common and perfectly normal. It is essential that you learn to accept your relative powerlessness when it comes to dealing with both the depression and the substance abuse. Your loved one, not you, must make the choice to get help and do the work to get better. All you can do is hope to influence his decision. Let him know how you feel. Encourage and reassure him that you care and that is why you are questioning his use of the substance. If you decide to pull back, explain why. Tell him that you do not want to be around him while he is drinking because you feel strongly that it is only hurting him. If he will listen, educate him about substance abuse and depression. Juan was able to use what he learned about drinking and depression to talk with George about his concerns, encourage him to get treatment, and ultimately take care of his own needs. Not only did he keep from taking on more responsibility than he should, but he also realized his own vulnerability to alcoholism and depression. He joined a support group, Adult Children of Alcoholics, and learned ways to protect himself from developing a drinking problem of his own. Throughout his journey through the SAD, he also learned how not to engage in the depressive dance and fall prey to depression himself.

11

Suicide

The sound of the phone ringing in the middle of the night awakened Mr. and Mrs. Ryan with a start. As Mr. Ryan reached for the phone, his thoughts were already filled with dread. The thought flashed through his mind that it would be bad news about his son, Gregory, who had been depressed. He was right. The caller was his son's wife, Susan, in tears, asking Mr. and Mrs. Ryan to come immediately to the emergency room. Gregory had taken an overdose of pills.

As the Ryans dressed and rushed off to the hospital, each silently worried about Gregory, his wife, and his three children. They knew their son had been depressed and they had been concerned about him, but neither of them suspected that he would ever resort to taking his own life. As they reached the hospital parking lot, Mr. Ryan finally broke the silence and said that Gregory had recently asked him a lot of questions about life insurance and making the proper investments for the children's futures. "Goddammit," he said, "I just assumed that Gregory was thinking ahead, not planning for a suicide attempt." Mrs. Ryan replied, "Yes, I feel as if I overlooked things too. Greg has seemed more withdrawn and hopeless lately, but I thought it would pass. I should have paid more attention." What neither was able to talk about in the car was their fear that Gregory would die.

In the hospital, they met Susan, who explained that Gregory was having his stomach pumped and could not be seen yet. She told them what had happened. She had woken up and noticed that Gregory was not in the bed beside her. She found him in the living room, passed out on the couch. When she was unable to wake him, she became frantic and called for an ambulance. She went with him to the hospital, leaving the children with a neighbor. Susan told his parents, "I know that Gregory has been having a difficult time with the depression, but I can't believe that he would do this! He's been talking about giving up and wanting to end it all, but I never thought he meant it." With that, she broke into tears and could not continue. What Susan could not verbalize was her feeling of terrible guilt that she had not paid closer attention to how awful Gregory must have felt. She was also terrified that he might not ever wake up. By the next morning, however, Gregory was conscious and in stable condition. The doctors told the family that he would survive but needed ongoing psychiatric care for his depression and suicidal feelings.

Susan and the Ryans were relieved, but all three of them had tremendous difficulty coping with the complicated feelings that Gregory's suicide attempt had stirred up. In the weeks that followed, Susan struggled with her guilt over not taking Gregory's depression seriously enough, and she worried constantly that he might try to hurt himself again. She also felt angry at him for not thinking about what would become of her and the children without him. She found herself walking on eggshells around him, worried that she might do or say something to upset him. Mr. and Mrs. Ryan avoided talking about the incident and spent more time apart than usual in the weeks following Gregory's suicide attempt. Mrs. Ryan blamed herself for not sensing how desperate her son had felt. She had always prided herself on being a sensitive mother, and after the suicide attempt, she said, "I feel like a failure because I didn't realize the state Gregory was in." For months afterward, Mr. Ryan was very uncomfortable around Gregory and never knew what to say to him. He did not think that he should bring up the suicide attempt because talking about it might "put the idea back in his head." Mr. Ryan was a very religious man and saw suicide as a cardinal sin. Instead of making Gregory feel guilty, however, he overcompensated by trying to joke with Gregory whenever they got together. On the inside, he felt sad and isolated from both his son and his wife.

No one—not Susan or Mr. or Mrs. Ryan—talked directly to Gregory about what led up to the attempt or what he was feeling or thinking about suicide now. Yet all three of them worried constantly about Gregory and the possibility that he would attempt suicide again. Gregory also felt unable to talk to any of them about the incident. He knew that Susan was both angry and worried about him, but he felt so guilty about trying to take his life that he avoided talking about it with her. He noticed that Susan did not push the subject either. As the weeks went by, Gregory pulled back from his parents as well. Beneath his father's jokes, he could sense intense disappointment each time he talked to him. He knew that his father had deep religious convictions and would never consider suicide. Greg worried that he had hurt his father by attempting it. Gregory's mother tried to talk to him a bit, but he did not want to hear either her pity or her lectures about how to cope with problems. No one on earth seemed to understand his pain.

This family's reaction is not uncommon. Suicide is frightening. Many family members and friends of depressed people worry that their loved one might hurt himself, and they feel tremendous guilt and anger after a suicide attempt, yet despite these strong feelings, suicide is rarely talked about. In our society, it has long been a taboo subject and is usually associated with shame and secrecy. Most religions view suicide as an unforgivable sin. Families often hide the real cause of death from even their closest friends because of the stigma attached to suicide. Many religions do not permit suicide victims to be buried near others in cemeteries.

There is no doubt that discussing suicide is upsetting and makes most of us uncomfortable. When a loved one is depressed, we usually avoid talking about it or even thinking about it. We tend to deny its possibility. As a result of this silence, many family members and friends do not have the opportunity to recognize the warning signs of suicide and figure out how to help. The reality is that suicidal feelings are an all-too-common aspect of depression. We must understand the risk of suicide and talk about it directly in order to help both ourselves and the depressed person cope with suicidal feelings.

Suicide is clearly the most devastating aspect of a loved one's depression. There are no easy answers and a lot of difficult issues to deal with. In this chapter, we take you through the phases of the SAD with your suicidal loved one. First, we help you through the Information-

Gathering phase by presenting facts about suicide, theories about why people try to kill themselves, advice on how you can cope with your feelings, and the important warning signs to look for if you are concerned that someone you love is suicidal. Then, we move into the Problem-Solving phase by going over specific guidelines designed to help you in your interactions with a suicidal loved one.

Facts About Suicide

In the United States, suicide accounts for at least 25,000 deaths each year—about 12 out of every 100,000 people. In fact, this statistic is probably a significant under reporting of the true number of suicides. Many suicides are reported as accidents or illnesses because of the social stigma attached to suicide or the possible loss of insurance benefits when a loved one kills himself. Many suicide researchers now estimate that closer to 75,000 Americans kill themselves each year. Three-quarters of those who commit suicide do so while depressed, and suicide is the major cause of premature death in people who are depressed. A person with recurrent depressions has a 1 percent chance of killing himself during an acute episode. A widely cited statistic is that 15 percent of people with major depression who are not being treated or whose depression does not respond to treatment will end their lives by suicide. More recent studies have suggested that the rate is more like 25 to 30 percent.

The risk of suicide varies by gender. Although women make three to four times the number of suicide attempts than men, men are three to four times more likely to complete a suicide successfully and die. There is some evidence that this sex difference stems from the different methods men and women use. Women are more likely to take pills or slit their wrists, actions that are not immediately fatal and can be thwarted if medical help is received in time. Men, on the other hand, are more likely to use more immediately fatal means, such as shooting themselves or jumping from a high building.

Suicide risk also varies by age. In children under age twelve, suicide is rare but does happen. It is the tenth leading cause of death in children one to fourteen years old, but this statistic is also probably an understatement of the true number of suicides because many are reported as accidents. About 12,000 children ages five to fourteen are admitted each year to psychiatric hospitals for suicidal behavior, such as voicing suicidal thoughts, making suicidal plans, and attempting suicide. Some estimates are that more than 1,000 teenagers a day attempt suicide in the United States alone, and 18 are successful. It is particularly difficult to recognize when a child or adolescent is suicidal because many of the warning signs look like common behaviors for this age group. Refer back to Chapter 4 if you are concerned that your child may be suicidal.

According to the National Institutes of Health, the suicide rate increases with age, and many studies have found that the suicide rate for single adults living alone is higher than for married adults. It may be that a single person who lives alone becomes more easily isolated without drawing the concern of others. Among older people (eighty to eighty-four years old), the suicide rate was 28.5 per 100,000 in 1994, more than double the rate in the general population. Elderly men are the most at risk for suicide. The combination of being elderly and being male increases one's suicide risk substantially.

Oddly, both research and anecdotal evidence indicate that many depressed people attempt suicide once they begin to feel better. One explanation is that a very depressed person is too passive and overwhelmed and has too little energy to take any action. Once the person begins to feel somewhat better and has more energy, the hopelessness may still be there, leaving him more vulnerable to carrying out a suicidal plan. In fact, the highest suicide mortality occurs during the six to eight months *after* the symptoms have begun to improve. It is important for family members and friends to know that the risk for suicide has not disappeared because the depressed person seems to be improving.

Why Do People Attempt Suicide?

A suicide attempt is usually the result of a complicated combination of emotional, social, and biological factors. It also tells us something about the depressed person's psychological state—that the person is trying to end unbearable emotional pain. An attempt may be a cry for help or the result of feeling that there is no other option. Because of depression and cognitive distortions, the depressed person may believe that there is no one to turn to. The fact that depressed people withdraw and reject offers of help contributes to feelings of isolation. Gregory felt that his problems were insurmountable and would never go away. He feared becoming a burden to his wife and his parents, as well as an embarrassment to his children. Feeling he had no other way out, Gregory made a suicide attempt. Afterward, he described the time leading up to the attempt as "the loneliest time in my life. I felt like no one could understand what I was feeling."

Many family members ask whether specific factors contribute to suicide or a suicide attempt. The answer is that probably certain life events and biochemical determinants can increase one's risk for suicide. Researchers have found some preliminary evidence that suicidality may have a biochemical basis in much the same way that depression does. In other words, a person may inherit a biological vulnerability to attempt suicide under extreme stress. Many researchers, however, have argued that suicidality is not inherited in and of itself; rather, a biological vulnerability to depression, which can lead to suicide, is inherited. Clearly, more research into the biological correlates of suicide and depression is needed to shed further light on this issue.

In terms of psychological factors, a substantial amount of research is devoted to the events and life circumstances that precipitate suicide. The findings indicate that most people can deal with isolated stressful or traumatic events fairly well, but when there is an accumulation of events or when one is depressed, normal coping strategies can be pushed to the limits. Before his depression, Gregory typically dealt with stress at work by talking over his problems with Susan, which helped him sort out his feelings and come up with solutions. But when he became depressed, he withdrew from her and was not able to cope with his work-related stress as well. Susan's response to his withdrawal was not to ask him as much about work, assuming that everything must be fine. When he began getting pressure from his supervisor to perform better or be fired, Gregory felt completely overwhelmed and alone. He could not tell Susan what was going on because he felt distant from her. They were locked in the depressive dance.

Different people vary in how much stress and what kind of stress they can deal with. Some are personally more or less vulnerable to particular stressful experiences, and some may find certain events stressful that others would see as positive experiences. There may be genetic and biochemical factors that can increase the risk of suicide. If a first-degree relative has killed himself, one's risk of suicide increases dramatically. Other risk factors that appear to contribute to suicidal feelings include significant changes in relationships, job, housing situation, financial situation, as well as significant losses or perceived abuses. Often a recent loss of position, either at work or in relationships, can precipitate suicide attempts.

In other cases, people kill themselves as a direct result of their symptoms. They are psychotic and either do not believe that they will die or believe that they are being ordered to die. A person who is experiencing a psychotic depression may not realize the consequences of his actions and jump off a roof because voices inside his head are telling him to. Or because of delusional ideas such as believing that he must die in order to save his family from some horrible fate, the depressed person will take his own life.

Other people try to kill themselves accidentally while trying to communicate something else. They may have wanted attention, hospitalization, or temporary relief from their symptoms but did not really want to end their lives. Rather than being delusional, they may be overwhelmed with pain and unable to ask directly for help. In the vast majority of cases, people who make a suicide attempt report afterward that they would not have attempted it if they were not in great distress and if they had been able to evaluate their options more objectively.

The Warning Signs of Suicide

It is difficult to know who will kill themselves and who will not. Some depressed people who seem suicidal never try to hurt themselves, while others who do not appear suicidal take their own lives. Although there are no definitive warning signs, most suicidal people give some signals that they are considering suicide. In this chapter, when we talk about someone as suicidal, we generally mean it in the broadest sense of the word—someone who is experiencing suicidal thoughts, has made suicidal plans, intends to commit suicide, or has attempted suicide.

Many people contemplating suicide let others know about their plans in the hope that they will be rescued. They may be intent on stopping the emotional pain but are not convinced that they want to die. They communicate their thoughts of suicide in subtle and not-so-subtle ways. In other cases, suicidal people may not want to be rescued and try to avoid giving any warning signs at all. Yet a knowledgeable observer can usually pick up on some behaviors that indicate suicidal ideas. If you are familiar with the following warning signs, you will be better equipped to identify suicidal thoughts and seek help for your loved one before it is too late. The presence of one or more of these warning signs does not guarantee that someone is suicidal, but if a loved one is exhibiting any of these signs, it is definitely worth exploring the question. In the last section of this chapter, we give specific advice about how to explore these issues with your loved one and how to get him the help he needs. Keep in mind that it is also important to pay attention to your own reactions and feelings when someone you love is suicidal. Use your feelings to help you assess for the presence of these warning signs and to evaluate when you need to ask for help for yourself.

Feelings of helplessness and hopelessness. A depressed person who experiences an overwhelming feeling of hopelessness may see no resolution to his problems and resort to suicide as a solution. You can evaluate his feelings of hopelessness by observing whether he can consider any alternatives to giving up completely. Does he try to solve problems or throw his hands up in despair? Listen for such comments as, "It won't matter anyway," or "What difference does it make?" or "I can't." Gregory's mother recalled that in her last visit with him before his suicide attempt, Gregory seemed particularly hopeless and said, "I don't even know why I bother trying anymore. Nothing ever changes."

Extreme withdrawal from friends, family, and usual activities. As you know by now, most depressed people tend to withdraw from those around them. When someone is suicidal, the withdrawal may be even more pronounced. He may have no interest in keeping up with anyone or doing anything. Sitting or lying in bed for hours at a time may indicate suicidal ideas. Some theorists believe that the suicidal depressed person withdraws to suppress his anger and then eventually acts on it, by the act of suicide. Others have suggested that the withdrawal may be an unconscious way of detaching and pulling back from family and friends in preparation for death. After Gregory's suicide attempt, Susan realized just how withdrawn and distant Gregory had been in the days lead-ing up to the attempt. Pay attention to whether your loved one is more withdrawn than usual.

Talking about suicide or ending it all. Do not believe the old myth that people who talk about suicide will not do it. They do try it, and too many of them succeed. A suicidal person may say, "Life is not worth it" or "Everyone would be better off without me." Take all mention of sui-cide or suicide threats seriously. Denying or minimizing someone's threat to kill himself can be dangerous. However, this does not mean that you shouldn't talk to your loved one about suicidal thoughts. In fact, in the final section of this chapter, we provide specific advice about how to bring the topic up, and we strongly believe that talking about suicide is an effective way to help your loved one. You are not going to be "putting ideas in his head," as Mr. Ryan believed. If your loved one begins to talk about suicide, you have to consider it as a warning sign that he is suicidal. In retrospect, Susan wished she had paid more attention to Gregory's talk of "wanting to end it all" rather than thinking it was just idle talk. If someone mentions suicide, sit up and pay attention.

Self-destructive or risk-taking behavior. Suicidal people often behave in a reckless manner that is a change from their usual behavior. A depressed person might suddenly start driving too fast, playing with guns, engag-ing in criminal activity, or taking other dangerous risks. It may be that the depression makes him feel helpless, and he truly does not care if he lives or dies. Or he may be taking risks as a way of ending his pain and suffering, without having to make an overt suicide attempt. There is no question that many deaths that are assumed to be due to accidents are successful suicide attempts made by depressed people in a self-destruc-tive state.

Giving away favorite possessions. Someone who is suicidal may give away cherished possessions or ask close friends to watch after children, pets, or plants if "anything happens to me." If your loved one is depressed and begins making out a will for the first time, you should pay atten-tion. He may be trying to straighten out financial arrangements and tie up loose ends in preparation for the suicide attempt. For example, after Gregory's suicide attempt, his father recalled that Gregory had been preoccupied with his investments and drawing up his will in the weeks before the incident. When Mr. Ryan thought back, he realized how insistent Gregory had been that all his papers be in order right away. It had not occurred to him that Gregory was preparing for his suicide, but Mr. Ryan wished he had paid closer attention to Gregory's behavior.

Sudden changes in behavior and mood. If your loved one has been down in the dumps and depressed and then suddenly becomes energetic and upbeat over the course of a day or two, you cannot rule out the possibility of suicide. Rather than really getting better, he may have made the decision to kill himself and feel relieved that the end is near. Or he may have more energy to act on a suicidal plan that he conceived of when he seemed more depressed. Look for other extreme changes in behavior. For example, you may notice that your loved one who has always been invested in his career is suddenly not interested in work. Any sudden changes in behavior should be cause for concern. However, you should try to distinguish these sudden changes in the mood of your depressed loved one from the more gradual changes typical of bipolar patients. In general, if the changes are extreme and come about quickly over a few hours or days, your loved one may be at risk for suicide. Bipolar patients are also at risk for suicide if they shift quickly from a depressed episode to a manic one. If you are concerned, your loved one should be evaluated by a mental health professional.

Increasing use of alcohol or drugs. Depressed people often use alcohol and drugs as self-medication for their depression, yet these substances typically make them feel more depressed and may increase the risk of a suicide attempt. One explanation is that drugs and alcohol tend to loosen inhibitions so that someone who is considering suicide may be more likely to attempt it when he is intoxicated. In addition, mixing alcohol and drugs, particularly prescription drugs, may be an attempt at suicide, either by overdose or by driving while intoxicated.

Identification with someone who has committed suicide or preoccupation with thoughts of death. If your loved one is preoccupied with thoughts of death or of someone who has killed himself, it indicates that death has become a recurrent theme in the depressed person's thinking. We all think about death and dying from time to time, but thinking about it to the exclusion of other things is a warning sign of suicide. Identifying with someone else who has killed himself should also be a red-light warning about suicide. There has been a lot of recent media attention paid to the idea of copycat suicides, especially in adolescents. Suicide researchers have suggested that someone who is depressed may model himself on others who have also coped with great stress and disappointment with suicide, whether the others are family members or people in the popular media. If someone close to the depressed person has killed himself in the past, the depressed person may consider it a way out for himself as well if things get too bad.

Clear plans. A definite and specific plan for committing suicide is a serious warning sign. Having a method, particularly one that is likely to be lethal, and access to the means of suicide is a strong predictor that your loved one may attempt it. Someone with a clear plan needs immediate psychiatric attention and should be brought to the nearest hospital emergency room right away. In the final section of this chapter, we provide more detailed strategies about talking to your loved one about getting help.

Previous suicide attempt. Anyone who has had a previous attempt is at risk for a future successful suicide. According to a number of different studies, from 45 to 60 percent of people who kill themselves have made at least one previous attempt. If your loved one exhibits any of the above warning signs and has had a previous suicide attempt, seek help immediately. Although we usually advocate teamwork and a collaborative approach with your depressed loved one, this is the time to take a more paternalistic approach. Get him help, whether he wants it or not.

How Suicide Affects Families and Friends

Suicide attempts, fatal or nonfatal, are tremendously traumatic for family members and friends. If a loved one succeeds in killing himself, the effects on those who care about him are devastating. Feelings of grief, guilt, anger, resentment, remorse, confusion, and great distress over un-resolved issues are very difficult for loved ones to cope with. The added stigma surrounding suicide can make it extremely difficult for family members to talk about what has happened. Although we will discuss some of the ways that a completed suicide can affect you and address how you can begin to cope with it, a full discussion of all the issues is beyond the scope of this book. If someone you love has indeed killed himself, we strongly urge you to turn to the Recommended Readings at the end of this book and consider getting some professional help to cope with your loss.

When a loved one makes an incomplete suicide attempt, as Gregory did, many of the same issues come up. Family members have difficulty coping with their complicated feelings and wonder what they can do to prevent a future attempt. There are no blueprints for how to proceed after a loved one's suicide attempt. It stirs up complicated feelings for everyone and can take a long time to recover from. You need to be aware of your own feelings during the Reaction stage, as well as during the Information-Gathering and Problem-Solving phases of the SAD. We cannot emphasize enough the importance of taking care of yourself when someone you love has made a suicide attempt.

Gregory's suicide attempt was stressful for all the Ryans. Mr. and Mrs. Ryan felt distant from each other and unable to bridge the gap that the incident had created. Mr. Ryan was disappointed in Gregory and felt guilty for feeling disappointed. How could he be disgruntled when his son was so clearly in pain, and shouldn't he just be relieved that Gregory was alive? Mrs. Ryan felt overly responsible and was un-able to shake her guilt that she should have been able to help Greg before it reached that point. She spent much of her time mulling over all of the conversations that they had over the months leading up to the attempt and wondering if she could have said something to pre-vent his attempt. Susan was probably the hardest hit of all. She was frightened and alone. She could not get past the idea that Gregory would leave her and the children. But what could she do with all of her anger at him? It did not seem right to burden him with how she felt. Obviously he was going through enough of his own pain. She worried constantly that the next time Gregory would succeed in killing himself.

When someone you love has attempted or completed suicide, there are natural reactions that you may have. You are responding to the trouble in your relationship, and you tend to respond with your knee-jerk reflex reactions. You may get mad or scared, or you blame yourself. Your reaction, whatever it is, is a natural part of the adjustment to a suicide attempt. Expect to have a whole range of different reactions in the weeks and months following your loved one's suicide attempt. Before we discuss what to do when someone you love is suicidal, you need to understand the common reactions to a loved one's suicidal thoughts or attempt. What's important to realize is that all of these feelings and reactions are natural.

You take it personally. If a loved one has attempted suicide or even just threatened to kill himself, chances are you will take it very personally. Rather than seeing it as an action that he has taken because of his depression, you will probably think about how you could have prevented it or what it means in terms of your relationship with the depressed person. It is ironic how painful a suicide attempt can be for those close to the depressed person when you consider how that same person probably believed that no one cared about him before he made the attempt. On the contrary, suicide attempts stir up a mixture of feelings for everyone involved.

When Gregory attempted suicide, his parents and Susan took it very personally. Mr. Ryan felt let down by his son. He wondered where he had gone wrong in raising a boy who would consider suicide as a way to cope with problems. Hadn't he instilled good religious values in his son? Mrs. Ryan felt guilty. Although she did not articulate it to anyone, she became more and more convinced that Gregory's suicide attempt could have been prevented if only she had paid more attention to her motherly instincts. Susan felt angry and frightened. If Gregory had tried to "leave her like that," what did it mean about the strength of their marital bond? If he really loved her, why would he ever consider killing himself and not being with her? For each of Gregory's family members, taking it personally hindered them in their ability to talk directly to Gregory about their feelings. Because they were so caught up in their personal reactions, they were unable to enter the Problem-Solving phase of the SAD.

You feel overly responsible. Many family members and friends feel responsible for what has happened to their loved one. A father of a young woman who killed herself told us, "I know it's all my fault. If only I hadn't divorced her mother." This man felt entirely responsible for his daughter's death even when other family members reassured him that many, many other factors had led to her suicide, most notably, her struggle with severe depression for many years. Yet it was almost impossible to convince this man that it wasn't all his fault.

If someone you love has tried to kill himself, you may feel like a failure. You may feel that you are to blame. In many cases, the people closest to the person who made a suicide attempt will blame themselves for not having done something to stop the person or for not noticing how desperate he felt. Both Susan and Mrs. Ryan felt terribly guilty that they had "allowed" Gregory to get to the point that he would take his own life. It is natural to feel responsible, but it does not help you move to the Problem-Solving phase with your loved one. You cannot collaborate with your loved one when you feel overly responsible for what has happened.

You feel angry. Many people struggle with anger after a suicide attempt. You may feel angry at mental health professionals for not preventing the suicide attempt or angry at the depressed person for inflicting such worry and pain on loved ones. Susan was certainly angry at Gregory for trying to take his own life. Yet the difficulty with feeling angry is that it can be very hard to express that anger, particularly when your loved one is recovering from the suicide attempt and may be in a fragile state. Instead, you may find yourself pulling back or withdrawing from the depressed person because of your intense anger. Mr. Ryan felt very angry at Gregory for what he saw as "committing a sin," but he felt unable to express his feelings.

Family members have asked us over and over again, "How can I let him know that I'm angry when he is going through so much pain?" We believe it is possible and beneficial to the relationship to express your anger but important to be watchful about how you act on your anger. In relationships, all of us sometimes cross over the line and act in a hurtful way when we are angry. When someone you love is suicidal, lashing out in anger may be dangerous because he is so vulnerable. You have to tread carefully and be very aware of how you act on your angry feelings. In the final section of this chapter, as well as in Chapter 7, we introduce you to specific ways to express your anger with your depressed loved one.

You feel ashamed. Shame is another common reaction to a suicide attempt. You may not want others to know that your loved one was suicidal. You may feel it reflects poorly on you. Mr. Ryan certainly did not want anyone at the family's church to know about Gregory's suicide attempt. He feared that others would see it as a shameful act. In addition, when someone you love has attempted suicide, some of your feelings may not feel "right" or acceptable. Many people close to a depressed person, particularly a person who has had a history of recurrent and severe depression, may have mixed feelings about suicide. If the suicide attempt is successful, loved ones may feel some relief at some level, because neither the depressed person nor those close to him will have to suffer with the depression anymore. If the suicide attempt is not successful, loved ones may feel regret that the depressed person was not able to end the long suffering with the depression.

These kinds of thoughts and feelings are understandable. At times, especially when we feel helpless and ineffective in alleviating pain, those close to a depressed person may wish that he would just disappear or die. Yet when he then attempts or completes suicide, we feel overwhelmed with guilt. However, wishing for an end to the pain and suffering that you feel and you see your loved one go through is very different than acting on that wish. The wish does not mean that you do not love the depressed person or that you are cruel and heartless. It just means that you are experiencing pain and feel helpless to ease the suffering of the depressed person.

As you pay attention to your own reactions to your suicidal loved one, remember that not one of your feelings is inappropriate and that a whole range of different feelings is to be expected. It will not help you or the depressed person to blame yourself for your reactions.

What to Do When Someone You Love Is Suicidal

Knowing what to do when you suspect that someone you love is suicidal is complex and intimidating. The fact that suicidal thoughts can lead to death makes it very anxiety provoking. Fortunately, in many cases, suicidal feelings will pass when the precipitating events pass or if their overwhelming nature dissipates. And even more encouraging, suicidal plans are often put aside if the person is able to make constructive choices about dealing with the crisis at hand rather than harming himself. How can you help? What should you do? And what shouldn't you do?

Gregory's family did not know how to react. Mr. Ryan refrained from talking to Gregory about it because his anger and disappointment would show and it would only "put ideas in his head." Instead, he avoided talking to Gregory at all. Mrs. Ryan was not sure that Gregory really needed professional help and felt uncomfortable with the stigma of his suicide attempt and need for therapy. However, she did not think she should tell Gregory about her opinions. Because of her own anxiety, she tended to chat incessantly about trivial matters whenever she saw him. Susan was terrified that Gregory would make another suicide attempt but did not know what to do to prevent it. She felt distant from him and worried that they were headed for a divorce.

As you read the following guidelines, be sure to keep part of the focus on yourself and your own reactions to your suicidal loved one. Suicide is a tough issue for all of us, and you should not overlook the stress it can cause you. Try to think back to the general guidelines we gave for when someone you love is depressed. Remember to learn all you can about suicide and have realistic expectations about what you can and cannot do in preventing a loved one's suicide. In addition, continue to offer unqualified support to your loved one, but be sure to maintain your own routine as much as possible and not take his behavior personally. Share your feelings with him in a constructive way. Finally, work as a team with your loved one. You will be much more successful coping with your loved one's suicidal thoughts or attempts if you can collaborate and come up with potential solutions to problems together.

Assess the risk of suicide. Use the research findings and warning signs we have outlined to help you determine if your depressed loved one is at risk for suicide. If you think that he might be at risk because one or more of the warning signs are present, he should be immediately evaluated by a trained mental health professional. If he is already seeing someone, inform the therapist immediately of your concerns. You may feel as if you are intruding or breaking your loved one's confidence by calling his therapist, but in this case, it is imperative that you let his therapist know your concerns. The professional will ask your loved one about many of the same warning signs. Is he having suicidal thoughts, feelings, or intentions? Does he have a plan for how he would do it? How readily available is the method? Is there a set time to attempt the suicide? Is there drug or alcohol involvement? Has there been a previous suicide attempt? Is his anxiety and frustration level so high that he may be desperate to relieve his feelings? If your loved one gives affirmative responses to any of these questions, the mental health professional will ask additional questions and then make a qualified decision about necessary treatment and precautions to prevent your loved one from hurting himself.

Talk about suicide. If you are concerned that your loved one may be suicidal, try to talk to him about it. Do not worry, as Mr. Ryan did, that asking someone if he has considered suicide will "put the idea in his head." That is a myth. Someone who is depressed and suicidal is already thinking about suicide and may be relieved to share his thoughts with someone else. Asking about suicidal feelings gives the person permission to feel the way he does and is an invitation to talk about it. Feeling understood can reduce the sense of isolation and help to relieve the immediate distress.

But how do you ask? Many of us understandably feel very anxious asking about suicide. Will we offend our loved one? How do we phrase it? The key is to be direct and compassionate. For example, you could say, "It sounds like you are feeling completely overwhelmed. Has it made you think about dying as a way to stop the pain?" or, "Have you ever felt so bad that you felt like hurting yourself?" or, "Are you feeling so hopeless that you're considering suicide?" The most appropriate way to raise the subject will differ according to the situation and your relationship with the depressed person. You will know best how to proceed. Just use your own intuition and understanding of the person to guide you.

Pay close attention to how the depressed person answers your questions. A person who is not feeling suicidal will usually be able to give a comfortable "no" and explain why he has reason to want to live. Someone who is contemplating suicide may not be able to answer the question as easily or as confidently. He may confess that he has indeed been thinking about it lately. If he does, be sure to ask, "What's your plan?" so that you can help ensure his safety until you get him professional help. Even if your loved one's answer is no, it can be helpful to ask what he would do if he ever got to the point where he was seriously considering hurting himself.

Whether he admits having suicidal thoughts or not, let him know that you are there and that he can always go immediately to a hospital emergency room or police station to get help. It is also important for you to acknowledge the changes in his behavior that you have observed and that have led you to worry about suicide. You could say, "You know, you seem different lately. I've noticed that . . . Should I be worried that you'll hurt yourself?" Let him know that you are concerned and want to help. Studies of adolescents who have attempted suicide have shown that many of them felt isolated and hopeless. They reported that their suicide attempt was more of an attempt to express their anger, frustration, and helplessness than to kill themselves. If their coping and communication skills had been stronger, they may have been able to speak out in a healthier, safer way. You need to let your loved one know that you are there to listen and will help him express himself in any way that you can. If someone tells you that he feels suicidal, listen. Then listen more. Tell him, "I don't want you to die. Let's talk about it." Although talking about suicide may not be a long-term solution, it can immediately reduce the feelings of isolation that often precede a suicide attempt and help to reduce the immediate risk of suicide.

Will your loved one get offended? In our experience, this does not happen very often, but offending the depressed person is something that many family members worry about. Most of the time, a depressed person who is not suicidal will just state, "No, actually I don't feel that bad. Suicide is not something that I'm considering." However, if you ask your loved one if he has considered suicide and he gets angry at you for asking, then you might say, "I'm sorry. I didn't mean to insult you. It's just that I've noticed you seem really down, and I was concerned that you might be thinking about suicide. I care about you and wanted to check in with you about this." A statement like this will usually calm an angry person. However, use your own intuition about your loved one's anger to guide you. Is he just angry because he cannot believe you think he'd kill himself? Or does he protest too much? If his reaction to your attempt to bring up the topic seems out of the ordinary or excessive, reconsider that he might indeed be suicidal.

Make a "no-suicide" contract. If your loved one is having thoughts of suicide, try to make a "no-suicide" contract with him: You and your loved one agree to join forces as a team against his suicidal feelings. In other words, you are fighting the depression together. When you make a no-suicide contract, ask the depressed person to promise you that he will not hurt himself until you get professional help for him or until the next time he sees you. As part of the contract, he must agree that if he feels that he wants to hurt himself, he will not do anything until he contacts either you or someone else who can help him. Your promise to him is that you will be available and help him in any way that you can. You let him know that he is not alone against the depression. It may even be helpful to put this kind of contract on paper. Although there is no guarantee that the person will not attempt suicide anyway, a contract can be very helpful in stopping people who might act impulsively or who feel so alone that suicide appears to be the only option. Suggest that the depressed person think of a list of five people whom he would talk to if he had no one else to turn to. Many suicidal people are so distressed that they cannot see anywhere to go to in the midst of a crisis. It helps to have a prepared list of people to approach.

Offer alternatives to suicide. If your loved one admits feeling suicidal, try to find out what aspects of his life are so terrible that he sees death as the only answer. Try to show him alternative ways of coping with his situation. Talk to him and try to engage in problem solving. The first step in constructive problem solving is to define what he sees as the problem. The second step is for the two of you to generate as many possible solutions to the problem as you can think of. And finally, help him to evaluate the pros and cons of potential solutions, and try at least one of them. Refer to our discussion of a family meeting in Chapter 4, and try this technique. You want to show him how change can be possible and offer alternatives to suicide, but also be careful not to come on too strong and overwhelm him with advice.

Stay alert. If someone you love is depressed and has suicidal thoughts, watch him, try to keep dangerous objects away from him, and make sure that either you or someone else stays with him until you can get professional help. If the depressed person is not talking about committing suicide immediately but admits thinking about it, you must also be alert. Watch for the warning signs and try to assess whether he sees no other way out of his pain. However, neither you nor anyone else can keep a twenty-four-hour vigil seven days a week. You need to get professional help for your loved one because you cannot possibly safeguard a suicidal person all of the time.

Seek professional help. This guideline is mandatory if someone is suicidal. You cannot rescue your loved one single-handedly from the grips of suicidality. In fact, you can be the most helpful by referring him to a professional for help. If he is already in treatment, contact his therapist immediately and let him or her know why you are worried about your depressed loved one. It is all right to break confidentiality with your loved one when you believe that his life may be in danger. Don't hesitate to call his therapist. You're not intruding. If he or she does not seem to be alarmed, emphasize that you believe this is a life-and-death emergency. In the very rare case that the therapist does not seem to understand the seriousness of your concerns, you can either take your loved one to the nearest emergency room or insist that he at least get a second opinion from another mental health professional.

In many cases, a suicidal person will refuse to seek help himself and resist going to see a professional, even when you suggest it. You must insist. Don't worry about being disloyal or going against his wishes. Although we usually suggest collaboration, suicide is a life-and-death emergency, and you cannot waste time trying to get consensus. You may have to take charge of the situation and get your loved one help against his wishes. Breaking a confidence to seek help might feel like a betrayal of your loved one's trust, but you must do it. Doing so could save his life. Because of the pessimism and cognitive distortions associated with depression, he may not believe that he can be helped, but there are effective treatments for suicidal feelings. Even if you think you have talked your loved one out of acting on his suicidal feelings, you must still get professional help. He may be just saying he won't do it to quiet you or he may reconsider in the near future and still act on his suicidal thoughts.

Most of the time, people who have suicidal feelings but no plan or intent to act on the feelings do not require hospitalization. However, if a plan or intent is strong, hospitalization may be necessary to reduce the risk of suicide. Depending on the laws in your state, you may be called upon to force your loved one into a hospital against his will. It is difficult to do, especially if the depressed person is begging you not to, but you have to consider it if it will save his life. If you think that your loved one may need to be hospitalized and he does not have a psychiatrist whom you can call, take the person immediately to the nearest emergency room. If no hospital is near, call the police. Most police officers are trained to deal with psychiatric emergencies and can help take your loved one to an appropriate place for treatment.

In ongoing psychological treatment for depression and suicidal feelings, your loved one will learn how to deal with his difficult issues more constructively and develop better coping skills to deal with problems that may arise in the future. Groups can also be very helpful to increase the sense of belongingness and being understood rather than feeling isolated and alone.

Get help for yourself too. Coping with a suicidal loved one is very difficult. If someone you love has committed suicide or made a suicide attempt, you have to find ways to deal with all of the complicated feelings that it stirs up. Trying to cope with it on your own is a mistake. You need the support and comfort of others, both friends and family close to you, as well as professional guidance. In our experience, family members and friends benefit greatly from survivors' groups and other support groups where they can relate to other people who have had similar experiences. The experience of being accepted and not judged can be extremely powerful. Often those close to suicidal people feel an intense burden of unresolved feelings and blame themselves. Individual and family psychotherapy can also be very helpful in coming to terms with a loved one's suicide attempt. Do not allow yourself to become one of the overlooked victims of depression. Get support for yourself during this difficult time.

The Ryan family was relatively lucky. Gregory's suicide attempt proved not to be fatal. They were able to get Gregory the help he needed and to learn more about the warning signs of suicide so that they could help to prevent a future suicide attempt. Over time, Mr. Ryan spoke to his clergyman about the incident and decided to talk to Gregory about the suicide attempt. The first time he brought the subject up, he found he had to force himself not to break into his usual joke-telling manner. He asked Gregory to come over and told him, "Look, I'm worried about you. When you tried to take your life, it really frightened me. I didn't know what to do or say. But now I think we should at least talk about it." Gregory felt tremendous relief that his father had not given up on him. He was able to tell his father about his feelings of desperation, and they discussed what led up to Gregory's attempt. Mr. Ryan told Gregory how his religious beliefs had initially made it hard for him to talk to Gregory but that he had realized that his relationship with his son was too important to him to ignore. This degree of closeness made it easier for Gregory to talk to his father in the future when he was feeling down.

Mrs. Ryan joined a local support group for family members of depressed people. Although she had always been somewhat skeptical about therapy and "psychobabble," she learned a lot about depression and got much needed support from other women who had gone through similar experiences with their family members. In particular, she learned not to feel as responsible and guilty about Gregory's depression. She came to understand that there might not have been anything she could have done to prevent his suicide attempt. As a result, she felt more able to talk to Greg directly about her concerns rather than make trivial small talk. In turn, Gregory reported feeling less alone and more understood by his parents than he had in years.

Susan had the most difficulty coping with Gregory's suicide attempt. After several months of keeping her anger and fears inside, she sought professional help for herself. In individual psychotherapy, Susan began to express all of the feelings she had kept hidden for so long. She learned skills to help her communicate more constructively with Gregory, and she began to trust her own judgment again for the first time in a long time. Rather than functioning as separate, isolated warriors fighting the depression, Gregory and Susan began to work together on the same side. She told him how angry and frightened she had been and he revealed how alone and depressed he had felt. They made a no-suicide contract, and worked hard to improve their relationship. For this family, knowledge about suicide and the ability to talk about it directly with Gregory helped them to safeguard their depressed loved one.

In the chapters to follow, we turn to the important aspects of finding help for both your loved one and yourself.

12

Psychological Treatments for Depression

Gary's wife, Sarah, had been seeing a therapist for nearly six weeks, and he was not very happy about it. His first gripe was that she had not told him she was going until after the first session. Sarah explained that she had met with a counselor in her employee assistance program at work who had referred her to the therapist. The two appointments happened over the course of only two days, and at first she told Gary that she was not sure why she had not thought to tell him about it. It simply didn't occur to her, in part, because of the depressive fog she was in at the time. Gary tried to accept this explanation but had lingering doubts about why she was being so secretive. These doubts worsened over the following weeks. He would ask how her session had gone, and she would give terse replies, such as, "It was fine." He complained to her, "I don't know what you can tell this guy that you can't tell me!"

A second problem Gary had with the therapy was that it did not seem to be helping fast enough. It was true that after the first session he saw definite improvement; Sarah came home smiling and hopeful. In fact, that was how the topic of her being in therapy had initially been broached. Gary remarked on her good mood, and she told him the reason was that she had gone to see a therapist and that she liked him. But by the third session, she was the same old Sarah he had been living with the previous month: feeling blue much of the day, extremely self-critical, no energy, and tired all the time.

Gary's other unanswered questions further undercut any confidence he felt in the therapy. Wouldn't antidepressant medication be quicker and more effective? Making matters worse for Gary was the fact that Sarah could not tell him the credentials her therapist had. She trusted the counselor at work to refer her to someone competent, so it never occurred to her to ask. Gary felt less inclined to be so trusting and repeatedly asked Sarah to find out her therapist's credentials. Sarah kept forgetting to ask, and this issue, along with her reluctance to go into much detail about what was discussed, were the catalysts for several arguments.

If you are close to someone who is in psychotherapy for depression, Gary's questions and feelings are probably familiar to you. They make sense. Of course, Gary was curious about what was going on in the therapy sessions. He and Sarah were each other's best friends. Since she had been depressed, Sarah had been telling Gary things she would not dream of telling anyone else—that she woke up every day feeling as if she would be better off dead and that she felt worthless. Now she was talking to someone else and less to him. He worried that she might not be telling her therapist about her constant thoughts of death or about how worthless she felt. Gary's questions about what was going on in the sessions and about whether antidepressant medication was indicated also make sense. He felt Sarah was desperate for relief and consequently vulnerable. Gary worried that she did not know her therapist's professional degree or whether he was licensed. (Refer to Chapter 14 for more on therapists' qualifications.) Gary had good reason to want to know the answers to these questions, but these concerns, as understandable as they were, were nonetheless leading to conflict in his relationship with Sarah. The depression had landed the two of them squarely in the middle of the Trouble and Reaction phases of the SAD.

The trouble they were having stemmed from some unacknowledged feelings Gary was having and from a breakdown in constructive communication. In this chapter, we give you the information you will need, and Gary could have used, to respond more constructively to the depression's effect on your relationship. We alert you to some of the common feelings people have when someone close to them is in psychotherapy for depression. We teach you skills to handle these feelings in ways that will benefit both you and your loved one, and ultimately these skills will reinforce your relationship. We give you guidelines to help you to identify problems quickly and to tackle them together. If you are reading this, you have obviously entered the Information-Gathering stage of the SAD and are ready for answers to some of your questions. Consequently, prior to giving you these guidelines, we turn to the information you will need to understand the role of psychotherapy in the treatment of depression.

Psychotherapies for Depression

The wide array of different antidepressants and therapies available can make treatment choices overwhelming. How can you know what kind of therapy is the best choice for your loved one? How do you make a decision about antidepressants versus psychotherapy? There are many issues to consider when you and your loved one are contemplating treatment options. The decision of whether antidepressants would be more or less helpful than psychotherapy alone can often be a difficult one. Many studies, including a landmark report in 1989 by the National Institute of Mental Health (NIMH), show that medications and psychotherapy are equally effective, except when the depression is very serious or if the patient is suffering from bipolar disorder. Medications are usually effective and therefore recommended for very serious depression because they can sometimes alleviate the most dangerous and painful symptoms in a matter of weeks. In practice, however, most practitioners use psychotherapy in conjunction with antidepressants. There are several reasons for this standard practice, including the fact that some researchers charge that the NIMH study was flawed. Critics argue that it inadvertently gave an advantage to the antidepressant medication condition. In fact, several other studies published more recently appear to support this claim; they too say that psychotherapy is every bit as effective as medication, even for cases of severe depression. Also, patients involved in both types of treatment simultaneously tended to do better than patients taking medication alone. Most clinicians agree that psychotherapy is, at the least, an important adjunctive treatment for patients who respond well to antidepressant medications.

We agree. Most people with depression suffer for months or years before seeking treatment. As a consequence, relationships, job performance, and the depressed person's self-concept are often harmed and in need of repair. Some patients on antidepressants report feeling much better but continue to harbor many self-doubts about themselves following the depression. Others complain that although the depression has lessened, the relationship troubles associated with the depressive period persist. In such patients, recovery is not complete. Psychotherapy can provide a forum for a full recovery from depression and all of its devastating effects on one's self and relationships.

Many people find therapy a helpful way to deal with their feelings of shame and embarrassment about having a mental illness and needing medication. Therapy also complements drug treatment by helping the patient to combat the impulse to discontinue taking the medication prematurely once she experiences some initial relief. Therapy provides a place to grapple with these issues, as well as with others about managing the illness. For example, people who are in psychotherapy and taking medication are more likely to be taught to identify the warnings signs of a relapse, the cycles and the patterns of their depression. Such knowledge gives them long-lasting control over aspects of the illness.

Surprisingly, although medicated patients in psychotherapy generally feel that their therapy is important to their recovery from depression, sometimes their therapists do not agree. For example, one study reported that 57 percent of people taking lithium felt psychotherapy was important, while only 27 percent of their therapists felt the same way. The majority of these therapists doubted the efficacy of the psychotherapy they were giving, despite good scientific evidence that psychotherapy works and the fact that they were therapists. We mention this study because the results speak to those of us who make up the depressed person's support system. Whether we are her loved one or her therapist, it is not uncommon to feel that we are not making a difference, even when the depressed person feels we are playing a crucial role in her recovery. Gary felt that he was no longer needed by Sarah and that he had no role to play in her recovery from the depression. To the contrary, Sarah revealed that during her time in psychotherapy, Gary's interest and supportive reassurances helped her tremendously. She added that having him at home with her in the evenings, even if they were arguing, kept her from feeling even more isolated and worthless than she already did. She appreciated the fact that Gary "stuck by her side."

Types of Psychotherapy

The decision of which therapy approach is better for your loved one depends largely on her specific needs, background, and the expectations that she has for the therapy. The decision of which therapy should be pursued, and whether to use antidepressants, should be explored with a trained mental health professional who is intimately familiar with different types of treatment. Do not be afraid to ask the therapist, if he or she is not a psychiatrist, whether he or she has also treated patients who are on medication. Find out this person's opinion about both medication and psychotherapy and ask for an explanation about which factors he or she would weigh in order to recommend one form of treatment over the other.

Practitioners of *psychodynamic therapy* assume that a depressed person is unconsciously mourning a loss in her life. The loss can be physical, as in the death of a loved one, or emotional, as when one is raised by a parent who is emotionally unavailable. The person feels depressed because she is not consciously aware of the mourning. In this model, therapy works by helping the person to become more fully aware of her past losses and thereby experience the depression for what it actually is—a constellation of memories of loss rather than the reality of her current life circumstances.

Within the psychodynamic approach are several major schools of thought focusing on different aspects of the depressed person's experience. The *classical* approach emphasizes exploring childhood trauma and understanding the defenses that have been developed to guard against direct awareness of these experiences. This approach focuses more on earlier childhood experiences and how they can affect current mood and functioning. The *relational* approach, also described in Chapter 8, focuses more on current events, self-concept, and interpersonal relationships.

Another form of psychodynamic psychotherapy, which is becoming increasingly popular, is *brief dynamic psychotherapy*. Treatment is usually limited to about thirty sessions or fewer, with the psychotherapist focusing on the crucial issues and feelings that he or she believes may have contributed to the depression, then trying to strike a balance between being supportive and asking difficult and probing questions. The patient and therapist together explore the issues and emotions underlying the depression, learn how these issues affect the patient's emotional states, and set up ways of coping and dealing with these emotions. One of the main differences between brief dynamic therapy and the other psychodynamic therapies is that it is time limited.

Despite their differences, all psychodynamic psychotherapies have several things in common. They all emphasize the curative role of the therapist-patient relationship and in this sense focus as much on the process of therapy as on the content. The therapeutic relationship becomes a microcosm of what the patient's experiences in relationships in her life are like more generally. She begins to experience the therapist, whom she actually knows very little about personally, in ways that are typical of her experience of other people in her life. This displacement of feelings is called *transference*. Because the feelings can sometimes be intense, and yet the patient realizes that they could not possibly be about the therapist because he or she did not do anything to warrant such feelings, the patient becomes aware of particular emotions and expectations that she brings to any relationship. The value of increased awareness of unconscious feelings and thoughts is emphasized in psychodynamic therapies.

Interpersonal therapy was specifically designed to treat depression. It is also time limited, with once-weekly sessions for three to four months. Practitioners of interpersonal therapy concentrate on the patient's relationships with peers, family, friends, and coworkers. The theory is that a person becomes depressed out of disappointment and frustration in her closest relationships. If the person can understand her effect on others, she can improve her relationship and alleviate the depression. In this form of treatment, the patient is encouraged to explore her behavior in relationships. She is taught how to identify conflicts, improve communication, and increase interaction when depressive isolation is a problem. Interpersonal therapy works well for people who find that their depression leads to a life of isolation or for people who find their depression seriously hinders their ability to communicate with their loved ones.

Behavioral therapy is based on the concept that we respond positively to positive reinforcement and negatively to negative reinforcement. A behavioral therapist assumes that since depressed people do not get enough positive reinforcement in their life, they should rearrange their actions to obtain more satisfaction and pleasure. Behavior therapy is based on behavior; instead of spending a lot of time talking about the history of the depression or the reasons behind it, focus is placed on coaching the patient to take actions that make her happier and to enhance her performance in social situations.

Cognitive behavioral therapy is a form of behavioral treatment that targets depressive thoughts, or cognitions, that lead to increased depression. The theory behind cognitive behavioral therapy is that depression develops because of errors in thinking and unrealistic attitudes about oneself and the world. The three major errors in thinking are undervaluing oneself, a negative view of one's current situation, and pessimism. Depression results from dissatisfaction with oneself, which comes from these errors in thinking. The cognitive behavioral therapist helps the patient to see that there is no evidence for her self-defeating beliefs. If the person's beliefs and attitudes are changed, the depression will be lifted. Alternatively, other theories argue that the self-defeating beliefs arise as a consequence of the depression rather than causing the depression. Often the patient is asked to keep a journal of her feelings and thoughts so she can more readily identify what she is feeling and what she is saying to herself in specific situations. The therapist encourages the patient to imagine herself in different problematic situations, to evaluate where the problem usually begins, and to practice positive thinking and future actions designed to prevent depressive thoughts from taking over. Studies of cognitive behavioral therapy show it tends to be more effective for depressions of briefer duration than for long-term depressions, in which the symptoms continue for two years or more.

Group therapy is a catch-all term for any therapy that involves a group of patients in treatment together. A group could employ any of the other orientations mentioned above, but what all groups have in common is that the experience of depression is shared with the other members. Groups can offer unique therapeutic experiences that are not possible in a relationship between one therapist and one patient. The benefits include the development of an empathic support system, a validation of feelings, and exposure to role models. Support groups can also be helpful for the loved ones of depressed patients; it can give them an opportunity to learn ways to cope with the feelings and conflicts that stem from being close to someone who is depressed.

Family and couples therapy can provide a forum in which people with depression and their loved ones speak openly about how the illness is affecting them and their interactions with one another. By establishing an atmosphere of respect and appreciation for each family member's experience, the therapist helps to create a safe environment in which difficult feelings and conflicts can be resolved constructively. The focus of treatment is the relationship(s) rather than the depressed person. In this book, you have learned about the ways in which depression can negatively affect relationships, leading the depressed person and her loved ones into a downward depressive spiral. Family and couples therapy is particularly effective in breaking this vicious cycle of depression. During sessions, the therapist uses techniques designed to break the cycle and teach family members how to communicate more constructively with one another and to problem-solve together. These new skills are practiced and honed during the treatment so that family members can use them effectively at home.

How to Choose

The results of studies that explore which therapies are the most successful in treating depression are often hard to interpret. A major problem is that researchers have not always defined clinical improvement in the same way, or adequately described how the therapies were conducted, or they have inadvertently given one treatment an advantage over the others. Nonetheless, the results of nearly all studies agree that engaging in some type of psychotherapy is definitely more helpful than going it alone.

The NIMH study comparing treatment of depression with antidepressants, interpersonal therapy, and cognitive behavioral therapy showed that all three treatments were helpful. The outcome of patients participating in interpersonal versus cognitive behavioral therapy did not differ significantly from one another. Medication appeared to be more effective in treating severe cases of depression, in comparison to the two psychotherapies studied; however, this finding may be flawed. So although the scientific debate may continue in some circles, we believe that one thing is clear: Psychotherapy and antidepressant medication work well together, and both forms of treatment can help to alleviate depression. In fact, a more recent study found that psychotherapy can reduce the risk of relapse after medication is stopped by up to 60 percent.

Where does this leave you and your loved one? Consultation with an experienced mental health practitioner will help you to determine which course to take. However, in order for this process to work well, the depressed person should be educated and actively involved in choosing the treatment rather than a passive recipient. You can help your loved one to be an active consumer of mental health services rather than a passive patient by encouraging her to ask questions and to learn all that she can about her treatment options. In the last part of this chapter, we give you guidelines to help you in this endeavor. But before you or your loved one can ask questions or choose a treatment, a mental health practitioner needs to be seen for a diagnostic and treatment evaluation. Choosing a practitioner you can trust and communicate well with is essential. We have devoted Chapter 14 to the question of where to find help for this type of consultation and encourage you to read it prior to seeking a referral.

Common Concerns and Feelings

Gary's questions and feelings about Sarah's therapy are ones that we have become very familiar with as therapists. Almost invariably, depressed people eventually reveal that someone close to them, often a spouse or partner, has had serious concerns about the therapy. Unfortunately, we typically do not hear about these concerns until long after they have caused trouble for the relationship. Once these feelings have been aired and dealt with constructively, they rarely have a negative impact on the relationship. Instead, the process of identifying and talking about such feelings often results in a positive effect, for both the relationship and the depression. Following are some common concerns and feelings you may also be experiencing. As you read the descriptions, ask yourself if you identify with any of them. If you do, read on to learn ways of dealing with the feeling constructively in your relationship with the depressed person in your life.

Feeling Rejected and Shut Out

Many people close to a depressed person who has recently started psychotherapy report feeling shut out. For example, until she started therapy, Gary had been Sarah's confidant. He provided her with a shoulder to cry on and comforting reassurances when she was feeling low. Although he was relieved that Sarah was finally getting some help for the depression, he felt a bit rejected when Sarah told him she would rather not talk about the therapy sessions. He had become used to his role in managing Sarah's depression and was caught off guard when it changed.

Making matters worse for Gary was the nagging suspicion that Sarah was not talking about the sessions because she was talking about him! Was she unhappy with him? Was she blaming the depression on their marriage? He wanted to push the issue and to insist that she tell him more about the sessions but worried that he would be pressuring her too much.

Skepticism about Psychotherapy or the Therapist

The entertainment industry has a penchant for portraying psychotherapy as a farce and psychotherapists as charlatans at best. Popular movies portraying psychotherapists having sex with their patients or stalking their patients do little to instill confidence in the profession. If popular movies were all you knew of the practice of psychotherapy, then your skepticism would be well warranted. Even when therapists are not portrayed poorly, the process, at least as Woody Allen's movies would have you believe, is depicted as interminable and useless against anxiety and depression. Unfortunately, this was all the exposure Gary ever had. He did not know anyone else who was in psychotherapy.

The fact that Sarah was reticent to talk about her sessions fueled his worry. He wanted Sarah to ascertain from her therapist the type and duration of psychotherapy he practiced. However, because Gary and

Sarah argued when they first tried to talk about it, his questions remained unanswered.

Even if you are already educated about the different forms of psychotherapy available for depression, you may still be skeptical about the therapist or the type of therapy being offered to your loved one. The skepticism will need to be resolved in a way that works for you and your loved one. If it is not resolved, it will fester in your relationship and likely add to your feelings of being shut out and to your loved one's feeling unsupported. In the latter part of this chapter, we describe how you and your loved one can constructively confront your skepticism.

Worry About How the Therapy is Progressing

Even if you are not skeptical about psychotherapy, you probably have worries about how the therapy is progressing. Gary was concerned that Sarah was not telling her therapist all that he needed to know in order to help her. In particular, he was not sure that she had told him about her intense feelings of worthlessness and her persistent thoughts of death. Sarah tended to put on a happy face to outsiders; few people had ever seen her as despairing as Gary had. He wanted to bring his concern up with her but felt reluctant to because he thought she would be offended. During some of their arguments, Sarah had complained that she felt Gary was patronizing her. For a short time, he considered calling the therapist, to make sure that he was aware of how badly Sarah had been feeling, but realized that this would lead to more conflict in their marriage when Sarah discovered what he had done.

He felt alone and burdened by her depression. One evening about three weeks into the therapy, Sarah complained of feeling hopeless. She admitted that as much as she liked her therapist, she was unsure if he could help her. Gary interpreted her comment as an opportunity to voice his own doubts and he said, "I've been thinking that maybe you shouldn't be seeing him." Unfortunately, this statement angered Sarah. She told him she did not want his advice; she simply wanted him to listen. What they both did not understand was that Gary was not giving advice so much as he was trying to be heard and included. That night, he lay awake while Sarah slept, worrying about what had become of their closeness and trust and about whether her therapist knew how badly she was feeling. Gary felt burdened and very much alone.

Problem Solving

Despite how it might appear, the relationship trouble Gary and Sarah encountered was *not* due to Gary's feeling rejected or to his having doubts about psychotherapy and the therapist. The trouble was a consequence of their not knowing how to problem-solve together about his feelings and questions. Here are some guidelines to help you problem-solve with a loved one in psychotherapy.

Communicate your doubts constructively. The general topic of how to communicate constructively was covered in great detail in Chapters 7, 8, and 9. We revisit it here because when a loved one is in psychotherapy, the people close to her feel as if they have no place or no role in the treatment. They feel that their doubts do not count. Consequently, they remain silent, and any negative feelings they have about the therapy grow. If you have doubts or questions, do not be afraid to voice them. Just remember to pick the time carefully and to focus on how *you feel* rather than what your loved one is doing. For example, Gary chose to tell Sarah of his doubts about her therapy at the same time she was feeling unsure. Because he voiced his worries when she was feeling especially vulnerable, neither of their doubts were assuaged. If he had waited until she was feeling stronger, he might have approached the subject more constructively. He could have said, "I know you like your therapist and he sounds like a caring guy, but I can't help but feel worried about his credentials. It would mean a lot to me if you could find out what kind of degree he has."

Ask to talk to the therapist together. If you still have doubts or questions about the therapy that your loved one cannot answer, then you might want to speak to the therapist directly. Sometimes even if you do not have any specific questions, you might want to meet the person to have a sense of who he or she is. Your loved one may be inclined to keep the therapist to herself, creating a hurdle for you to cross before the two of you can talk to the therapist together. This was the case with Gary and

Sarah. When he asked to see the therapist, Sarah replied, "I don't see why you need to see him. What we talk about doesn't really concern you. Besides, he told me that I should try and keep what we talk about in our sessions between him and me. He said talking about our sessions with other people dilutes the therapy." Gary felt rejected and hurt and ended the conversation abruptly by saying, "Never mind." If instead he had started by saying that he knew that psychotherapy was a private affair and that he respected that, Sarah may have felt less of a need to put up a boundary. He could have said, "I know it's important that you and I don't talk much about your sessions and I can see why. I don't feel a need to know about what you say. I have to tell you that I do feel nervous about the therapy though. I know you're not, but it's hard for me not to because I really don't have much of an idea as to what goes on there or what the overall plan is. I would really like us both to talk with your therapist together for one meeting so I can learn more about the therapy he's giving you. How would you feel about that?" If Gary had first reassured Sarah that her privacy would be respected and that he understood how she felt, she may have been more open to hear about how he was feeling and to meeting with her therapist together.

Give encouragement. Being supportive does not mean that you should be untruthful. Early on in her therapy, Sarah had doubts about whether her therapist could help her. Gary was certainly in no position to encourage her with reassurances that this therapist was good. He was struggling with doubts of his own. However, he was in an excellent position to help her to problem-solve about her doubts. Encourage your loved one to ask her therapist questions. There is no reason to be in a therapy without having some understanding of how it is designed to treat the depression. Encourage your loved one to get educated and to make an educated decision about continuing or stopping any treatment.

During the course of her therapy, Sarah and Gary learned to work more closely to resolve questions each of them had about the treatment. In fact, Gary's worry that Sarah had not been telling her therapist just how hopeless she was feeling was confirmed when the two of them met him. Gary described how worried he had been about Sarah. When her therapist asked Gary what he was worried about, he turned and asked Sarah if he could tell the therapist about the previous morning. When she gave her consent, Gary answered, "Just yesterday she woke up in tears. She was inconsolable. She said that she thought she would be better off dead! Sometimes I get terrified that she will kill herself!" Sarah's therapist remarked that he had not known about the depth of her hopelessness. What followed was a frank discussion about suicidal thoughts. The therapist was able to confirm his earlier impression that Sarah was *not* actively suicidal (not planning to kill herself). This conversation reassured Gary tremendously. Moreover, Sarah and her therapist realized that there was an important aspect of her illness that they had not been talking about because of Sarah's shame. She said, "I didn't tell you about how bad it gets because I don't want to come in here and complain constantly. I guess I am ashamed when I cry like that. It makes me feel like I am a baby."

Much can be accomplished when you speak openly with your loved one about any feelings and questions you have about therapy. It can help you to be a more supportive and effective caregiver, while simultaneously helping you to cope with any reactions you might be having yourself. Sarah and Gary reached the Problem-Solving stage by learning to speak openly with one another about the treatment Sarah was receiving. Although many of the problems and solutions applicable to psychological treatments are relevant when a loved one is taking antidepressant medication, there are many questions that are unique to the medical treatment for depression. The next chapter addresses the questions that commonly come up when a loved one is taking medication for depression.

13

Medical Treatments for Depression

Linda and Harold had been dating for six months and seemed very much in love, but Linda was concerned that Harold seemed disinterested in sex. He had never even tried to initiate anything more than a goodnight kiss. When she asked Harold, he was vague, and Linda was left with the nagging suspicion that he was not telling her something. She worried that he was not attracted to her, but Harold assured her that he was attracted to her. He just needed more time before he would feel comfortable being sexually intimate.

His explanation added to Linda's concern when she remembered that he had told her that he had been sexually active within one month of the start of his last relationship. Feeling unable to trust his explanations anymore, she confronted him. Harold reluctantly revealed that he had been telling Linda white lies because he was ashamed to talk about the real reason he was holding back sexually. He worried that once Linda knew the reason, she would have nothing to do with him.

Harold was taking Prozac. In the year that he had been on this medication, he had had great difficulty achieving an orgasm. When he started taking it, he had been dating his previous girlfriend, and their sex life had become a "disaster." Harold worried that if he and Linda made love, he might not be able to have an orgasm, and he did not want to be in the position of having to tell her the reason. He had told her that he sometimes gets moody but had never revealed that he was taking medications for depression. He worried that she would see him as "damaged goods" now that she knew the depth of his bad moods. Linda tried to reassure him that she did not see him this way, but she was left with new worries, new questions, and serious doubts about the relationship.

Linda had many questions she wanted to ask Harold but felt she could not because it would hurt his feelings. Was the antidepressant making him high? Was it addictive? Would he always be on it? She had seen him drinking wine and wondered if that was okay when taking this drug. Could he father a child without risk of birth defects? If he stopped taking it, would it change his personality? And most worrisome to Linda, would she have even fallen in love with Harold if he was not on an antidepressant?

Questions like Linda's are common and frequently asked by people who know someone taking antidepressant medications. Whether it is your romantic partner, relative, employee, or friend, you are affected when someone you know is receiving a medical treatment for depression. Your relationship is affected as well.

Many people close to someone taking antidepressants worry about the effect of these medications. The worry is understandable but often unnecessary. The quickest cure for such worry is education. For this reason, we begin by teaching you about the various forms of medical, or somatic, treatments currently available to treat depression. Medical treatments include a variety of medications and electroconvulsive therapy (ECT). We answer the most commonly asked questions, including those Linda raised. We give you guidelines to help you handle the special problems that can arise in a relationship when someone is receiving medical treatment for depression. We also teach you how to help yourself with the problems you may encounter personally when someone you know is receiving treatment.

What You Should Know About Medications for Depression

All physicians are legally qualified to prescribe antidepressant medications, but not all are equally adept. The question of where to find the right kind of help is so important that Chapter 14 is entirely devoted to this issue. As a rule of thumb, a psychiatrist is the best professional to supervise a treatment course with antidepressant medication; however, many general internists and family physicians do prescribe antidepressants. In addition, primary care physicians are becoming "gatekeepers" for mental health services due to managed care requirements that you receive a referral from your primary doctor before seeing a psychiatrist or psychologist. Although it is always preferable to see a physician with advanced training in psychiatry when taking antidepressant medication, it is not always possible. Because your loved one may have to ask his primary care doctor for a mental health referral or may receive antidepressant treatment from a physician who is not trained in psychiatry, it is especially important that you and your loved one are actively involved in the treatment plan. You need to know how to judge if the physician your loved one is seeing is adept at diagnosing and treating depression.

Be as educated as you can, regardless of whom your loved one is seeing. It is even more important that the person taking the antidepressant be as educated as he can be. Frequently depressed people are not as active in their treatment as they could or should be. If someone you know is depressed and considering taking antidepressant medication, encourage him to learn as much as he can before starting.

Among the several excellent resources available for learning about psychiatric medications we particularly recommend *The Essential Guide to Psychiatric Drugs*, by Jack Gorman. Many people turn to the *Physician's Desk Reference* (PDR) to obtain information on drugs, interactions with other medications, and potential side effects, but the PDR was written for professionals with a background in science or medicine. Consequently, it is easy for people without this background to misinterpret some of the information printed there. For example, reading that headache is listed as having occurred in 20 percent of the patients studied while taking Prozac, you might erroneously conclude that anyone taking Prozac would have a 20 percent chance of having this effect. However, the PDR also reveals that 16 percent of the patients on placebo, from the same studies, also reported headaches. Since a sugar pill and Prozac resulted in essentially the same percentage of cases reporting the symptom, it cannot be said that Prozac causes headaches.

Antidepressants: Indications, Common Side Effects, and Addictive Qualities

Drug	Use[a]	Anticho-linergic[b]	Sedative	Insomnia	Weight gain	Dizzi-ness	Addictive
New							
Effexor	M,A	—	—	✓✓	—	—	—
Prozac[c]	M,A	—	—	✓✓	—	—	—
Zoloft[c]	M,A	—	—	✓✓	—	—	—
Paxil[c]	M,A	—	—	✓✓	—	—	—
Serzone	M	—	—	✓✓	—	—	—
Desyrel	M	—	✓✓	—	—	✓✓	—
Asendin	M	—	—	✓✓	—	—	—
Welbutrin	M,B	—	—	✓✓	—	—	—
Cyclic							
Tofranil	M,P,B	✓✓	✓	✓	✓✓	✓✓	—
Norpramin, Pertofrane	M,P,B	✓	—	✓	✓	✓✓	—
Elavil	M,P,B	✓✓✓	✓✓	—	✓✓	✓✓	—
Pamelor	M,P,B	✓	✓	✓	✓	✓	—
Sinequan, Adapin	M	✓✓	✓✓	—	✓✓	✓✓	—
Surmontil	M	✓✓	✓✓	—	✓✓	✓✓	—
Ludiomil	M	✓	✓✓	—	✓	✓	—
Vivactil	M,A	✓✓✓	—	✓✓	—	✓	—
MAOIs							
Nardil	A	✓	✓	✓	✓✓✓	✓✓✓	—
Parnate	A	—	—	✓✓	—	✓✓✓	—
Stimulants							
Dexedrine	A	—	—	✓✓	—	—	✓✓✓
Ritalin	A	—	—	✓✓	—	—	✓✓

Note: Likelihood of the side effect: ✓=Low; ✓✓=Moderate; ✓✓✓=High; —=None, or almost none.
[a]: M=major depression; P=psychotic depression; B=bipolar depression; A=atypical depression.
[b]: Dry mouth, constipation, blurry vision, difficulty urinating.
[c]: Serotonin specific reuptake inhibitor.

We recommend starting with books like the *Essential Guide to Psychiatric Drugs*, written for a lay audience.

The table of antidepressants, modified from Dr. Gorman's book, lists four major classes of antidepressant medications: cyclic antidepressants, monoamine oxidase inhibitors (MAOIs), stimulants, and the "new" antidepressants. Those listed are the most widely prescribed. Although we have listed the most common side effects in the table, other problems not listed can also occur. One notable problem associated with taking SSRIs such as Prozac or Zoloft is difficulty achieving orgasm, which can lead to a loss of interest in having sex. In our case example, Harold was suffering from anorgasmia (or ejaculatory delay), which, in one study of males, occurred in 15 percent of patients taking Zoloft compared to only 2 percent of patients on placebo. Similar rates have been reported from studies of other SSRIs. However, Effexor is reported to have less of this type of side effect. Although not technically an SSRI or a tricyclic, Effexor acts on the same neurotransmitter systems as these two classes of antidepressants.

In our example we purposely focused on SSRIs such as Prozac because these are currently the most widely prescribed medications. They are popular because they have very few side effects, not because they are generally more effective than the other types of antidepressants. Among the newest of the new antidepressants are Effexor and Serzone. These drugs are designed to work on the two neurotransmitter systems that have been implicated in depression. While cyclic antidepressants work on the norepinephrine system and SSRIs focus on the serotonin system, Effexor and Serzone target both. For this reason, they are sometimes referred to as serotonin specific norepinephrine reuptake inhibitors (SSNRI). Although Serzone is technically an SSNRI, it has relatively little effect on the norepinephrine system. Some studies have suggested that because they act on both types of neurotransmitters, the SSNRIs may have a broader application than either the cyclics or SSRIs. If your loved one has not responded to an SSRI or a cyclic, it might make more sense to switch to an SSNRI rather than trying a second or third SSRI or cyclic. Don't assume that your loved one's doctor is necessarily up to date on what is available. With the rapid pace of development of new psychiatric drugs, it is not always easy to stay abreast of recent developments.

Most of this chapter is devoted to medical treatments for depression. However, a brief discussion of treatments for bipolar disorder, in which mania is a prominent feature, is in order. Because bipolar disorder involves the two opposite ends of the emotional spectrum, depression and mania, treatment can often involve two very different kinds of medication. Antidepressant and mood stabilizer medications (lithium carbonate and various anticonvulsant medications, such as Depakote, originally used to treat epilepsy) are frequently used in concert during the acute phase of the illness.

Treatment with lithium requires ongoing monitoring of the level of lithium in the blood. Lithium and Depakote are both very effective treatments for bipolar disorder. In our opinion, because they can be so effective, failure to treat a bipolar patient with either lithium or Depakote, provided there are no known health risks such as an allergy, is malpractice. Treatment for the depressed end of the spectrum is also helped by mood stabilizers, but only during the maintenance phase of treatment (after the depression has lifted). During the acute phase, when a bipolar patient is depressed, antidepressant medications are often indicated, along with a mood stabilizer.

The following guidelines, with modifications, are drawn from *The Essential Guide to Psychiatric Drugs*. These guidelines assume that a course of treatment with medication has been decided upon. Because we have already described the circumstances in which we would recommend medication alone or as an adjunct to psychotherapy in Chapter 12, we will not revisit the issue here. However, if you have skipped to this chapter without reading Chapter 12, go back and read it; much information that is relevant to the topic of psychiatric medications is presented there.

Suggested Treatment Plan for Major Depression

1. Make sure that your doctor has considered the possibility that other medical illnesses or drug side effects could be causing the depression (e.g., hypothyroidism, treatment with certain cardiac medications, hormonal therapies, steroids, etc.) and that the appropriate tests have been done.
2. Carefully evaluate for suicide potential; hospitalize if necessary.

3. If over fifty years old, have an electrocardiogram; some medications, in some people, can affect the heart.
4. Begin an SSRI, Effexor, or Serzone.
5. Start at a low dosage and gradually increase the dosage to the therapeutic level.
6. Wait four to six weeks for a response. If there is no response, consider other medications as primary or adjunctive treatments.

Suggested Treatment Plan for Bipolar Depression

1. Make sure that your doctor has considered the possibility that other medical illnesses or drug side effects could be causing the depression (e.g., hypothyroidism, treatment with certain cardiac medications, hormonal therapies, steroids, etc.) and that the appropriate tests have been done.
2. Carefully evaluate for suicide potential; hospitalize if necessary.
3. If over fifty years old, have an electrocardiogram; some medications, in some people, can affect the heart.
4. Begin lithium or Depakote and an antidepressant (one of the new or cyclic antidepressants are all reasonable choices).
5. Watch for development of signs of mania.
6. Stop the antidepressant as soon as the depression resolves, but remain on lithium indefinitely to prevent future depressions and manic episodes. ·

Suggested Treatment Plan for Psychotic Depression

1. Make sure that your doctor has considered the possibility that other medical illnesses or drug side effects could be causing the psychosis and/or depression (e.g., brain tumor, hypothyroidism, abuse of certain illicit drugs, certain cardiac medications, hormonal therapies, steroids, etc.) and that the appropriate tests have been done.
2. Carefully evaluate for suicide potential; hospitalization often is advised.
3. If over fifty years old, have an electrocardiogram; some medications, in some people, can affect the heart.
4. Begin a tricyclic antidepressant (imipramine, desipramine, and

nortriptyline are good choices) and an antipsychotic drug (e.g., Trilafon, Haldol, or Stelazine).

5. Wait four to six weeks for a response. Stop the antipsychotic drug when the hallucinations and delusions are completely resolved.
6. If there is no response, consider electroconvulsive therapy.

Suggested Treatment Plan for Atypical Depression or Dysthymia

1. Make sure that your doctor has considered the possibility that other medical illnesses or drug side effects could be causing the depression (e.g., certain cardiac medications, hormonal therapies, steroids, hypothyroidism, etc.) and that the appropriate tests have been done.
2. Begin an SSRI, Effexor, or Serzone.
3. Start at a low dosage and gradually increase the dosage to the therapeutic level.
4. Consider psychotherapy in addition to medication.

Common Questions About Antidepressant Medications

It is natural to have questions when someone you know is taking antidepressant medications. In our example, Linda had questions that were anxiety-provoking. Some common questions are answered below; however, bear in mind that any question you have is important, no matter how trivial it may seem to you or to others. If we have not addressed your question(s), ask your loved one's doctor, read the readings we recommend, and do not hesitate to ask questions. You should also feel free to contact us at the World Wide Web site listed in this book.

Do antidepressants make you high? No. Antidepressant medications help to bring you out of a depression and are also used to keep you from becoming depressed again. It is true that some stimulants like Dexedrine can make you feel "high." Although stimulants are sometimes used to treat atypical or treatment-refractory depressions (those that do not respond to the usual treatments), technically they are not antidepressants. Stimulants should be reserved for people who have not responded to adequate trials of several antidepressant medications and who have also not responded to psychotherapy.

Can you feel sad when taking antidepressants? Yes. People taking antidepressant medications still experience the normal range of emotions. They cry, get angry, feel anxious, and laugh like anyone else. Some patients, particularly those with bipolar disorder, may complain of feeling that their emotions are muted when first recovering from an acute episode of depression or mania. However, they are usually referring to a loss of pathological mood states, such as mania or severe depression, rather than a loss of normal highs and lows.

Do antidepressants change your personality? No. But the answer to this question depends on how you define "personality." Most psychologists agree that personality refers to long-standing, stable characteristics or traits—traits that emerge in childhood and persist throughout a person's lifetime. Sometimes when someone has been depressed or manic for months or even years, we mistakenly see such temporary pathological mood states as enduring traits. When treated, it appears as if a personality change has occurred. The usually pessimistic person suddenly (over the course of four weeks or so) becomes more hopeful. But what is changing is the temporary mood state, not the traits that make up one's personality.

Do antidepressants cause birth defects or affect fertility? No, as long as the woman stops the medication before trying to get pregnant. There is no evidence that antidepressant medications have any long-lasting effects that would complicate a pregnancy. However, women are always strongly advised to discontinue such medications as early as possible during pregnancy because we do not know what, if any, detrimental effects can be incurred by the fetus. Since such studies are almost impossible to conduct and we may never know, common sense is the standard—better safe than sorry. Ideally, a woman who is considering having a child should stop taking the antidepressant before she starts trying to become pregnant. This should always be done in consultation with her psychiatrist. In some cases, when prophylactic treatment with antidepressants is being used to ward off a recurring severe depression (e.g., with concomitant suicidal risk or severe social dysfunction), the potential risks and benefits of discontinuing the medication must be weighed carefully.

How long do antidepressant medications take to work? Everyone is different. Some people take months to respond, while others notice improvement in just a couple of weeks. Research on this topic reveals that there are particular periods of time that are typical and that represent what we call an adequate trial. Only after receiving an adequate trial should you conclude that a particular medication will not work. Adequate trials average around six weeks. You should ask your loved one's physician about what the *Physician's Desk Reference* indicates an adequate trial is for the particular medication taken.

How do we know when a medication has worked? Your loved one should feel well, not just slightly better, when antidepressant treatment is working. Some people have been depressed so long they have forgotten what it is like to feel well again. Take the time to review with your loved one the symptom list we gave in Chapter 2. If the medication is working, both you and your loved one will notice significant improvement. Sometimes its easy to be fooled into thinking the medication has worked when some symptoms show improvement. For example, if your loved one has better energy, concentration, and is sleeping better, the two of you might come to the conclusion that the medication has worked fully. In this senario it has not. You will see improvement in all of the relevant symptoms, including mood, when an antidepressant has worked.

If one medication does not work, should a different one be tried? Yes. Research shows that many people respond differently to different antidepressant medications. For example, if a trial with an SSRI has failed, an SSNRI could be tried.

Can antidepressants make you suicidal? No. You may be familiar with media reports claiming that Prozac makes people suicidal, but this question has been examined scientifically, and there is absolutely no evidence that this is true. Some clinicians nevertheless believe that people prone to suicide may become more at risk for attempting suicide as their depression begins to lift. This may be particularly true in the beginning phases of treatment with SSRIs, which are typically faster acting than the other types of antidepressants. We have found that some severely depressed people, with preexisting suicidal thoughts, can feel more energetic and less slowed down cognitively when they start medication; however, they continue to feel dysphoric, negative about themselves, and pessimistic about the future. They mistakenly believe that the medication has "worked" as much as it will and that no further improvement is possible. With reinforced pessimism and increased energy, they are at greater risk for acting on their suicidal thoughts. If your loved one is in a similar situation, educate him and encourage him to give the medication an adequate trial before concluding that it will not help. If a particular medication does not work, educate him about the fact that another medication should be tried.

How long should someone stay on a medication that works? Most psychiatrists recommend staying on a medication that has worked for a minimum of four to six months. For people with recurrent depression, many psychiatrists recommend an indefinite period of time.

Can you drink alcohol when taking antidepressants? Yes, but in moderation. As we discussed in Chapter 10, alcohol can lead to increased depression. However, many physicians do inform their patients that drinking in moderation is not a problem when taking antidepressants. Drinking in "moderation" can be a gray area, especially for someone who has been medicating depression with alcohol for years. The best course of action is to be honest with the treating psychiatrist about how much alcohol is being consumed. If your loved one refuses to talk about it, chances are that he should not be drinking. In general, it is best not to drink excessively when taking antidepressant medications so that the depression is neither masked nor exacerbated by the alcohol. MAOI medications have certain dietary restrictions, which include red wine. If your loved one is taking an MAOI, he should not drink red wine under any circumstances because this type of antidepressant interacts negatively with tyramine, an amino acid that exists in many foods, certain beers, and red wine. The interaction can cause a hypertensive crisis, resulting in chest pain, nausea, vomiting, and possibly death.

What You Should Know About ECT

ECT is without a doubt the most misunderstood treatment for depression. We all grow up learning that electrical shocks are dangerous. We buy plug guards so children do not stick their fingers or objects in electrical outlets. We do not work on broken electrical appliances ourselves for fear of being shocked. We stay away from trees during an electrical storm for fear of being struck by lightning. So why would we voluntarily want to shock a loved one? To make ECT even more frightening, we have gratuitous, inaccurate depictions of it in popular movies like *One Flew over the Cuckoo Nest.* If this is all that a person knew of ECT, he would indeed be crazy to submit to it! However, there is more to know about ECT.

ECT is safe and effective, and can be the treatment of choice for some forms of depression. It may surprise you that ECT is by far the most successful treatment for major depression. Someone with major depression has approximately a 90 percent chance of recovering following a course of ECT. In patients where a rapid recovery from depression is indicated, such as individuals who refuse to eat and are extremely malnourished, ECT can be the treatment of choice. In addition, there is good evidence that ECT is the best treatment for psychotic depressions and depressions that do not respond to psychotherapy and medication.

Here are some answers to common questions about ECT.

Does ECT damage the brain? No. There is absolutely no evidence that ECT causes brain damage. This question has been studied extensively by scientists.

What are the side effects? The main side effect of ECT is short-term memory loss, usually for events occurring just prior to the treatment. After several treatments, patients may develop amnesia for recent events. Numerous research studies show that by one month after a treatment course of ECT, memory impairments have disappeared in the great majority of patients. Other research shows that memory problems can be reduced to a bare minimum by choosing the right type of ECT. Just as there are different types of medication and varying dosages, there are different types of ECT that can be given at varying dosages. For example, unilateral (only one side of the brain) versus bilateral (both sides of the brain) ECT can result in differing side effect profiles. Also the type of electrical wave form used (e.g., square wave) can influence how easily a brain seizure is triggered. Cerebral seizures have been shown to be indispensable to achieving a therapeutic effect. Because anesthesia is used, the seizure is confined to the brain and does not result in bodily convulsions. Other side effects of ECT are those associated with general anesthesia and would be a factor in any procedure requiring it.

If after reading this chapter you still find yourself doubting the efficacy and safety of ECT, we suggest you contact the NIMH, which has excellent reading materials on its efficacy and safety. Also, refer to our list of World Wide Web links at the end of the book for information. You owe it to yourself and your loved one to be as educated as possible about the facts. After learning all that you can, you may or may not come to the same conclusion we have: that ECT can be a safe and effective treatment for depression. But how will you know unless you are familiar with all of the facts?

Does the person convulse and feel pain? No. Many years ago, before anesthesia was given, this was true. Modern ECT treatment, however, is monitored by an anesthesiologist and does not result in bodily convulsions, associated injuries, or pain. In fact, the effects are so minimal that it can be done on an outpatient basis. After the therapy, some people complain of feeling tired and fuzzy for the rest of the day because of the anesthesia and the ECT itself.

When should ECT be given? Most clinicians agree that ECT should be used only after psychotherapy has been tried without success and several good trials of antidepressant medication have failed. Despite its efficacy, ECT is reserved as a last-ditch effort, mainly because many people are frightened by it and will consider it only if other treatment approaches have not worked. In addition, anesthesia associated with ECT treatments does pose risks. Individuals requiring a rapid recovery due to other health risks and patients with psychotic depression are particularly good candidates for ECT.

Medical Treatment for Depression and Your Relationship

When someone we care about is receiving treatment for a serious illness, it can raise a lot of fears and hopes. Regardless of the type of illness, we worry that he may not recover fully, or we may have unrealistic expectations for recovery. Medical treatment for depression is no different. Unlike many other illnesses, however, treatment for depression can cause unique problems in relationships. Shame, fear, ignorance, and old-fashioned ideas can result in trouble for relationships in which someone is receiving antidepressant treatment.

Harold's shame about being on an antidepressant medication and his lack of education about alternative medications that would not have resulted in anorgasmia kept him isolated from Linda and created trouble in their relationship. He had not reflected much on how being on an antidepressant made him feel about himself. If he had stopped to think about it, he would have come to understand that he felt ashamed and inferior. Harold was holding on to old-fashioned ideas about depression and its treatment. Rather than seeing himself as having the courage to seek help when he could not resolve the depression on his own, he saw himself as inferior.

Because Linda did not know about antidepressant medications, she found herself worrying needlessly. Her worry led her to question whether she had fallen in love with the "real" Harold or an artificial version of him, produced by a drug. Because Harold had difficulty talking about being on medication without feeling as if he was somehow defective, Linda could not bring herself to talk with him about her worries. Once the "cat was out of the bag," and she knew he was on medication, the two of them were caught in a cycle of shame and fear. Neither knew how to talk further about it without feeling worse. Although they had moved through the Trouble, Reaction, and Information-Gathering stages of the SAD and had learned helpful information about depression, they had not yet acquired the communication strategies that would enable them to enter an effective Problem-Solving stage.

Try to keep the following guidelines and communication strategies in mind if someone you know is either taking antidepressant medications or contemplating such treatment.

Learn all that you can about antidepressant treatments. If you have more questions after reading this book, read the literature we recommend and browse the web sites we list at the end of this book. Educate yourself about medical treatments for depression so that you and your loved one will not suffer needlessly from misconceptions.

Have realistic expectations about the treatment. Many people understandably want immediate relief and become impatient if after two to three weeks, no improvement is seen. In our experience, unrealistic expectations about the time it takes to respond have led many individuals to discontinue treatment prematurely. This is unfortunate for two reasons. First, the depressed person does not get better when he could have. Second, he erroneously comes to believe that he never responded to that particular medication. Be sure that you know the range of response times, not just the average. Once you know the upper limit, encourage your loved one to stay on the medication for as long, or nearly as long, as that period of time, to give it an adequate trial.

Give unqualified support. Let the depressed person in your life know that you are glad to see that he is doing something constructive about the depression. Share your knowledge about antidepressants, and encourage him to talk about his feelings concerning the medication. If you have a negative attitude about antidepressant medications, you will have a very difficult time giving unqualified support. Hopefully, after educating yourself fully, you will appreciate the potential of medication to help alleviate the depression.

Express your feelings about the treatment. Let your loved one know your fears and concerns. If you have questions that he cannot answer, find out the answers together. Try to approach any discussion of your negative feelings about medical treatments with an open mind. Eventually Linda was able to tell Harold her worry that she may not really know him and that she fell in love with an "artificial" Harold.

Because she opened the discussion in a nonthreatening way—"I've never known anyone on Prozac before. I guess I am worried that it really changes people into someone they're not. What has it been like for you?"—Harold was able to reassure her that he believed that not only had he not changed, but that for the first time in a long time, he felt he was back to his old self. Several months later, Linda asked Harold's sister the same question, and she confirmed his observation.

Do not take side effects or therapeutic effects personally. Linda took Harold's apparent disinterest in sex as a personal rejection. This is not an uncommon reaction. Many people take the side effects of antidepressants personally, believing it is their fault or that it means something about their relationship. Alternatively, sometimes it is the therapeutic effect of medication that people take personally. For example, several parents have told us that they felt as if they somehow failed their child because medication could do what they could not do in lifting the depression. If you have read the first several chapters of this book, you know that depression is a serious and biologically based illness. The most well-meaning parents cannot cure a major depression. Only treatment can.

Ask for help. If you have questions about the treatment a loved one is receiving, ask him if you can speak to his psychiatrist so that you can learn more about his treatment. Be sure to let your loved one know that you are doing this for yourself, as well as for him. If you more fully understand the details and potential side effects of the medication, it will reduce the risk of misunderstanding with your loved one.

Work as a team. When someone you love is undergoing a medical treatment for depression, be sure that both of you are as educated as you can be about the risks and benefits of any treatment option presented. Work together to make treatment choices and monitor the response, or lack thereof, to the treatment. Keep a detailed history of which medications have been tried in the past, at what dosages, and for how long. This kind of information can be indispensable to the psychiatrist who will refer to the history for tailoring treatment.

We gave you a lot of information in this chapter to help you understand the types of medical treatments for depression that are available; however, we do not want you to lose sight of the importance of paying attention to your own needs. Ask questions, voice your concerns, and learn how to communicate your feelings about the treatment in a manner that will be constructive for you and your relationship with your depressed loved one. The more tuned in you can be with yourself, the healthier will be your relationship's adaptation to the depression. It will help to lessen the depression's effect on you and your loved one.

Although we have discussed the various treatments available for depression, we have not distinguished among the different types of mental health professionals who deliver those services. In the last chapter, we give you the information you need about where to find help, from whom you should seek it, and how to go about doing it. In particular, we return to the topic of how to help your loved one make the decision to seek the most appropriate treatment for his depression. We also give you advice on how to find help for yourself and your relationship.

14

Finding Help for Your
Loved One and Yourself

Finding help is one of the most unsettling aspects of caring about someone who is depressed. Most loved ones have many unanswered questions about finding help. When should I get help for her? Whom should I call: a psychologist, psychiatrist, social worker, counselor, or even clergy? Where should I look? How can I decide? Will the professional include me in the treatment? How can I learn more about depression? And, most important, how can I talk to my depressed loved one about going to an appointment with a professional?

These are good questions. The fact that treatments for depression can be so varied and are offered by so many different professionals makes it difficult to decide whom to see. And even if you do decide which kind of professional to consult, it is hard to know how to find a qualified professional whom you can trust. In this chapter, will answer these and other common questions. We will help you learn more about the various professionals who can help both your loved one and yourself, where to find more information and help for the depression, and, finally, how to talk to your loved one about getting help.

There is help. You do not need to deal with your loved one's depression all alone. With adequate treatment, nearly all depressions can be effectively treated. You have to ask for help, for the sake of both the depressed person and yourself.

When to Get Help for Your Loved One

Studies have shown that very few people snap out of a depression without treatment. In fact, all types of depression can benefit from treatment. Major depression that is untreated usually lasts from six months to a year. Even if a depression does lift on its own, research indicates that, without treatment, half of the people who have one depressive episode will have another. After two episodes, the chances of having a third episode are even greater. After three episodes, the chances of having a fourth depression are almost 90 percent. Clearly it makes sense to get help for your loved one as early as possible in the course of her illness, both to alleviate her pain and to prevent recurrence.

Dysthymia (chronic low-grade depression), which we discuss in Chapter 2, can last for years or even a lifetime if it is untreated. Without treatment, dysthymia will continue and probably become more debilitating over time. Manic depression will also continue to worsen if it goes untreated. Often the depressed lows become increasingly worse and the shifts from mania to depression become more frequent and severe. In fact, whatever form of depression your loved one is suffering with, clinical studies have shown that treatment tends to be more successful the earlier it is begun.

Most experts agree that depression should be treated when it causes prolonged interference with social and work activities and day-to-day functioning. However, treatment should also be sought when the depressed person's subjective distress becomes severe, even if she appears to be functioning at an adequate level. Many depressed people are good actors and able to put on a good show while at work or at a social gathering, even when they feel most depressed. If someone you love acknowledges that she feels terrible and wants help, do not try to talk her out of it because she seemed fine the day before. Take her at her word, and support her in finding help for the depression.

When to Get Help for Yourself

Getting help for yourself when someone you love is depressed can be equally as important as getting help for her. As we have stressed throughout this book, depression affects not only the depressed person but those close to her as well. If you are in a relationship with a depressed person—your spouse, your parent, a friend—you are likely to have difficulty coping with the depression. As you move through the phases of the SAD, you will undoubtedly experience a whole host of reactions and feelings. If you find that your loved one's depression is "contagious" and you see depressive symptoms in yourself, then you owe it to yourself to get help. But even if you are not depressed, you can benefit from professional help. If you are having any difficulty keeping up with your usual routine or even just having more frequent arguments with your loved one, consider seeing someone.

You may want to discuss with your loved one the possibility of attending a meeting or two with her therapist. In our practices, we often find it helpful to have a family member attend several sessions with the depressed person to discuss the family's adjustment to the depression or to answer any questions the family member might have about the treatment. However, it is important to respect the relationship between your loved one and her therapist. Do not expect to attend every session unless it is explicitly discussed. You might say to your loved one, "I have some concerns about what it means for you to be depressed. Do you think it would be all right if I met with you and your therapist once to talk about it?" If your loved one refuses, accept her decision. You can still get help for yourself, separate from her treatment. If she agrees, you might want to think ahead of what kinds of questions you have about your loved one's treatment. You might also bring up any concerns you have about how the two of you are getting along.

Other possibilities for getting professional help include individual psychotherapy, family and couples therapy, and group therapy or support groups. Individual psychotherapy can help you cope with the strong negative feelings you might have about a loved one's depression, as well as help you learn to collaborate more effectively with her. Family or couples therapy can help you and your loved one communicate more constructively and begin to problem-solve as a team rather than as isolated opponents. And group therapy or support groups can be very helpful in reducing your sense of being the only one in the world coping with a loved one's depression. You can learn invaluable strategies from other people who have been in similar situations. Do not make the mistake of assuming that just because your loved one is in treatment, you do not need to be. Getting help is not a sign of weakness but a sign of strength.

What Kind of Professional Should We Look For?

If we polled the family members and friends of depressed people, this question would probably be the most frequently asked one. Whom should she go see? How do we tell the difference between the different kinds of professionals? And how do I know my loved one isn't seeing a quack or someone incompetent to treat this illness?

Someone who is depressed should see a mental health professional, if at all possible, rather than a physician who is not a mental health expert. In some areas of the country, there are few mental health professionals, so you may have no other choice than to see a general physician. Many general physicians, particularly in rural areas, are well versed in treating depression and may do a fine job. However, it is preferable for your loved one to see someone who has experience in diagnosing and treating depression. It is worrisome to us that according to a recent statistic of the Department of Health and Human Services Depression Guideline Panel, 60 percent of antidepressants are now prescribed by primary care doctors with little or no formal training in treating depression. We strongly recommend that you choose a professional who has experience and is qualified to treat depression.

A loved one may resist seeing a mental health professional because of beliefs that only "crazy" people go to such professionals. At the end of this chapter, we give you specific advice on how to talk to your loved one about getting help, especially if she is resistant to the idea. If she continues steadfastly to refuse to see someone trained in mental health, it may be worthwhile for a general physician to evaluate her and perhaps decide to start her on antidepressant medication. Once the depression lifts a bit, your loved one may be more willing to consider other forms of treatment, such as psychotherapy as well.

If it is the first time your loved one has sought professional help for a depression, the therapist will probably insist that she see a medical doctor early in the treatment for a complete checkup to rule out any medical conditions that could be the underlying cause of the depression. The exam will probably include a physical, as well as blood and urine analysis to check for low thyroid, mononucleosis, anemia, diabetes, or hepatitis. If the physician suspects that one of these medical conditions may underlie the depression, further medical examination may be indicated. Because depression runs in families, the doctor may ask your loved one about any family history of depression. It is particularly important that the physician be told about any medicines, both prescription and nonprescription, that your loved one has been taking, as well as any recent changes or stressors in her life.

If the medical doctor rules out medical causes of the depression, then it is time to see a mental health professional. If you do not already have someone to consult, your general physician can usually refer you to an appropriate professional. The choices include social workers, psychologists, psychiatrists, as well as many other kind of counselors. Many family members do not fully understand the differences, particularly between psychologists and psychiatrists. Before we give you more advice about choosing a professional, you need to have a clear understanding of the differences and similarities among the different professionals.

Psychotherapists are those in the general category of practicing psychotherapy. Unfortunately, there are no rules or restrictions about who can call themselves a psychotherapist. This is a generic term that does not require any training or certification to be used. The only information that the title conveys is that the person practices some form of psychological therapy. A psychotherapist's education, training, and qualifications can range from the extreme of a highly trained doctoral-level psychologist to someone with a high school degree and a summer course in psychotherapy. If you are referred to someone who calls herself a psychotherapist, be sure to ask questions about her background and qualifications to determine if she does indeed belong to one of the following professions.

Social workers usually have at least two years of postgraduate training, known as an M.S.W. (master's in social work), as well as additional fieldwork. Some social workers also have advanced training in psychiatric settings and may have a specialty, such as marital and family therapy. They cannot prescribe medication but are trained in psychotherapy and are particularly well versed in acquiring concrete social services for patients and their families. In most states, social workers must be licensed or certified by the state in order to be in private practice. Social workers reach different levels of expertise, with each level having its own initials after their name. For example, a social worker who has earned a bachelor's degree uses the label B.S.W. A master's degree is an M.S.W., and a doctoral degree is a D.S.W. The profession is licensed in most states, indicated by the initials L.C.S.W. (or a variation, such as C.I.S.W., L.M.S.W., L.I.S.W., and B.C.S.W.). Generally certification means that the person has the minimum of a master's degree and two years of experience and has passed an exam. You can contact the National Association of Social Workers (NASW) at (800) 638-8799 to learn more about your state's certification process.

Psychologists have six to eight years of postgraduate training in psychology, including a clinical internship and completion of a doctoral dissertation. Psychologists typically hold either a Ph.D. (doctor of philosophy) or Psy.D. (doctor of psychology) degree. They cannot prescribe medication but are highly trained in both diagnosing depression and treating depression with psychotherapy. They are also the only mental health professionals who are qualified to administer psychological tests. With the advent of better and more effective antidepressant medications, more and more psychologists are working closely with psychiatrists to treat depression in a team approach. In fact, a small group of armed forces psychologists have been given limited prescription privileges through a government study to evaluate the ability of psychologists to prescribe psychiatric medications. A large number of psychologists are lobbying for prescription privileges, and it is likely that in the future, more and more psychologists will be able to prescribe. In most states, psychologists must be licensed by the state to practice psychology. Licensing tells you that the professional has completed a doctoral degree, has several years of supervised experience, and has passed the licensing exam. You can contact the American Psychological Association at (202) 335-5500 to find out more about requirements for licensing or you can call your state education department, division of professional licensing services, for the requirements in your state.

Psychiatrists have an M.D. degree, meaning that they have completed medical school and a residency training program in psychiatry, as opposed to another specialty, such as pediatrics or internal medicine.

Currently, psychiatrists are the only mental health professionals who can prescribe medication (other than the small group of psychologists in the armed forces). Not all psychiatrists have much experience or training in providing psychotherapy, but some do. In the past decade or so, psychiatric training has emphasized the physical causes of depression and treatment with medication. As a result, the psychiatric community is increasingly divided among the biological psychiatrists, who believe that most depression has a biological cause and should be treated as such, and the older, more traditional psychiatrists, many of whom are psychoanalysts, who practice psychotherapy and favor more psychological causes. However, some psychiatrists do both, and many will work closely with a psychologist or social worker who is providing the psychotherapy portion of the treatment. In most states, psychiatrists are licensed medical doctors but may or may not be board certified in psychiatry and neurology. Board certified means that the doctor has met certain requirements for a specialty as required by the American Board of Medical Specialties. Generally these requirements consist of having a medical degree, completing a residency, successful performance or competency, two years of experience in the specialty, and passing a written, and sometimes oral, examination. You can contact the American Psychiatric Association at (202) 682-6066 or your state education department, division of professional licensing services, for the requirements for licensure in your state.

Counselors is a general term used to describe a wide range of different mental health professionals. Their training and experience can vary greatly, but most counselors have experience working with people with a mental illness and a bachelor's or associate's degree in psychology, counseling, or a related field. They often work in clinic or institutional settings, along with the other mental health professionals. They may or may not practice psychotherapy. Some counselors offer supportive counseling, particularly to adolescents. Other counselors hold a C.A.C., which means that they are certified to counsel people on alcohol and drugs, but the majority of counselors do not hold any professional certification. In most states, there are no uniform licenses or certifications required to call oneself a counselor.

Members of the clergy can also offer help to your depressed love one. Many people, particularly if they have never been seen by a mental health professional before, feel more comfortable talking to their religious leader, whom they trust, about what is bothering them. If your loved one is reluctant to get help from a "shrink," seeing a clergy person may be less threatening. Of course, a member of the clergy cannot prescribe medication and is often not trained in dealing with depression, but talking to this person may be a good first step toward seeking other kinds of treatment. A member of the clergy may also help to ease the burden you are feeling and remind you to take care of yourself too when someone you love is depressed. He or she can almost always refer your loved one to other professionals for treatment.

Social workers, psychologists, and psychiatrists may work in a clinic or hospital setting or may have a private practice in which they accept various forms of medical insurance. They may all practice any or all of the different types of treatment we discussed in Chapter 12: cognitive-behavioral treatment, interpersonal therapy, family therapy, and group therapy. Unlike other illnesses, when a medical doctor usually oversees the care of a patient, even if he sees other health care professionals, depression is different. The mental health professional who is coordinating the care may be a social worker or psychologist, who consults with a psychiatrist, rather than the other way around.

How Do We Make a Choice?

What kind of professional to choose depends on a great many factors, including the severity of the depression, the person's preference for medication or psychotherapy (or both), and finances. Generally, if the depression is severe, medication should be considered and that means your loved one should see either a psychiatrist for medication or a psychologist or social worker for therapy who is willing to have your loved one also seen by a psychiatrist for medication. Your loved one's preference for treatment should also be considered. In the last section of this chapter, when we discuss how to talk to your loved one about treatment, we come back to the importance of matching the kind of professional to your loved one's beliefs and biases about mental health treatment.

Whatever type of professional you choose, you should feel comfortable that this person is well trained and experienced. Social workers, psychologists, and psychiatrists must be licensed in order to practice in most states. The rationale behind licensing professionals is that it guarantees the public a standard of training and experience, provides self-regulation of the professions, and includes a mechanism for disciplinary action and peer review. Look for a license on the professional's wall or ask if he or she is licensed or certified by the state. You can also call your state's department of education to check on the licensing status of any professional.

In terms of cost, psychiatrists tend to be the most expensive, with fees varying a great deal by area of the country. According to the American Psychiatric Association, a psychiatrist's average fee ranges from about $150 to $200 or more an hour. Generally a social worker charges about half a psychiatrist's fee, with a psychologist's fee somewhere in the middle. Fees tend to be significantly higher in private practice settings than in either clinic or hospital-based outpatient settings. Fees also tend to be higher in large urban areas and much lower in rural or less populated areas. In many parts of the country, sliding-scale services are available at clinics where the fee is based on income and slides up or down accordingly. If you live near a major medical center or university, your depressed loved one may be able to participate in an ongoing research study. Such sites may offer state-of-the-art treatment at little or no cost to you. However, your loved one has to be willing to be part of the study and probably take part in some extended evaluation and follow-up questions.

As our health care system continues to undergo restructuring, it may be more difficult to afford good mental health care. Mental health coverage has always been more restrictive than the coverage for medical treatment of any illness. As managed care companies become more and more prevalent, you may find that you have to pay more out of pocket for treatment for depression. In some states, insurance companies are already excluding some mental health providers, such as social workers, from reimbursement. Be sure to check with your insurance company to see what kind of treatment is and is not covered before you make any decision about treatment. You can also talk to any mental health professional whom you are considering consulting to see what kind of cost he or she expects you will have to incur above and beyond your insurance.

How do you decide whom to make an appointment with? Treatment for depression is complicated and so highly subjective that it is impossible for us to say that one specialty is superior to another. We, as psychologists, have a personal bias that psychologists are among the best trained to treat depression, especially if they work in concert with a psychiatrist who can prescribe medication. Psychologists are highly experienced in the art of psychotherapy and are especially trained to understand the development of personality and relationships. However, a social worker or a psychiatrist would probably not agree with us. What we can say is that one of the most crucial parts of choosing a mental health professional is that you and your loved one feel confidence and trust in the person whom you select. The depressed person needs to feel comfortable talking to this person about her symptoms, her feelings, and her innermost thoughts. It is our firm belief that no matter what kind of treatment or what kind of professional a depressed person sees, a large part of the success of treatment is the relationship between the depressed person and the professional. The depressed person needs to feel able to express herself and explore her feelings with the professional. She should feel that the professional is genuinely understanding and cares about her.

In choosing a mental health professional, you should also not feel that any decision is irrevocable. We usually recommend that patients have a consultation meeting with any new therapist to discuss the problem and see if they can work together. In this kind of meeting, the patient has a chance to check out the therapist and decide if she feels comfortable talking to him or her. If not, it may be useful to set up another consultation with a different therapist. Even when you or your loved one has made a decision to work with a specific person, we often recommend an evaluation period of about a month. During this period, patient and therapist have a chance to get to know one another and see if their styles click. All of the research on the outcome of psychotherapy has indicated that the relationship between the therapist and patient is the number one factor that predicts whether treatment will be successful. If either you or your loved one feels that the therapist is not a good match, speak to the therapist about your feelings, and he or she can either allay your anxieties or refer you to someone else.

There are also other factors to consider. First, is the mental health professional willing to explore a variety of treatment options? Depression is a complicated illness and often requires a multitude of treatment techniques. You want your depressed loved one to work with someone who is willing to try more than one approach if the initial attempt does not help alleviate the depression. Another question is whether the professional resists the idea of the depressed person's seeking a second opinion about treatment. Even if the relationship is good, if the depressed person is not feeling better within four to six months, it may be worth considering trying another professional with different areas of expertise or some additional treatment. For example, if your loved one is so severely depressed that she does not even have the energy to talk to her therapist, it might make sense to have her also take medication. As psychologists, our rule of thumb is that if someone is not making progress in psychotherapy because her depressive symptoms are making it impossible for her to think clearly or work constructively in therapy, we will strongly recommend antidepressant medications, in addition to the psychotherapy. If the medication begins to work and the depression lifts a bit, the person can benefit from psychotherapy, geared toward issues such as her feelings of inadequacy, relationship difficulties, and cognitive distortions.

You might also ask the professional if he or she is open to meeting with the depressed person's family and friends, interested in educating you about her condition, and helping you in the way you relate to her. As you know by now, depression affects both the depressed person and those around her, so any professional who is willing to include you in the treatment is probably well aware of the secondary effects of depression. View the mental health professional as your ally in the fight against depression rather than as your enemy. He or she wants to help your depressed loved one and has the same goal of helping the depressed person feel back to her old self. You may not want to or need to be privy to the details of what goes on in the treatment, but it is entirely appropriate for you to be informed about the treatment options and progress.

Where Should We Look?

Finding help is likely to be easier than you imagine. Fortunately, there is an abundance of good written information about depression and resources that are available to refer you to qualified mental health professionals. A good first step is to call your family doctor or general internist. It is important for your loved one to have a full physical examination, especially if it has been years since her last checkup, to rule out any physical problems that could be causing the depression. But even if your loved one has had a recent physical or no physical basis is found for the depression, your family doctor can usually refer you to someone with whom he or she has a good working relationship and respects as a mental health professional. He or she may also be able to talk with you and your loved one about the possible treatment options.

Another option is to look for help at local universities, hospitals, and institutions. Many universities have a psychology department that may have an in-house clinic or be able to refer you to licensed psychologists who are graduates of their program. Many medical schools and centers have affiliated clinics and private practice groups. Health maintenance organizations and managed care companies will be able to refer you to providers. It is very appropriate for you to ask for the qualifications of professionals to whom you are referred.

Try to become familiar with all of the mental health services in your area. Even if your loved one refuses treatment or a particular kind of treatment at this time, it is important for you to know where to get help when a crisis arises or when she agrees that she needs help. Sometimes just having a name or a place to go will make it that much easier for the depressed person to seek help. It is much more difficult to find help when you are in the middle of a crisis. And even if your loved one continues to turn down help, you may be interested in seeking help for yourself. Most of the mental health services that are available for depressed people offer mental health treatment for you as well. Ask about services available to help family members cope with a loved one's depression.

If you need help and are looking for a service that does not seem to be available, don't clam up about it. You can get excellent recommendations from friends, neighbors, or acquaintances. Tell others about what you are looking for. You may feel, as many of the family members in our case examples did, that you do not want others to know your "dirty laundry," but you would be surprised at how many people have had to seek some sort of mental health treatment for a family member at one time or another. The more people who know what type of help you need, the more likely it is that you will find someone who can truly help you.

If you still feel uncomfortable telling acquaintances in your community about your loved one's depression, ask a local librarian for appropriate resource books or telephone lists. You can even tell the librarian you are doing some research for a paper or are just gathering information for "a friend." As you search for the appropriate treatment for your depressed loved one, realize that you may have to devote some time to making phone calls before you find what you are looking for. Help for depression is available, but you have to search it out. In the next section, we provide a list of resources that can supply you with more information about depression, treatment referrals, and access to local support groups for your loved one and for yourself.

What Resources Are Available?

In the United States, we are fortunate to have a number of excellent information centers, research institutes, and consumer advocacy groups dedicated to understanding and treating depression. The following list is not exhaustive, but it consists of the organizations and resources that we believe will be the most helpful for you. Write to or call any of them for more information about depression and their activities. Remember that the more information you have about depression and its treatment, the better able you will be to problem-solve with your depressed loved one. Armed with knowledge and working as a team, you can win the fight against the depression.

National Alliance for the Mentally Ill
2101 Wilson Blvd., Suite 302, Arlington, VA 22201
(703) 524-7600 or (800) 950-NAMI (6254)

NAMI is the best source for support and educational materials about depression. It was formed in 1979 by families of mentally ill people who were frustrated by the lack of services, treatment, research, and education available for mentally ill people and their families. It has grown to be an influential and large advocacy group with local chapters in almost every major city, as well as in many smaller towns. People who join NAMI or FAMI (the associated Family Alliance for the Mentally Ill) are usually understanding and caring people who have had very similar experiences to your own. Many chapters offer family support and education groups. Some have hot-lines for you to call during a crisis and can offer referrals to treatment and other helpful services.

If someone you love is depressed, we recommend getting on the mailing list of NAMI, as well as joining your local chapter. If you call the toll-free number, you can find out details about your local chapter of NAMI and whether there are support groups in your area. NAMI also has many books and pamphlets about depression available at a discounted price. If you belong to your local chapter, you can usually borrow books and tapes. One of the best is *Coping with Depression*, a twenty-four-minute video by the State of Iowa Department of Human Services and Mental Health Institute that describes depression from the perspective of both the depressed person and family members. The video focuses on medical treatments, coping strategies, support groups, and working together with the depressed person to problem-solve more effectively. NAMI also has a newsletter, the *Bond*, which offers support and resource information for families affected by mental illness.

Depression Awareness, Recognition, and Treatment (D/ART)
National Institute of Mental Health,
5600 Fishers Lane, Rockville, MD 20857
(800) 421-4211

This organization can give good general information about depression, its signs and symptoms, and the latest in treatment options. D/ART publishes some excellent booklets and brochures about depression that you can request. One that we particularly recommend is *Depressive Disorders: Treatments Bring New Hope.* This organization's materials are usually quite brief and easy to read, which is particularly good for friends and relatives who may not want to or be able to read a whole book about depression.

National Foundation for Depressive Illness (NAFDI)
P.O. Box 2257, New York, NY 10116
(800) 248-4344

NAFDI is a nonprofit organization that focuses on educating the public about the symptoms of depression and updating professionals in their recognition and appropriate treatment of depression. They can send clear and concise brochures and pamphlets about depression, as well as refer you to mental health professionals in your area.

National Depressive and Manic Depressive Association (NDMDA)
730 North Franklin Street, Suite 501, Chicago, IL 60610
(800) 82N-DMDA (826-3632)

This organization consists of depressed people and their families who try to educate the public about depression and manic depression and help others find treatment. The central branch responds to requests for referrals in other areas of the country and can refer you to a local qualified mental health professional. Its quarterly newsletter provides up-to-date information and research findings about depression and manic depression. The newsletter is free with membership in the association.

Lithium Information Center
8000 Excelsior Drive, Suite 302, Madison, WI 53717
(608) 836-8070

This center, part of the Department of Psychiatry at the University of Wisconsin, is a well-known resource for information about the use of lithium in the treatment of bipolar disorder. The center can send informational materials, as well as a book by Bohn and Jefferson, *Lithium and Manic Depression: A Guide,* which we suggest in the Recommended Readings in this book. If you have questions about lithium use, the staff is knowledgeable and can answer your questions or refer you to some other appropriate source.

Depression After Delivery
P.O. Box 1282, Morrisville, PA 19067
(215) 295-3994

This organization is a lay group offering printed information to help those suffering from postpartum depression. It can also provide a list of support groups, as well as a roster of women in your area who have suffered from postpartum depression and who would be willing to talk to you. This organization is particularly helpful in reducing the social isolation and feelings of excessive guilt that plague women who suffer from postpartum depression.

National Organization for Seasonal Affective Disorder (NOSAD)
P.O. Box 40133, Washington, DC 20016

NOSAD is a relatively new organization geared toward the study of and education of the public about seasonal affective disorder. If your loved one is suffering from this kind of depression or you think she might be, NOSAD can send useful information about diagnosis and treatment. Material about light treatment for this type of depression can be especially helpful.

American Association of Suicidology
2459 South Ash, Denver, CO 80222
(303) 692-0985

This organization offers a variety of printed suicide prevention materials, primarily for use in schools and other institutional settings. It can also refer you to local suicide hot-lines and support groups.

Suicide Research Unit
National Institute of Mental Health
5600 Fishers Lane, Rockville, MD 20857
(301) 443-4513

This is the department of the National Institute of Mental Health (NIMH) that specializes in studying all aspects of suicide. Although it cannot provide treatment referrals, this resource is very helpful if you are interested in learning more general information about suicide prevention.

There are hundreds of suicide crisis centers in the United States staffed by volunteers trained to establish rapport and avert a potential suicide. They are knowledgeable about the various helping agencies in your area and can usually guide the caller to the appropriate facility. Look in your local telephone book for the number of the nearest hot-line center. If your loved one is depressed and potentially suicidal, you may even want to give her the number or leave it by the telephones in your home.

American Psychological Association
750 1st Street, N.E., Washington, DC 20002
(202) 336-5500

American Psychiatric Association
1400 K Street, N.W., Washington, DC 20005
(202) 682-6066

These two organizations are the national associations of the professions of psychology and psychiatry, respectively. They can send information about depression and its treatment, as well as refer you to their qualified members in your area. The American Psychological Association publishes fact sheets (*Facts about Depression* and *Facts about Manic Depression*) that may be of interest to you.

Support organizations are another important resource. In most communities, there are local and regional support groups for those suffering from depression, as well as for their families and loved ones. Contact your local NAMI office for information about local support groups or look in your local newspaper or community newsletter for announcements of meetings.

How Can I Talk to the Depressed Person About Getting Help?

This is the last question about finding help in this chapter, but certainly not the least important or the least difficult to answer. As someone close to a depressed person, you can have a critical role in whether your depressed loved one gets the help she needs. You need to encourage her to participate in and cooperate with whatever treatment she is involved in. Your support can help the treatment succeed in alleviating the depression. If you give your loved one mixed messages about getting help or if you constantly question the treatment decisions of the professional, you will undermine the chances for successful treatment.

Communicating What You Have Learned to the Depressed Person

You want the depressed person to have some of the same knowledge that you have found during the Information-Gathering phase of the

SAD. You want her to understand that there are effective treatments available and to know that you care about her and want to see her feel better. To communicate what you have learned, we recommend that you be as direct and compassionate as possible. An approach that seems to work best is to set some time aside to sit down and talk with the depressed person. Do not have this conversation during an already heated discussion or fight or when one of you is rushing off to work. Instead, make the time to explain calmly to her that you have noticed changes that concern you. Tell her that you think that she might be depressed and you want to help her get the appropriate treatment so she can feel better. You might say, "You know, I've noticed that you seem down and blue lately. You don't seem yourself. I wonder if you're depressed. I think it might be worth seeing a professional to see if they can help you."

In many cases, a statement like that is all it takes. The depressed person is relieved that someone has noticed the changes and is willing to have you help her get into treatment. It doesn't always go so smoothly, however. Your loved one may reply, "I'm having a hard time lately, but it will pass. I don't think I really need to see a professional. Just give me some time, okay?" or "What are you talking about? I'm fine. I don't need a shrink! You're the one who's crazy!" If this is the response, your next step is a little trickier. You need to emphasize that you are genuinely worried about the person, that you do not think it means she is crazy to see a mental health professional, and that you respect her opinion. In many cases, the cognitive distortions that go along with depression make the person feel so hopeless that she assumes that nothing will help her pain. You need to point out how there are some very effective treatments for how she has been feeling. You could tell her that you have learned a lot about depression over the past several days and you think that it's worth finding out more about some of the treatments that seem to really work. You might even ask the person who is skeptical about a "shrink" to try it for you, if for no other reason. Explain to her that it would help you if she went to see someone because you are truly worried about her and want to at least know that there is nothing to worry about.

In any discussion of this kind, ask the depressed person what she thinks would be most helpful. Remember, she is depressed, not incompetent. Treat her with respect for her opinion. What does she think of depression? Does she believe that she is not depressed? How does she account for the changes you have noticed? How does she feel about therapy? About medication? People vary in their comfort levels with psychotherapy and medication. Some think that if they take medication, it indicates that their depression is "biological" and that takes away some of the stigma of having an "emotional problem." Others would prefer to talk to someone and are very frightened by the prospect of putting "chemicals" in their body. And still others are willing to consider both talking therapy and medication but are concerned that others will think they are "crazy" if they see a mental health professional. In talking to your loved one, you need to take her beliefs and biases into consideration. An ardent vegetarian who does not even take aspirin when she has a headache is not likely to agree to take Prozac. And a private, reclusive man who does not believe in burdening others with his problems may be much more comfortable taking a pill than revealing his innermost feelings to a therapist. Let your loved one know that her preferences and feelings are very important. You want to work with her to get her the kind of help she wants.

The issue of confidentiality may also be important. The depressed person may want to get help but not want you to be involved in finding her help because she does not want you to know everything about the treatment. You must let her know that you respect her privacy and confidentiality. You can say, "I want to know something about how the treatment is going, but I don't expect to know all of the details of what you talk about with your therapist." Such a statement may decrease her fears about your involvement in the treatment and make her feel more comfortable in getting help.

Talking to the Depressed Person Who Is Resistant to Treatment

If after following our advice and having several discussions with your loved one about treatment, she still refuses, then you are coping with someone who is resistant to treatment. Maybe she is not depressed. However, if you are basing your concerns on your new knowledge about the signs and symptoms of depression, chances are that she is depressed but unable to acknowledge it. In this case, you should continue to talk to your loved one about getting treatment.

Refer back to Chapter 7 for strategies on communicating effectively with your loved one. Follow the Do's and Don'ts of Constructive Communication when you talk about treatment. You may want to pay special attention to the gender differences in communication. If you are a woman trying to talk to a depressed man about getting treatment, try to follow our advice on the five most effective ways to communicate with a depressed man. The first step is to suggest that your loved one at least learn more about depression. If she believes that she is not depressed, it may be useful for her to become more educated about the signs and symptoms of depression. You can provide some of the pamphlets and brochures we have described or even give her Chapter 2 ("How to Recognize If Someone You Love Is Depressed") from this book to read. Sometimes a depressed person is not familiar enough with what depression is to recognize it in herself.

It may also help to have power in numbers. If other people in your loved one's life are similarly concerned, ask them to help you talk to her about treatment. Have a family meeting in which you each take a turn to tell her your concerns. Preface all your comments with the fact that you are doing this because you love her and want to help, but do not come on too strong, especially if you think your loved one is likely to become defensive. Cornering her with a room full of people may only make matters worse. Try to be sensitive to your loved one's threshold for confrontation.

Finally, use your own feelings and reactions to guide you as you talk to your loved one. You might say, "I know that you don't think you're depressed and I respect that opinion. But I have learned a lot about depression lately, and I'm worried that you might be depressed. It would mean a lot to me if you would at least be willing to be seen by someone. It would give me peace of mind." It may be helpful to have several of these conversations over the course of days or weeks. In most cases, a loved one will eventually come around and agree to at least one appointment.

In the first example we used, in Chapter 1, Jane went through a similar difficulty with her depressed husband. As you may recall, Jane was a thirty-six-year-old advertising executive who had been feeling overwhelmed. In addition to her full-time job and taking care of two children, she had begun to assume many of her husband's usual chores around the house. She noticed that her husband was not sleeping well, felt unmotivated and tired, and complained of feeling blue. Jane knew that he was not feeling well and felt badly for him, but she was beginning to resent him.

Suspecting that her husband was depressed, Jane set out to educate herself about depression. She went to the library and contacted various depression organizations in her area. She read books, pamphlets, and other written material. With this new information, Jane became convinced that her husband was depressed and needed treatment. When she sat down with him to discuss her concerns, he was defensive and denied feeling depressed. He explained that he had just been tired lately and certainly did not need or want any professional help. When Jane told him what she had learned about depression, he refused to listen and left the room.

At first, Jane felt defeated. How would she ever get him to listen? She decided not to give up and to continue to try to talk to her husband about depression. She left some of the written material around the house that evening. Several days later, her husband admitted to Jane that he had "looked over a pamphlet or two" and thought he might be depressed. However, he was adamant about not wanting to join the "Prozac generation" just because he was a little down. Jane said that she would try to find out more information about other treatment options.

The next weekend, after dinner, Jane told her husband that she had learned about psychotherapy that could help with depression. She had also been given the name of a qualified and licensed psychologist in their town. At first, her husband was angry and insistent that he did not need help. When Jane told him that it would mean a lot to her for him at least to try to get some help, he began to reconsider. Jane then added that she was finding it hard to concentrate on her job because of worry about her husband, and he recognized how hard the changes in him had been on her. He agreed to see the psychologist and began a treatment of cognitive-behavioral therapy. Although the therapist suggested that Jane's husband meet with a psychiatrist to discuss the possibility of medication, he refused. After several months of therapy, Jane's husband's mood improved, his activity level was back to normal, and he was able to discontinue therapy.

Jane was eventually successful, but not everyone is. It may be that no matter how much you talk to your loved one or try to help educate her about depression and the effective treatments that are available, she refuses to consider treatment. In this case, you may want to seek some treatment or a support group for yourself. Hearing the details about what your loved one is like and why she refuses treatment may enable a mental health professional or other people in a support group to give you more specific advice.

There is one important caveat: *If someone you love is suicidal or showing one or more of the warning signs of suicide that we discussed in Chapter 11, seek professional help immediately.* It does not matter if she is reluctant or even outright refuses. This is a matter of life and death. Do not worry about her anger or about betraying her confidence. If she is already in treatment, call her mental health professional immediately. That is completely ethical and appropriate. If she is not in treatment or you cannot reach the professional, take your loved one directly to a hospital emergency room or call 911.

Having read this chapter, you and your loved one are now well armed in the fight against depression. You have learned about the differences among the various mental health professionals, where to look for help, and what resources are available. Most important, you have learned strategies for talking to your depressed loved one about getting help. We have also reminded you to remember your own needs. Not only your loved one can benefit from treatment. Consider getting help for yourself during this difficult period whether or not your loved one is in treatment. If you want to stop the depressive dance, all it takes is one person's changing steps. If you begin to dance in a new pattern, your loved one may follow your lead, and the two of you will begin to dance productively.

Afterword

Our hope is that after reading this book, you feel empowered to give your needs the attention they deserve, to counter the negative effects of depression on your relationship with your loved one, and to not become one of the overlooked casualties of this disorder.

As your relationship with your loved one adapts to the depression, we encourage you to practice the guidelines we have given you. Remember to use your own feelings and reactions to the trouble in your relationship as an important source of information that you can use to help your loved one and yourself. We have emphasized the value of being educated and informed about depression and its effects on relationships. By now, you know our biases and have read what we have to say on the topic of depression and relationships, but much of the work lies ahead of you. Having read this book is a critical first step toward protecting you and your loved one from engaging in the depressive dance. The next step is to make a commitment to practice the strategies that you have learned. Ideally, you and your depressed loved one will practice these guidelines together, but even if you have to go it alone, remember that by changing your own steps you can break the depressive cycle. If you change the way you interact, your depressed loved one will naturally respond differently. You will have to break the cycle repeatedly for long-lasting change. Two steps forward and one step back is the rule, not the exception, when trying to change a relationship pattern.

When you picked this book off the shelf, you were aware or suspected that there was trouble in your relationship because of depression. Your relationship had already passed through the Trouble and Reaction phases of the SAD. You were reacting to the changes caused by the depression. When you read this book, you learned important facts about depression and its effects on relationships. We have described this type of learning process as characteristic of the Information-Gathering phase of the SAD, but remember that these stages sometimes recur even after you have successfully moved on to the next stage. In fact, the Information-Gathering stage is one that you will visit repeatedly throughout the course of your loved one's depression. As you begin problem solving with your loved one in earnest, you will need to continue to gather information. Throughout your loved one's depression, remember to:

• Learn all you can.
• Have realistic expectations.
• Offer unqualified support.
• Keep your routine as much as possible.
• Share your feelings.
• Don't take the depression personally.
• Ask for help.
• Work as a team.

Most important, remember that depression is difficult for you as well as for your depressed loved one. The processes of working with your loved one collaboratively against the depression not only will help his recovery and your relationship but will also be intrinsically rewarding. You will both feel less alone, more connected, and more hopeful. Our experience has taught us that there is every reason to feel optimistic. You now know what you can do when someone you love is depressed.

Recommended Readings

Berger, D., and Berger, L. *We Heard the Angels of Madness: A Family Guide to Coping with Manic Depression.* New York: William Morrow, 1991.

A family's account of an eighteen year old's return from college and onset of his manic-depressive illness. Gives an excellent description of a family's view of bipolar depression, as well as some practical advice about understanding manic depression and seeking appropriate treatment for your loved one.

Bernheim, K., Lewine, R., and Beale, C. *The Caring Family: Living with Chronic Mental Illness.* New York: Random House, 1982.

This book is a bit old and some of the discussion is outdated. In addition, it does not focus on depression per se but discusses mental illness in broad strokes. It nevertheless offers good advice to families regarding the feelings and practical problems that come up when someone you love has a chronic mental illness.

Bohn, J., and Jefferson, J. *Lithium and Manic Depression: A Guide.* Madison, WI: Lithium Information Center, 1992.

This very helpful resource about lithium for treating bipolar disorder is available from the Lithium Information Center, Department of Psychiatry, University of Wisconsin, 600 Highland Avenue, Madison, WI 53792. The center will also answer questions about lithium use.

Fran, R. *What's Happened to Mommy?* New York: R.D. Eastman Publishing, 1994.

This book is written for children whose mother is depressed. It was designed to help educate and raise awareness about depression in families. We recommend it to help promote useful discussion between parents and children about what depression is so that children do not blame themselves for their parent's condition.

Gorman, J. M. *The Essential Guide to Psychiatric Drugs.* New York: St. Martin's Press, 1990.

If someone you love is taking or considering taking medication for depression, we recommend this excellent reference book. Dr. Gorman provides both a general discussion of psychiatric drugs and specific information about medications used for depression.

Recommended World Wide Web Sites for Dealing with Depression

When Someone You Love is Depressed
http://www.simonsays.com
The first self-help book written by psychologists with a World Wide Web site allowing readers to "speak" directly with the authors. The authors' Web site is a place where readers can ask specific questions, learn from the answers the authors give to other readers, and meet other readers dealing with similar problems.

Depression FAQ (Frequently Asked Questions)
http://avocado.pc.helsinki.fi:81/128.214.75.66/%7Ejanne/asdfaq/
Describes different types of depression, their causes and treatments. Also contains a list of book and Internet sources related to depression.

Internet Depression Resource List
http://earth.execpc.com/%7Ecorbeau/
Provides links to depression-related and mental health Internet sites.

World Wide Web Mental Health Home Page
http://www.mentalhealth.com/
Provides information on detection, treatment, research, medications, magazine articles, and personal accounts of overcoming depression.

Wing of Madness: A Depression Guide
http://users.aol.com/DebDeren/depress.htm
"A guide by a layman for laymen." Provides a depression screening, recommended reading, and accounts of personal experiences with depression, and discusses children and depression.

Depression Is a Treatable Illness: A Patient's Guide
http://www.mentalhealth.com/bookah/p44-dp.html
Answers common questions about depression and provides detailed information on causes of depression, diagnosis, treatment types, antidepressant medication, psychotherapy, light therapy, choosing a treatment, and talking to friends and children about depression.

Walkers in Darkness
A supportive and active mailing list for sufferers of depression and affected friends. To get on the list, e-mail majordomo@world.std.com with the words "subscribe walkers [your e-mail address]" in the body.

America Online Depression Mutual Support Group
Provides online support group meetings for America Online users. (Other online services may have similar support groups.) For a schedule of meeting times, enter the keyword PEN (Personal Empowerment Network), click on "Chatrooms," and click on "Depression Mutual Support."

Index

Acknowledgment, 125
Adapin (Sinequan), 217
Adolescents, 65, 81
    characteristics of depression in, 68–69
    peer groups and, 140
    suicide in, 181, 187, 194
Advice, giving of, 123, 130
Aggressive behavior, 67
Alcohol, antidepressants and, 224
Alcohol abuse: see Substance abuse
American Association of Suicidology, 246
American Psychiatric Association, 237, 245
American Psychological Association, 33–34, 236, 247
Amish people, 164–65
Amphetamines, 165: see also Stimulants
Anger, suicide and, 184, 190–91
Anhedonia, 23, 24, 167–68
Antidepressants, 56, 214–24, 241: see also specific types
    for children, 75–76
    common questions about, 220–24
    implications for relationships, 226–30
    indications, side effects, addictive qualities, 217
    prescription privileges for psychologists, 236
    psychotherapy and, 202–3, 207–8
    qualifications of professional prescribing, 234
Appetite, weight changes, 24, 25
    in children, 66
    substance abuse and, 168
Asendin, 217
Atypical depression, 26
    antidepressants for, 220
    characteristics of, 27, 32

Behavioral therapy, 206
    cognitive, 206, 207

Biochemical factors, 21–22
    in childhood depression, 69
    in postpartum depression, 36
    in suicide, 182, 183
Biological psychiatrists, 235
Bipolar (manic) depression, 26
    antidepressants for, 219–22
    characteristics of, 27, 28–30
    financial changes and, 46–47
    professional help for, 232
    resources for, 245
Birth defects, antidepressants and, 221
Blame, 112–13
Board certification, 235
Bohn, J., 243
Brief psychodynamic therapy, 204–5

Cancer, 20
Causes of depression, 21–23
Children, 39, 63–85: see also Adolescents
    antidepressants for, 75–76
    causes of depression in, 69–70
    characteristics of depression in, 66–67
    effect of depression on family, 70–72
    professional help for, 72–76, 81
    psychotherapy for, 74–75
    research on depression in, 64–65
    suicide in, 64, 65, 67, 180–81
Classical psychodynamic therapy, 204
Clergy, 237–38
Clinical depression: see Unipolar depression
Cocaine, 165
Cognitive behavioral therapy, 206, 207
Cognitive distortions, 108, 117, 196
College roomates, 6
Communication, 12–13, 115–33
    breakdowns in, 116
    concerns about psychotherapy and, 211
    do's and don'ts of, 125–27
    gender and, 116, 119, 127–31

Communication (*continued*)
    general guidelines for, 120–25
    practice in, 118
    about substance abuse, 172–73, 174
Concentration problems, 24, 25, 66
Contagious depression, 6, 49, 71–72, 152,
        231
Coping with Depression (video), 244
Copycat suicides, 186–87
Counselors, 235
Couples therapy, 207, 231
Criticism, 168
Cyclic antidepressants, 216, 217

Defensive behavior, 170–71, 173
Definitions of depression, 19–21
Delusions, 30, 32, 183
Denial, 20–21
    of substance abuse, 165
Depakote, 218
Depressed mood, 23, 24, 167–68
Depression After Delivery, 245–46
Depression Awareness, Recognition, and
        Treatment (D/ART), 242
Desyrel, 217
Dexedrine, 217, 220
Diabetes, 20
Diagnosis
    of childhood depression, 68
    failure of, 19–20
*Diagnostic and Statistical Manual of Mental
        Disorders* (DSM-IV), 66
    on major (unipolar) depression, 23–25
    on manic episodes, 29–30
Dilemmas of helping, 151–53
Divorce, 4, 69
Dopamine, 22
Drug abuse: *see* Substance abuse
DSM-IV: *see* Diagnostic and Statistical
        Manual of Mental Disorders
Dysphoric mood states, 19
Dysthymia, 26
    antidepressants for, 220
    characteristics of, 27, 30–31
    professional help for, 230

Effexor, 217, 218
Elavil, 217
Elderly, 39: *see also* Parents
    relationship with physicians, 88–89,
        95–96, 99
    suicide in, 181
Electroconvulsive therapy (ECT), 215,
        223–25
Empathy, 125
    gender and, 128, 129, 131
    mirroring and, 139

Empty nest, 38, 44
Endocrine system, 22
Essential Guide to Psychiatric Drugs, The
        (Gorman), 216, 218
Expectations, realistic: *see* Realistic ex-
        pectations
Expression of feelings, 9, 124–25
    delaying, 110
    friend's depression and, 104
    helping and, 158–59
    about medical treatment, 227
    parent's depression and, 99
    partner's depression and, 52
    sexual problems and, 57–58
    suicidal behavior and, 192

Failure-to-thrive, 65
Family Alliance for the Mentally Ill
        (FAMI), 242
Family history, 22, 235
    childhood depression and, 69–70
    of substance abuse, 172
Family therapy, 233
    childhood depression and, 75, 81–82
    communication in, 118
    described, 207
    suicidal behavior and, 197–98
Fatigue, lack of energy, 24, 25, 67
Fearfulness, 66
Feelings, 11: *see also* Expression of feel-
        ings
Fertility, antidepressants and, 222
Financial changes, 46–47
First-degree relatives, 22, 183
Friendship, 101–14
    research on depression and, 105–6
    vicious cycle of depression in, 106–8

Gender, 32–34
    bipolar depression and, 29
    childhood depression and, 65
    communication and, 116, 119,
        127–31
    dysthymia and, 31
    helping and, 152–53
    professional help and, 248
    substance abuse and, 33, 165
    suicide and, 180, 181
    unipolar depression and, 28
Generalizations, 114, 127
Generation gap, 89–93
Genetic factors, 21–22
    in childhood depression, 69–70
    in postpartum depression, 36
    in substance abuse, 164
    in suicide, 182–83
Gray, John, 116

Group therapy, 233
  for children, 75
  described, 206–7

Hallucinations, 32
Heart conditions, 20
Help, asking for, 9, 159–60
  childhood depression and, 80–82
  medical treatments and, 230
  parent's depression and, 93–95, 99
  partner's depression and, 53–54
  sexual problems and, 58–59
Helping, 147–62
  dilemmas of, 151–53
  guidelines for, 156–61
Helplessness, feelings of, 23, 184
Hormonal changes, 34, 36
Humor, 126, 132
Hyperactivity, 24, 67
Hypoactivity, 24
Hypothyroidism, 22

Idealization needs, 140
Immune system, 88
Individual psychotherapy, 231
  for children, 81
  suicidal behavior and, 197–98
Infants, 64–65, 68
Information-Gathering stage, 12, 16, 40
  characteristics of, 17
  communication and, 118
  described, 8
  friend's depression and, 103
  parent's depression and, 87
  suicide risk and, 188
Insurance company reimbursement, 237
Interpersonal therapy, 205, 207
Isolation, 23, 154
  parents and, 94

Jefferson, J., 243

Kitchen sinking, 127, 131, 132

Learning, 9–13
  childhood depression and, 77
  feelings to listen to, 11
  about medical treatments, 226
  reactions to watch for, 10–11
  about suicide, 192
Licensing of professionals, 234, 237
Life events, 23
  positive, 23, 28
  suicide and, 182
Life stages, 39
Listening, 121
Lithium, 203, 219

Lithium and Manic Depression: A Guide
  (Bohn & Jefferson), 243
Lithium Information Center, 243
Ludiomil, 217

Major depression: *see* Unipolar depression
Manic depression: *see* Bipolar depression
Manic episodes, DSM-IV criteria for,
  29–30
MAOIs: *see* Monoamine oxidase inhibitors
Masked depression
  in children, 65
  substance abuse and, 33
Medical treatments, 214–30: *see also* Antidepressants; Electroconvulsive
  therapy
Medication (non-psychiatric) side effects,
  88, 89, 233
Men, communicating with, 130–31: *see
  also* Gender
Menopause, 37–38
Midlife crisis, 38
Mirroring needs, 139, 141
Mitchell, Stephen, 138
Monoamine oxidase inhibitors (MAOIs),
  216
  dietary restrictions, 224
  indications, side effects, addictive
  qualities, 217

Name-calling, 126–27
Narcissism, 135–38
Nardil, 217
National Alliance for the Mentally Ill
  (NAMI), 241–42
National Association of Social Workers
  (NASW), 234
National Depressive and Manic Depres-
  sive Association (NDMDA), 245
National Foundation for Depressive Ill-
  ness (NAFDI), 244–45
National Institute of Mental Health
  (NIMH), 202, 207, 225
National Organization for Seasonal Af-
  fective Disorder (NOSAD),
  246
Needs, 134–46
  idealization, 140
  meeting, 140
  mirroring, 139, 141
  relational psychology on, 138–42
  selfishness and, 135–36, 142
  striking a healthy balance in, 142–46
  twinship, 140, 141
Negative attributions, 117
Neurotransmitters, 22

New antidepressants, 216, 217
Nonverbal behavior, 120–21
Norepinephrine, 22
Norpramin (Pertofrane), 217
No-suicide contracts, 195

Pamelor, 217
Parents, 86–100
    generation gap and, 89–93
    relationship with physicians and,
        88–89, 95–96, 99
Parnate, 217
Partners, 43–62
    financial changes and, 46–47
    helping, 153–54
    role changes and, 46
    routine changes and, 47
    social life changes and, 47
    special aspects of relationship, 45
Paxil, 217
Peer groups, 140
Personalized reactions, 9
    to child's depression, 79–80
    helping and, 159
    to medical treatment, 229
    to parent's depression, 99
    to partner's depression, 52–53
    to sexual problems, 58
    to suicidal behavior, 189, 192
Pertofrane (Norpramin), 217
Physical illness, 20, 67
Physicians
    antidepressant therapy and, 215–16,
        234
    elderly and, 88–89, 95–96, 99
Physician's Desk Reference (PDR), 216
Positive life events, 23, 28
Postpartum depression, 26
    characteristics of, 27, 34–37
    resources for, 243–44
Postpartum psychosis, 36
Premenstrual dysphoric disorder, 37
Premenstrual syndrome (PMS), 37–38
Preschool children, 65, 68
Prevalence
    of bipolar depression, 29
    of childhood depression, 64–65
    of dysthymia, 31
    of elderly with depression, 39, 95–96
    of substance abuse with depression,
        164, 165
    of unipolar depression, 28
Problem solving
    concerns about psychotherapy and,
        211–13
    gender and, 128, 129, 131
Problem-Solving stage, 12, 16

communication and, 117, 118, 119
components of, 18
described, 8
friend's depression and, 103
partner's depression and, 49–55
substance abuse and, 170
suicide risk and, 188
Professional help, 231–52: *see also* Med-
        ical treatments; Psychotherapy
    available resources, 243–47
    for childhood depression, 72–76,
        81
    cost of, 237
    finding the appropriate professional,
        241–43
    indications for, 232
    for oneself, 197–99, 232–34
    persuading depressed person to ac-
        cept, 247–52
    selecting the appropriate professional,
        238–41
    for substance abuse, 173, 174, 237
    for suicidal behavior, 196–97
    types of, 234–38
Prozac, 31, 214–15, 216–218
    suicide and, 222
Psychiatrists, 216, 236–37, 240
    biological, 237
    fees of, 239
Psychoanalysts, 237
Psychodynamic therapy, 204–5
Psychological treatment: *see* Psychother-
        apy
Psychologists, 236, 240
    fees of, 239
Psychosis, 30
Psychosocial factors, 21–22, 69
Psychotherapists, 235
Psychotherapy, 200–213
    antidepressants and, 202–3, 207–8
    for children, 74–75
    choosing the appropriate type, 207–8
    common concerns about, 208–11
    types of, 204–7
Psychotic depression, 26
    antidepressants for, 219–20
    characteristics of, 27, 32
    electroconvulsive therapy for, 224
    suicide and, 183

Questionnaires
    on child's depression, 73–74
    on identification of depression, 41–42
    on parent's depression, 97–98
    on partner's depression, 60–61

Reaction stage, 12, 16, 25, 141

childhood depression and, 67–68, 70–71
described, 7–8, 17
identifying depression in, 39–40
parent's depression and, 87, 91, 92, 94
partner's depression and, 48–49
substance abuse and, 169
suicide risk and, 188
Realistic expectations, 9
of children, 77
helping and, 156
of medical treatments, 226
of parents, 93, 96
of partners, 50
sexual problems and, 56–57
suicidal behavior and, 192
Red wine, monoamine oxidase inhibitors (MAOIs), 224
Relational Concepts in Psychoanalysis (Mitchell), 138
Relational psychology, 138–42, 204
Research
on childhood depression, 64–65
on depression effects on others, 5–7
on friendships and depression, 105–6
on substance abuse, 164–65
Responsibility, taking of, 126, 190
Restlessness: *see* Hyperactivity
Ripple effect, 45–46
Risk-taking behavior, 185
Ritalin, 217
Role changes, 46
Routine, changes in, 47, 70
Routine, maintaining
child's depression and, 79
helping and, 157–58
parent's depression and, 96
partner's depression and, 51
sexual problems and, 57
suicidal behavior and, 192

Seasonal affective disorder (SAD), 26
characteristics of, 27, 31–32
resources for, 246
Selective serotonin reuptake inhibitors (SSRIs), 216–18, 223
Self-destructive behavior, 185
Self-image, 66
Selfishness, 135–36, 142
Self-medication, 33, 164, 167–68
Sensate focus exercises, 59
Serotonin, 22
Serzone, 217
Sexual problems, 4, 44, 55–59
antidepressants and, 56, 214–15, 216–19
Side effects: *see also* specific types

of antidepressants, 217
of electroconvulsive therapy, 225
of non-psychiatric medication, 88, 89, 235
Sinequan (Adapin), 217
Sleep disturbances, 24, 25
in children, 66
substance abuse and, 168
Social life, changes in, 47, 70
Social support, 23, 48, 103, 105, 108–14
effects of, 153–55
giving, 109–14
importance of, 108–9
Social workers, 235–36, 240
fees of, 239
Spouses: *see* Partners
SSRIs: *see* Selective serotonin reuptake inhibitors
Stages of adaptation to depression (SAD), 7–9, 16–19: *see also* Information Gathering stage; Problem Solving stage; Reaction stage; trouble stage
children and, 84
partners and, 45
professional help during, 233
Stimulants, 216, 221
indications, side effects, addictive qualities, 217
Stress, 22–23
childhood depression and, 69
gender and, 34
suicide and, 182–83
Stroke, 20, 88
Substance abuse, 163–76
effects on relationships, 169–70
encouraging loved one to seek help for, 170–76
gender and, 33, 165
identification of, 165–67
professional help for, 173, 174, 235
research on, 164–65
as self-medication, 33, 164, 167–68
suicide and, 168, 186
Suicide, 177–99
antidepressants and, 223
assessing risk of, 192–93
in children, 64, 65, 67, 180–81
copycat, 186–87
effect on families and friends, 187–91
in the elderly, 181
number of deaths caused by, 180
offering alternatives to, 195–96
in psychotic depression, 32
reasons for, 181–83
resources for at-risk individuals, 246

Suicide (*continued*)
    substance abuse and, 168,
        186
    talk about, 193–95
    in unipolar (major, clinical) depres-
        sion, 24, 25
    urgency of obtaining professional help,
        252
    warning signs of, 183–87
Suicide Research Unit, 246
Support: *see* Social support; Unqualified
        support
Support groups, 233
Surmontil, 217
Sympathy: *see* Empathy

Tannen, Deborah, 116, 128
Task Force on Women and Depression,
        American Psychological Associa-
        tion, 33–34
Teachers, 80–81
Teamwork, 9
    children and, 82–84
    helping and, 160–61
    medical treatments and, 230
    needs and, 143–44
    parents and, 99–100
    partners and, 54–55
    sexual problems and, 59
    suicidal behavior and, 192
Teenagers: *see* Adolescents
Tie-breaker rule, 145–46
Tofranil, 217
Transference, 205
Treatment: *see* Professional help
Trouble stage, 25
    in bipolar depression, 28
    in childhood depression, 67–68,
        70
    described, 7, 16–17

identifying depression in, 39–42
    parent's depression and, 94
    partner's depression and, 48
    substance abuse and, 164,
        167
Twins, 22
Twinship needs, 140, 141
Tyramine, 224

Unipolar (clinical, major) depression,
        19
    antidepressants for, 219
    characteristics of, 26–28
    DSM-IV on, 23–25
    professional help for, 232
Unqualified support, 9
    for children, 77–78
    helping and, 157
    during medical treatment, 229
    for parents, 96–99
    for partners, 50–51
    sexual problems and, 57
    suicidal behavior and, 192

Vivactil, 217

Welbutrin, 217
Withdrawal, 184
Women, communicating with, 129–30:
        See also Gender
*Women Are from Venus and Men Are from
        Mars* (Gray), 116
World Wide Web, 256
Worthlessness, feelings of, 24, 25, 111,
        168

You Just Don't Understand (Tannen), 116,
        128

Zoloft, 216–18, 217